T0386243

THE SMALL STATES CLUB

ARMEN SARKISSIAN

The Small States Club

How Small Smart States Can Save the World

HURST & COMPANY, LONDON

First published in the United Kingdom in 2023 by
C. Hurst & Co. (Publishers) Ltd.,
New Wing, Somerset House, Strand, London, WC2R 1LA

Copyright © Armen Sarkissian, 2023

Printed in Great Britain by Bell & Bain Ltd, Glasgow

The right of Armen Sarkissian to be identified as the author of
this publication is asserted by him in accordance with the Copyright,
Designs and Patents Act, 1988.

A Cataloguing-in-Publication data record for this book
is available from the British Library.

ISBN: 9781787389403

www.hurstpublishers.com

To my family
and to my country, Hayastan,
this book is dedicated with love and hope.

CONTENTS

CONTENTS

LIST OF ILLUSTRATIONS

1. At my desk in Yerevan, Soviet Armenia, with the IBM PC XT machine on which we perfected Wordtris. 1980s.
   Credit: Office of President Armen Sarkissian
2. Meeting Mrs Thatcher, who as Prime Minister had put me on the spot, in her retirement. Early 1990s.
   Credit: Office of President Armen Sarkissian
3. En-route to Armenia with Shirlene Sarkissian, better known as Cher, with a humanitarian mission in the winter of 1994.
   Credit: Office of President Armen Sarkissian
4. With Bill Clinton in London. Late 1990s.
   Credit: Office of President Armen Sarkissian
5. Presenting credentials to Her Majesty Queen Elizabeth II following my recovery. October 1998. PA Images / Fiona Hanson.
   Credit: Office of President Armen Sarkissian
6. His Royal Highness Charles III, one of the most humane monarchs in the world, visited Armenia in 2013 as my guest.
   Credit: Office of President Armen Sarkissian
7. Being inaugurated as the Fourth President of Armenia. April 2018.
   Credit: Office of President Armen Sarkissian

LIST OF ILLUSTRATIONS

LIST OF ILLUSTRATIONS

ACKNOWLEDGEMENTS

This is not a scholarly book; it is a collection of reflections stemming from my experiences.

Over the years, I've had the privilege of learning, observing, interacting and traveling, all of which have shaped the thoughts in the following pages. And throughout this journey, my family have been my constant companions. I give thanks for the support and love of my grandparents, parents, sister, my beloved wife, sons and grandchildren, and the many friends I've made from the age of 7 to 70.

I am grateful to people from all walks of life—politicians, academicians, scientists, Nobel laureates, craftsmen, and the men, women and children who approached me on the street and struck up a conversation—who have imparted valuable lessons to me through their thoughts, generosity and kindness.

I record my deep appreciation for my brilliant publisher and editor, Michael Dwyer of Hurst & Co, for his insights and guidance in bringing this book to life. Finally, let me express my gratitude for the leaders of small successful states: their wisdom, friendship and leadership have made this book possible.

1

INTRODUCTION

THE POWER OF SMALL

Long before I became the president of a small state, I was an ordinary citizen of an immense power. I did not choose my side. My parents, members of the great Armenian diaspora, had relinquished a promising future in Europe to return to their ancestral homeland. But the Armenia in which they landed was not an autonomous nation; it was one of the fifteen so-called "republics" that constituted the Union of Soviet Socialist Republics. And thus my parents, who had sacrificed so much to reclaim Armenia, had to contend with their only son being claimed at birth as the citizen of a superpower.

The USSR, besotted with scale, was innately hostile to the small. Despite its global ambitions, the communism which animated the USSR was not a capacious ideology capable of breeding an inclusive nationalism. Successive Soviet leaders had made sustained efforts to stamp on national differences in the hope of spawning a new species of citizen whose identity would be defined primarily by the dogma of the super-state. Could one, in such a place, affirm one's distinct heritage without being seen to be undermining the cohesion of the Soviet Union?

I found myself unexpectedly forced to confront this quandary during Mikhail Gorbachev's state visit to Britain in the 1980s. I was a young researcher at Cambridge University and had been summoned along with another Soviet scientist working at Oxford University to a reception at the Soviet embassy in London. We were brought there, really, to be put on show for the British guests as model products of Soviet education. We were introduced to the great and the good, and everyone seemed impressed. But one guest, sharp as a razor, got the better of the hosts by engaging with me beyond science. "Young man," she asked me within the earshot of Gorbachev and his entourage after a brief discussion about music, "do you feel Armenian or do you feel 'Soviet'?"

The questioner was Margaret Thatcher, and the question was no less provocative for being posed in a humorous vein. I felt a measure of admiration for her forthrightness and a current of trepidation rising within myself. To say that I felt Armenian could induce the dangerous perception that I was rubbishing the Soviet identity imposed on me right in front of the custodian of the Soviet state, and that too on foreign soil. To claim that I felt Soviet, on the other hand, would amount, in my own head and heart, to a craven repudiation of my parents' sacrifice and my patrimony— one of the oldest civilisations in the world whose existence, after interminable attempts to snuff it out, seemed to me like nothing less than a miracle. "I am of course Armenian, madam Prime Minister," I answered matter-of-factly, but added hastily that I was also a grateful Soviet citizen who had received an excellent education back home. The visitors from Moscow, alarmed for a moment, puffed their chests with pride at hearing this.

Mrs Thatcher, perhaps sensing my predicament, did not press me further at the time. But she told me years later that she understood what I had felt: that Soviet identity was irreconcilable with the pre-communist identities of its "republics" because the survival of the former was predicated on stifling the latter. And it is this tension between the expansionist large state and the permanently besieged small fragments of which it was composed that precipitated the disintegration of the Soviet behemoth. The experiment to create a communist colossus by usurping the territories of states, effacing their particularities and recasting their populations as identical ideological ciphers—after years of seemingly unstoppable success—collapsed spectacularly against the aspirations of smaller nations to revive their suppressed self-dignity and restore their selfhood.

It was the Armenian quest for self-determination that initiated the unravelling of the Soviet Union. In February 1988, well before cries for independence rang out in Georgia and the Baltic states, Armenians in the province of Nagorno-Karabakh staged the first public protest in contravention of the Kremlin's policy. Karabakh, a historically Armenian territory, is known to Armenians as Artsakh. Despite its history and demography, the region was bequeathed to Soviet Azerbaijan in 1921 by Joseph Stalin, who believed that disrupting cohesive national and ethnic communities was the best way to keep diverse populations in check. After endless appeals to Moscow had gone unanswered, the local Armenians, taking advantage of the reforms initiated by Gorbachev, formed the "Karabakh Committee" and demanded the unification of the territory with Armenia. Within days, a million people took to the streets of Yerevan—the Armenian capital—to rally in peaceful solidarity with the Armenians of Karabakh. The Karabakh soviet, the local parliament, voted to join Armenia. Its vote was followed by a similar ballot by the Communist Party of Karabakh. Never before had a local parliament and party—instruments created explicitly to enforce Moscow's edicts—dictated *their* will to Moscow. The ordinary people of Artsakh then voted overwhelmingly in a referendum to dissolve Moscow's artificial cartography, secede from Soviet Azerbaijan and assert their Armenian identity. All of this was unprecedented in Soviet history and unthinkable up to the point that it transpired. The politburo's attempts to break up the protests and seize the airport in Yerevan with force led to bloodshed. For the first time, Moscow was openly castigated, while members of the Karabakh Committee who had issued the call for unification with Armenia acquired the status of heroes.

For the duration of its existence, the Soviet Union had seemed to its inhabitants an immortal leviathan. This view did not arise from any dispassionate assessment of its strengths but was formed entirely by long immersion in the perception of its invincibility. The entity we were coerced into calling our homeland was fortified by such formidable structures that even the revelations about the Communist Party's ideological bankruptcy and the depredations of the KGB—the dreaded Soviet security agency—could not incite doubt about their durability. As a scientist and a professor of theoretical physics, the prospect of the sudden demise of this gargantuan empire encased inside seemingly impregnable layers of protection would have seemed too fantastic for me to consider seriously. But unbeknown to me, and even to its almighty rulers, the minute particles that made up the USSR were engineering its implosion. The template for its ultimate dissolution was forged by tiny Armenia's irrepressible desire for freedom.

Eventually, small republics such as Armenia, Georgia and Lithuania launched the process of swift secession from the Soviet Union, leaving Gorbachev as a commander without an army, secretary without a party or politburo and president without a country. In 1991, Soviet bank accounts were seized, its foreign ministry abolished and all the buildings that lent grandeur to the Soviet capital of Moscow—from the Kremlin Museum to the Lenin Library, from the Bolshoi Theatre to the Pushkin

Museum of Arts—were reclaimed for Russia by Boris Yeltsin's decrees. Gorbachev's own office in the Kremlin—and the Kremlin itself—was slowly wrested from him. The only possession that gave Gorbachev gravitas in his bitterly humiliating final hours in office in the dying hours of the USSR was the *chemodanchik*—the small box containing the nuclear launchpad which, if activated, could annihilate the world.

On the evening of 25 December 1991, Gorbachev settled into a room in the Kremlin that had been redecorated to resemble his old office. A CNN news crew from America, handpicked by the last Soviet leader to document his precipitous exit, crowded the space, outnumbering the indifferent local journalists. Gorbachev pulled out a Soviet-made pen from his pocket to sign his letter of resignation, but the pen did not work—a final demonstration of the communist enterprise's decrepitude. Tom Johnson, a CNN executive from New York, offered his Mont Blanc. Gorbachev signed the document, and seconds before 7pm, went live on TV to announce his departure and the effective end of the Soviet Union. Stripped of all authority by this point, Gorbachev drew some solace from the assurance given to him that the Soviet flag would fly above the Kremlin until midnight on 31 December 1991, before being lowered and replaced by a Russian flag against a backdrop of fireworks. But Yeltsin, furious at not finding a positive mention of his name in Gorbachev's televised speech, commanded a pair of guards to pull it down seconds after the broadcast ended. At precisely 7.32pm, the Soviet standard bearing the hammer and the sickle was brought down from the illuminated flagpole over the Kremlin. Gorbachev's last wish in office, to keep the Soviet flag as a souvenir, was denied.

The high drama unfolding in Moscow was not the "end of history" for me or my compatriots. It was the beginning of something new, something excitingly and terrifyingly unknown. My life was shaped by the Soviet Union's inequities, but also opportunities, particularly in education. I lost my father to cancer when I was ten, and my mother toiled hard at two jobs to give me and my sister the opportunities normally unavailable to people from our background. The hardships of my youth, combined with the absence of a level playing field, made me fiercely competitive, and I excelled in science. As a doctoral candidate in my early twenties, I won the prestigious Lenin scholarship for achievements in this apolitical discipline. And this recognition came, in addition to something approaching academic celebrity, with a monthly stipend fatter than the salaries of my professors. In the early 1980s, I was invited to do research at Cambridge University. But exiting the Soviet frontiers was a luxury available only to a tiny elite. I was blocked repeatedly from travelling, but I persisted. Finally, on the recommendation of two revered academicians—Anatoly Logunov, the rector of the Moscow State University, and his counterpart at the Yerevan State University, Sergey Hambartsumian—my application was approved in Moscow. My wife and two young children, however, were kept as hostages to ensure my return.

Having flown from an oppressively drab Moscow, Britain instantly dazzled me. The streets were brightly lit, the stores overabundantly stocked, the people genial. In England I got my first glimpse of the evil West—and drew my first breath of freedom. And what *was* freedom? For me, it was the noise of people speaking freely, reading newspapers that openly castigated politicians and the serenity of a society unfamiliar with surveillance. My first proper stop was Colchester, in Essex, where we were taken, ostensibly, to be trained in English. The real reason, of course, was to be observed. Since I had been taught English from an early age, I had no trouble with the course and moved on quickly to my next stop: Jesus College, Cambridge. With its cobbled streets, slender medieval alleys, flat-bottomed boats floating down the river Cam, courtyards and quads, and at the centre of it all, the eight-centuries-old university, it was impossible not to be captivated by the city.

Cambridge held a special place in my heart before I set foot in it: Newton and Darwin had been trained there, John Harvard called it home before he moved to Massachusetts, and Byron—who had lived among Armenian monks and mastered their language—had written his earliest poems at the university. But nothing had quite prepared me for the absence of hierarchy in Cambridge. I was embraced without a hint of condescension by such luminaries as Stephen Hawking and Sir (now Lord) Martin Rees. A litany of Nobel laureates would discuss theoretical physics with me over lunch as if I were their equal. It was a world apart from the Soviet Union; the equality Moscow praised in theory was put into practice at Cambridge.

I spent my days at seminars and in the library reading rooms, where I devoured journals that would have been impossible to find in Yerevan and Moscow. In the evenings, after dining at the college, I discussed and debated music, politics and science with other students. It was in Cambridge that I was introduced to Britain's national cuisine—Indian food—by a dormmate who was the nephew of the Nobel-winning theoretical physicist Subrahmanyan Chandrasekhar. I joked that if there was a Nobel prize for cooking, the young Subrahmanyan would have won it. Some years later, I had the honour of introducing the older Subahmanyan to Armenian cuisine when I hosted him in Yerevan. At weekends, I boarded the train to London and feasted on its culture. I went to the theatre, opera, galleries and libraries.

England taught me to be financially prudent. Even though the Soviet embassy took half my stipend—it was an unspoken rule, and one had to comply with it—I saved enough to buy presents for my family and an IBM computer for myself. A member of the Armenian diaspora I had befriended warned me that the authorities would seize my machine the moment I landed in

Moscow. So he offered a generous way out: he bought me the cheaper Toshiba computer, which I donated to the Yerevan State University, and the authorities let me keep my computer.

Upon returning home, I founded the Department of Computer Modelling of Complex Systems—what we would today call Artificial Intelligence—at the Yerevan State University and began applying my problem solving experience in theoretical physics to other fields. By the beginning of the 1990s, as Gorbachev's attempts to reform the Soviet Union loosened the state's suffocating oversight of life, I had co-invented and sold to an American company a hugely successful video game— *Wordtris*—and was dividing my time teaching between Yerevan and London.

On 21 September 1991, the day that Armenia voted to leave the Soviet Union, my exultation was bound up with consternation. Armenia's historic territory had been devoured by imperial powers over long and harrowing centuries of foreign rule. The modern Armenian state rising from the detritus of the Soviet Union was going to be one-thousandth the size of the empire it was leaving. It had no seaport and few resources. Its industry, deliberately designed to be dependent on other Soviet republics, was already in a dire state. It had no autonomous relations with the world outside and was still bruised by the 1988 earthquake, which had killed more than 40,000 people—a calamitous number in a land of 3.5 million people. Armenia had been among the first Soviet republics to be electrified. But now, following the closure of its nuclear plant in the jittery aftermath of the earthquake, it had to import energy via the territory of its hostile neighbours. In the blink of an eye, Armenians were making the transition from subjects of a veritable superpower that possessed the capability to end organised human life to citizens of a small state flanked by immense historic adversaries with a long history of trampling on Armenians. Even as they rejoiced in their freedom, Armenians,

INTRODUCTION

with their inimitable gift for gallows humour, asked if they were not hurtling from the Space Age to the Stone Age.

Since I had by then established strong relationships with people and institutions in the West, particularly in the United Kingdom, I was asked by the inaugural president of Armenia, Levon Ter-Petrosyan, a fellow academician, if I might consider setting up Armenia's embassy in London. It would be our newly liberated nation's maiden diplomatic mission on any foreign soil. I was thirty-eight years old and responsible for a young family. My mathematical cast of mind would ordinarily have resisted the invitation to undertake an assignment outside my specialism. But this was no ordinary moment. To say that each of us had a patriotic obligation to serve our newly reincarnated nation is not to peddle a platitude: it is to state a plain fact. I agreed.

On a chilly autumn afternoon, armed with a letter of accreditation from Armenia's foreign ministry, I arrived at the Foreign and Commonwealth Office in London. It would be an understatement to say that officials at the FCO were astonished to see me on their doorstep. Having dealt with the great power that was the USSR, they were still figuring out ways to proceed with the multiple small states re-emerging on its former territory. There was no protocol in place. I was the first person from a post-Soviet state to land at the FCO. But if my interlocutors remained unfazed when I introduced myself as "the chargé d'affaires of Armenia", it was because even those coming to grips with the fallout from the Soviet Union's dissolution were familiar with Armenia. As an antique civilisation with a vast diaspora, Armenia wielded disproportionate soft power.

In the four years after raising the Armenian flag in London, I proceeded, with the help of the Armenian diaspora, to open embassies in Paris, Brussels, Berlin, Athens, and Rome—and was appointed Armenia's envoy to Belgium, the European Union,

NATO, the Netherlands and the Vatican—before being recalled and elected prime minister of Armenia in 1996.

We will revisit Armenia—the world's oldest Christian country that is at once an ancient civilisation, a small state and a global nation—later. I relate this story at the outset to emphasise that I write this book from a unique vantage point: that of someone who was born and raised in a seemingly indestructible superpower and went on to help steer the course of an apparently untenable small state.

During my lives as a scientist and diplomat, businessman and politician, I have unceasingly marvelled at the tenacity of small states. Even as a young Soviet citizen, I studied the small states in my atlas with admiration. In a world where the Soviet Union—the largest state in the world—spoke of a constant threat to its existence and maintained the largest army and nuclear arsenal on the planet to safeguard itself, how did small states preserve their sovereignty and independence?

Their survival has always been predicated on overcoming insuperable odds. When the modern state came into existence with the Peace of Westphalia in 1648, as Dr Matthias Maass has shown, there were 400 small states. Hundreds of them were swallowed up or extinguished by the antecedents of today's great and middle powers. Some 265 small states vanished from the face of the earth between 1791 and 1812. Today, there are roughly 150 small states—a seven-fold increase since the establishment of the post-war order in 1945. But their survival can scarcely be taken for granted in an increasingly pluri-polar world whose order, institutions, and norms are being torpedoed by the velocity of political, geopolitical social, and technological transformation.

Across the world, from Africa to Eurasia and America to Asia, in every significant sphere, large states are again engaged in antagonistic competition, and the world order that has prevailed since 1992 is becoming rapidly obsolete.

INTRODUCTION

Before we can ask what this means for small states, we must answer what we mean by a "small state". Although most readers will have a common-sensical conception of a "small state", there is no standard definition built on universal consensus. The most common definition is a negative one: small states are those that are not great powers—a category characterised by features such as possession of aircraft carrier(s), weapons of mass destruction and permanent membership of the UN Security Council. By this hard power-prioritising standard, however, Germany would qualify as a small state despite being, by a combination of factors, Europe's foremost power. Another definition measures small states by their material capabilities—population, wealth, power projection—but this is complicated by the fact that many "small" underdeveloped countries have large populations and project power disproportionate to their wealth, while many "great" powers have relatively tiny populations and barely any military power.

Since this is not a scholarly book, we are emancipated from rigid definitions. Small states, as I see them, are not unlike my own country: small in size and population (say up to or under 15 million), dismissed at birth, often (but not always) without many or few resources and locked into conflict or surrounded by hostile powers. Many small states are microcosms of the problems that afflict their larger counterparts—they are beset by ethnic strife, political turmoil and economic mismanagement—but their ability to address their problems is often frustrated by difficulties peculiar to them.

If there is an overwhelming priority or a paramount preoccupation common to all small states, it is survival. The world has never been structured to facilitate the survival of small states, and treating them as disposable has been the norm through most of recent history. Survival, therefore, has largely depended on the will and skill of small states themselves. As an

11

Armenian, I am always alert to the hazards of over-dependence on the goodwill of others. At the same time, I am conscious that hard force alone has seldom saved small states from the designs of large powers or from coalitions determined to injure or wipe them out. In other words, while I am wary of depending on others, I am acutely aware of the limitations of relying solely on military power. This is an important reason why small states tend for the most part to be averse to conflict: war imposes a disproportionate toll on them. There will always be exceptions to the rule, but small states generally tend to promote peace—or at least strive to create conditions to avert the outbreak of fighting.

To preserve themselves, small states must be agile, adaptable *and* adroit. Internally, as Aristotle said of the city-states in the third century BCE, they must train their populations to be "jacks-of-all-trades". Externally, they must exert themselves to mobilise an international order reinforced by institutions and equipped with the means to uphold its rules. In short, small states must also be *smart states*. In international relations, as the Harvard political scientist Joseph Nye argues, there are three kinds of power: hard power, which involves coercion; soft power, which flows from a nation's cultural output; and a hybrid, or what I'd call "smart power", which amalgamates components of hard *and* soft power.

Throughout my career, I have seen the improbable rise of small states that were born in impossible conditions and written off before they could learn to crawl. The United Arab Emirates, for instance, was dismissed even before its visionary founder, Sheikh Zayed, had unified the dusty emirates that made up the Trucial States. Today, five decades after its inauguration in 1971, the UAE is not only an international cultural hub and a centre of commerce—it is also home to the world's unlikeliest green city.

The future of Singapore, similarly, was in grave doubt once Britain withdrew its forces in 1971, exposing it to the whims of the great and middle powers surrounding it. Lee Kuan Yew, the city-state's father, reacted to this crisis by aggressively superintending Singapore's transformation into an economic force in the world and a diplomatic trouble-shooter in the region.

At its independence in 1966, Botswana, which receives training in governance from Singapore, had exactly eight miles of tarred road in the entire country. Its land was either dusty or swampy and the people scraped a living from agriculture. Today, Botswana is a model of economic prudence and efficient governance in Africa. With a population under 2 million, its low taxes, high income (at $6,000, its per capita income is larger than Malaysia's), excellent healthcare and openness to foreign talent have made it the envy of others. Those who attribute Botswana's success solely to one resource—diamonds—overlook the dexterity and dedication with which it has diverted the income from that resource into the development of its people rather than the enrichment of its rulers.

As a diplomat and later prime minister and president, I floated the idea of a club of such smart small states—an informal international platform to share ideas, advance the interests of its members, act as a conduit between them and large states, foster peace, and promote scientific and economic partnerships and collaboration. The proposition encountered stiff resistance from established groupings because they tend, understandably, to be wary of encouraging the birth and growth of any forum they fear might challenge them. This fear is unfounded. A club of small states will find ways to accelerate rather than hamper cooperation with and between small, middle and great powers. Large states desire dominance. Small states seek stability. And since peace is the condition of the survival of small states, a body that champions them would also naturally be an evangelist for amity among nations. It would help minimise, if not eliminate, any scope for misunderstanding and misadventure.

We inhabit a world in which, for the first time, long marginalised voices have acquired the capability to amplify themselves and be heard. An individual with a smartphone has the power to break news and to shape trends. A small, tech-savvy state can now remotely sabotage and paralyse large states. Technology has eroded the capacity of large powers to remain the predominant centres of progress and achievement. Where once large powers shaped the fate of the world, today small nations are endowed with the prowess to compete with them. To take an example, Israel, with a population smaller than North Carolina's, is spearheading a technological revolution in Asia. The nation that gave us the USB stick and the pillcam—a swallowable miniature camera that has transformed gastroenterology—has established itself as a start-up nation that is home to 60 of the world's top 500 tech giants.

Small states, often overlooked in favour of their larger counterparts, can navigate the complex challenges of the twenty-first century in smarter ways than the traditional great powers. Smallness is often regarded as a weakness; it can be a strength. It may induce insecurity in states, but it also endows them with an instinct for survival. Large states are ponderous; small states can be nimble and adaptive.

Eight of the top ten nations on the Bloomberg Innovator Index are small states. Singapore, a consistently high-ranking state on the index, is a world leader in medical innovation. Despite being home to only 7 per cent of Germany's population, it accounts for more patents in healthcare than its European counterpart. It has converted its curses—its location and limited resources—into opportunities to become one of the most prosperous countries in the world.

Sweden, home to under 11 million citizens, has emerged as a captain in the fields of technology, R&D and innovation. It has more technology hubs per capita than any part of the world save Silicon Valley. Having given the pacemaker and Skype to the world, it is now leading the planet in cutting-edge work in robotics, nanotechnology and digital engineering. Even the stars are no longer beyond the reach of small states. In 2021, the UAE, home to just over 9 million people, successfully orbited its 'Rashid' Rover, developed by the Mohammed Bin Rashid Space Center (MBRSC) in Dubai, around Mars—catapulting itself into an exclusive league once occupied by great powers. In 2022, the tiny state of Qatar hosted the FIFA World Cup, the greatest sporting and entertainment event in the world—another first for a small state.

Animated by a survival instinct unique to them, small states are showing themselves capable of things that were once the sole preserve of large powers. Whether it is through their ability to allocate their scarce resources and innovate against the odds, or their commitment to global collaboration, small states can be powerful forces for good in our interconnected world—provided that the world is willing to learn from them.

International institutions, however, are not only behind the times but actively resist change. They reflect the realities of the world in which they were born and can seem archaic in the world as it is. Multilateral institutional arrangements, from the United Nations Security Council to G7, remain captive to the geopolitical dynamics of a bygone era. Those who dominate these structures are naturally opposed to reform—and inimical to new ideas. The existing international institutional framework ensures more often than not that in any contest between what is beneficial for the world and what seems advantageous to the dominant global powers, the latter prevails. It is sobering to remember that the most consequential and wasteful post-9/11 military campaigns that plunged substantial segments of the world into chaos and carnage were waged by large powers with the imprimatur or acquiescence of international organisations.

Stability, constancy, the rule of law, peace and predictability are imperative for the success of small states. And a club of such states would help smaller nations exert greater influence in cultivating the climate essential for global security, progress and prosperity. In doing so, it would also temper the aggression and destructive impulses of large powers.

Who would belong to such a club?

The book that follows tells the story of nine small countries that dot Europe, Asia and Africa that would qualify as founding members. I have selected these states because I have studied their progress closely—but also because their travails and successes, individually and collectively, carry indispensable lessons for small (and even large) states operating in a world in flux. I have interacted extensively with many of the leaders and key figures in these nations. Not every country I examine will feature every virtue prized by every society: some states are not fully democratic, others place too much emphasis on technocracy and none is perfect. The chapters that follow are not *arguments* for why these states are entitled to belong in or lead the Small States Club. They are my impressions of these places, based on my extensive observations, and are thus personal and idiosyncratic. Some aspects of some of these states may not endear them to some people; I am conscious of the criticisms that can be levelled at them, but they are not the subject of this book. I may consider the flaws in a future study. I believe that despite their shortcomings, they can teach us something valuable about surviving and succeeding in an inhospitable world—and making it safe for all who inhabit it.

2

SINGAPORE

THE POWER OF LEADERSHIP

Singapore begins to astonish visitors even before they have set foot on the island. The first intimation of what is to come is the hospitality onboard the city-state's flag carrier, Singapore Airlines. Its aircraft, belonging to a fleet that is refreshed every decade, are always among the most advanced in the industry. The cabin crews, put through the most thorough training programme of its kind, deliver a service that is unparalleled in the skies. To land in Changi airport, situated on the eastern tip of Singapore, is to encounter a model of efficiency. Since its inauguration in 1981, Changi has won more than 660 "best airport" awards from around the world, and with good reason. The place is designed so ergonomically that it takes the visitor about 30 minutes to check in to a downtown hotel from the moment he or she steps off the plane. The roads outside the airport are among the cleanest in the world; there is no litter in sight. And in the unlikely event that you spot a pothole, the authorities will fill and smooth it out within 48 hours of being notified.

You can relish a Singapore Sling at the Raffles Hotel, the birthplace of the cocktail; enjoy chilli crab, the "national dish" born of Malay and Chinese influence, at one of the salubrious hawker centres replete with ethnic food stalls; and marvel at the breath-stopping prosperity all around you. How did this island—burnt to its foundations by the Portuguese in 1613, inhabited by Sea Gypsies and settled by scattered fishing communities, colonised by the British in the nineteenth century, tinier than New York City, bereft of any natural resource, and teeming with a multiplicity of once mutually hostile ethnicities—establish itself, within a few decades of its founding as a modern state in 1965, as one of the world's most affluent countries, a financial, manufacturing and entrepreneurial entrepot, and one of Asia's most formidable military powers?

To appreciate Singapore's achievement—which has no parallel in modern history—we must consider the condition of the island before it became a sovereign state. A visitor to Singapore in 1960 would have been struck most of all by its wretchedness. He would have been surrounded by swamps, besieged by swarms of mosquitoes and assailed by the stench emanating from the densest slums in the world at the time. Plumbing and electricity were princely extravagances, families shared crammed tin-roofed shacks with strangers and most people lived ten to a room. There was no sanitation. And the squalor became a feast for diseases. Illnesses like tuberculosis and cholera were rife, and infant mortality rates—at 34.9 deaths per thousand live-births—were among the highest in the region. It was not uncommon for entire families to be wiped out by sickness. Clean water was also a luxury most Singaporeans could scarcely afford. In areas where water was rationed, families had to depend on dirty, contaminated sources. The result was diseases like dysentery, which further exacerbated the already dire living conditions.

SINGAPORE

Our visitor in 1960 would have struggled to find anything approaching a cohesive nation among the squatters' settlements, the pig farms and the fishing villages that dotted Singapore. The inhabitants of the island he met would have identified themselves not as Singaporeans but as members of their respective ethnic communities—Chinese, Malay, Indian. Commercial cooperation between these three groups, which collectively accounted for a majority of the country's citizenry, was laced with suspicion and resentment that often erupted into violence. To top it all, a section of the state's Chinese populace, inspired by the revolutionary fervour of China, agitated for a communist state.

Singapore's modern political consciousness can be traced to the 1900s, when fervent local support for the Xinhai Revolution, which ended imperial rule in China, kindled political activism among the local populace. The Malayan Communist Party (MCP) was born out of this ferment in 1930. Once Malaya achieved self-government, the MCP's agitation prompted British authorities to declare a state of emergency that lasted until 1960. As demonstrations and strikes against British rule became the norm, new political parties appeared on the scene. One notable party was the Labour Front, which, led by the charismatic David Marshall, was founded in 1954. Another was the People's Action Party (PAP), which rose under the astute guidance of Lee Kuan Yew, a Cambridge-educated lawyer of Chinese descent. The PAP's founding members comprised passionate political activists from Singapore's three major ethnic communities, and their backgrounds ranged from law to journalism to trade unions.

In its formative years, the PAP set forth a compelling vision which it shared with the voters in its 1954 manifesto. It promised to achieve and preserve Singapore's independence by merging with the Federation of Malaya, pledged to establish a democratic and socialist government, and committed itself to fostering a harmonious and egalitarian society that celebrated its multi-ethnic composition. The early development of Singapore's politics was governed by dynamic individuals and their resolute pursuit of a common destiny for the nation. Their aims encompassed not only independence but also social progress and a society that embraced diversity. These foundations would shape Singapore's future.

The PAP first participated in the general elections for the Legislative Assembly in 1955. It was a crucial moment that set the stage for their meteoric rise. It was in the subsequent general elections of 1959, however, that the PAP achieved an awe-inspiring feat. With an impressive 43 out of 51 seats in the Legislative Assembly, they had a clear mandate to form the government. At the top of the PAP sat Lee, the party's general secretary, who became Singapore's maiden prime minister.

In the intense negotiations with London that followed, Singapore made significant strides towards self-governance. Internal affairs were entrusted to the Singaporean government; the British controlled defence and foreign affairs. In 1958, a year after Malaya, Singapore's large neighbour, achieved independence, Singapore signed the Constitutional Agreement on Independence with Britain. And yet, even after gaining full sovereignty, Singapore opted to retain British troops on its soil for a time. This decision not only served as a safeguard against potential threats from neighbouring states, but also allowed for continued close ties with London. Besides, the British military base, bringing with it an abundance of employment opportunities, bolstered Singapore's economy.

Singapore's smallness, however, seemed incapable of supporting its nascent statehood. And so, in 1963, hoping to stave off extinction, it voluntarily merged into Malaysia. It was a choice driven by the belief that, as part of a large state, Singapore would profit from a security blanket, a big market in the hinterland and the conditions to realise its true potential.

But that experiment lasted less than two years. The Malays— Malaysia's "children of the soil"—felt threatened by the surge in Chinese citizens triggered by the union with Singapore. Deadly race riots between Malays and Chinese, raging through Singapore in 1964, validated such fears. In 1965, Singapore was summarily ejected from Malaysia in one of the rarest instances—if not the only instance—of a country expelling its constituent state.

Disgorged and discarded even after offering itself up to a larger neighbour, Singapore seemed doomed. What conceivable future did its two million citizens have? One option was to emigrate and find work elsewhere. After all, most of the people who made up Singapore were descended from forebears who had migrated to the place from China, Malaya and India just over a century before to scratch a living or make a fortune. They had been administered as members of a British possession from 1819—first as workers in an ambitious port city overrun by vice, and later as colonial subjects with the accoutrements of a state— before being surrendered to the Japanese in 1942. The Japanese had then exposed them to a brutal occupation, singling out the Chinese for savagery, before the British, desperate to reclaim the territory, rained down enough bombs from the skies to reduce so much of Singapore more or less to rubble. Now, in 1965, Singapore was truly alone, in a region in which once glorious states, from Funan to Champa, had vanished without a trace.

The options before Singapore were stark. It had to fortify itself from within—or wither away. Even the most optimistic observer of Singapore at the time would have considered its mere survival a miracle. Enter Lee Kuan Yew, the founder of modern Singapore and its first prime minister. Lee was not content with survival. He wanted his speck of a country to become a bastion of stability and prosperity at home—and a leader and a model for the region and the world. Lee arrived at this audacious plan *after* his ambition to integrate Singapore into Malaysia had resulted in utter failure. It was not unreasonable to dismiss him as delusional. But Lee got to work with what he had. And what he had was a largely destitute island splintered by race.

His first challenge, then, was to harmonise the clashing ethnic factions into a coherent nationhood. Singaporean national identity was not bound by ancient history. It was forged by the steely determination of its unyielding leader. Its basis was not the past, but a vision of the future. Himself of Chinese descent, Lee subordinated his identity to the overarching Singaporean identity he preached to his compatriots. "If you want a Chinese chauvinistic society," Lee told university graduates a year after Singapore's foundation, "failure is assured".

There would be no ethnic favouritism in the Singapore envisaged by Lee and his comrades, and the island would henceforth exert its energies on converting its perceived weaknesses into its greatest strengths. Lee's foreign minister and closest friend, Sinnathamby Rajaratnam, articulated his boss's vision:

> History has brought all these diverse peoples from all over Asia to this little island. They will live here for all time as Singaporeans. That is why we don't go about shouting "Chinese unite!" and "Malays unite!" and "Indians unite" ... We are trying to show that a multiracial Singapore can function as a harmonious political unit; that cultural differences need not lead to cultural cannibalism; that a multilingual society makes for intellectual enrichment ... that a country with no natural resources of its own can, through the mobilisation of its intellectual and labour resources, give its people generally a better life.

The leaders of the PAP claimed to be socialist, and Lee was widely perceived as genuinely embracing socialism during the early years of his party's rule. His brand of socialism, however, was geared to the project to cultivate national characteristics and usher in prosperity. Lee subsequently acknowledged that shortly after assuming power, he veered away from the notion of a welfare state. The challenges of implementing a welfarist model within the confines of a small state seemed to him overwhelming and even self-defeating, and he immediately re-examined the benefits of the state's adoption of socialist ideology.

The evolution of Lee's view of socialism and the welfare state is one instance of the pragmatic approach that typified his leadership. Appreciating the realities and constraints faced by Singapore, he recalibrated his early beliefs. Such flexibility and willingness to reassess and revise ideas has become a hallmark of Singapore's governance model, and it has helped to place the island on its distinctive trajectory of success.

With the benefit of his first-rate education in England and a keen understanding of the realities of both peace and war, Lee painted for Singaporeans a vivid picture of the future he claimed was within their reach: a thriving economy, advanced industries, a robust military, an educated populace, full employment and a well-oiled state machinery. This lofty vision was accompanied by a sober acknowledgement of the fact that its realisation would depend on superhuman effort and total internal stability. Pragmatism thus swiftly became a defining feature of Singapore's government and set it profitably apart from the rigid doctrines of Chinese communism that prevailed in the 1960s. Lee, who scorned naïve idealism, epitomised Singapore's commitment to rationalism. By defying dogma and embracing a results-oriented approach, Singapore's leadership demonstrated its clear commitment to achieving tangible outcomes for its people while at the same time shielding their country from the lethal ideological currents sweeping the region and positioning it as a beacon of success in South East Asia.

The fixation on stability also made it easier to portray opposition parties advocating for a more vibrant multiparty democracy within Singapore as radicals out of touch with the genuine concerns of the people. Both foreign and domestic critics calling for greater transparency and accountability in governance—albeit without explicitly framing their arguments in the language of liberal democracy—were swiftly brushed aside as uninformed or insensitive to Singapore's unique circumstances. The implication always was that such ideals were irrelevant, ill-suited, and potentially perilous to Singapore in the context of its distinct history and geopolitical challenges.

The principle of adherence to pragmatism permitted Singapore's leaders to sidestep ideological debates and focus on what they deemed to be the urgent needs and priorities of the nation. Critics urging change were met with a calculated scepticism, and their idealistic demands painted as incompatible with the messy Singaporean reality. This approach, while effective in silencing dissenting voices, also fostered a contentious environment where competing viewpoints were marginalised in favour of a "pragmatic" pursuit of Singapore's best interests. Lee and the PAP certainly exhibited a strategic talent for framing criticisms and aspirations for change as detached from the pulse of the people or ignorant of Singapore's unique circumstances. And the insistence on pragmatism not only shaped the country's developmental trajectory but also reinforced the government's grip on power.

What distinguished Lee was how he deployed that power: he never used it to enrich himself or his family or cronies. In fact, he did the opposite. Corruption was a deep-rooted malady Singapore had inherited from its colonial economic model. Lee led a frugal life. I was startled by the modesty of his house when I visited Singapore in 2021. His everyday life, while in office, resembled that of a hyperactive CEO. His life in quasi-retirement (he never fully retired) resembled a middle-class retiree's. In the early years and decades of Singapore's birth, Lee played an instrumental role in cleaning up the country. He launched a comprehensive anti-corruption campaign immediately after Singapore gained independence. His objective was to eradicate corruption once and for all. Corrupt officials and their family members were stripped of immunity. The judiciary was empowered to confiscate illicit gains. Salary increments were introduced to deter corrupt practices among public servants. The result: personal integrity, rectitude and accountability entered the public consciousness as non-negotiable national values of Singapore, and the island went from being numbered among the most hopelessly venal states in the world to being ranked alongside the least corrupt countries on earth.

In the late 1960s, the government introduced affordable housing programmes to meet a growing demand. It gave dignity to Singaporeans, improved their quality of life, evened the field and reconfigured the social landscape. Once people had a roof over their head, one of the most basic necessities of life, they had to be put into productive work if the country's economy had any hope of growing. The government prioritised job creation and industrialisation. It also devised ways to make idleness constructive by introducing universal conscription to boost the island's security. Individuals of all ages and genders were expected to perform military service in a bid to foster a sense of collective duty and national pride among Singaporeans.

When evaluating Singapore's rapid development, it is crucial to acknowledge the state's powerful grip on the country's liberalisation and transformation. This exercise of absolute control had both positive and negative implications. On the one hand, viewed through the lens of pragmatism—a relentless pursuit of clearly defined goals—the government's complete command facilitated robust state-led growth and impressive economic achievements that allowed Singapore to excel on the global stage. On the other hand, the government's total control curtailed democratic processes, restricted certain freedoms, imposed limits on political pluralism and made the country resemble a one-party state.

This duality, a complex interplay between state control and societal dynamics, shapes Singapore's trajectory. As the nation grapples with the tension between centralised authority and calls for greater political participation and freedom, striking a delicate balance becomes imperative. Navigating this terrain will determine not only the future success of Singapore but also the extent to which its citizens can exercise their democratic rights and contribute to the vibrant tapestry of a diverse and inclusive society.

When assessing the pragmatism adopted by Singaporean policymakers, it becomes evident that their decision-making is driven by an "ends justify the means" approach. This pragmatic orientation often places technological rationality at the forefront, overshadowing moral, political and aesthetic considerations. And what is the overarching aim of this pragmatic outlook? Sustained economic growth.

One notable outcome of such an outlook is the preponderance and prominence of economists and like-minded thinkers among key public administrators. These individuals prioritise decision-making based on cost-benefit analysis, assuming that people will respond rationally to incentives and deterrents. Their emphasis on economic rationality can sometimes result in a dismissive attitude towards alternative viewpoints offered by the public, for in their estimation the latter's perspective is not formed on the basis of a comprehensive understanding of the broader picture. The selection and advancement of public administrators hinges on their proficiency in utilising policy development tools and methods generated and prized by the system. This approach, while having proved efficient to date, may inadvertently breed disregard for alternative views and thus stifle the diversity of perspectives needed for robust decision-making. In the pursuit of competence and effectiveness, the pragmatic approach risks sidelining the valuable input of those who challenge the prevailing orthodoxy.

Another obvious danger is that "pragmatic" politicians, animated by a value-neutral outlook, may find themselves compelled, when challenged, to flavour their policies with ideals, values and principles popular at any given time among the populace. This strategic manoeuvre, intended to garner widespread acceptance and secure successful policy implementation, may blur the line between genuine conviction and expedient manipulation, potentially compromising the integrity of their policy frameworks. As Singapore continues to navigate the complex terrain of pragmatism, it is crucial to strike a delicate balance between technical efficacy and inclusive decision-making. Embracing alternative perspectives, upholding democratic values, and ensuring the active participation of citizens will promote a more robust and resilient governance model—one that can effectively address the varying needs and aspirations of Singaporean society.

Singapore created an official culture and value system from a calculated intertwining of Western and Asian influences. In their striving for a cohesive national identity, policymakers meticulously crafted an ideology that blended elements of Western rigidity with traditional Asian virtues. This deliberate fusion created an image of the quintessential Singaporean citizen—characterised by individualism, thrift, diligence and deference to authority.

In this carefully constructed framework, certain values were consciously discarded. Asian superstitions, for instance, found no place in the Singaporean ethos. Similarly, the Confucian disdain for merchants and soldiers was deemed incompatible with the Singaporean conception of progress and prosperity. Western liberal ideals associated with individualism, freedom, equality, and scepticism of government were also regarded as inappropriate for the Singaporean context and carefully sidelined.

Constitutionally, Singapore is a vibrant multicultural mix. Its population can be neatly categorised into three major groups: the Chinese, constituting a significant 74 per cent of the population; the Malays, making up 14 per cent; and the Indians, comprising 9 per cent. Alongside these larger groups, smaller communities of Europeans, Arabs, Jews, Armenians and others contribute to the rich diversity of the nation. Religion, too, is variegated, with adherents of Buddhism, Islam, Christianity and Hinduism dotting the cultural landscape. The origins of this diverse population trace back to the island's colonial beginnings in 1819 when the English established a foothold that eventually became part of the Straits Settlements colony in 1826.

In his memoirs, Lee candidly acknowledges the profound effect of racial clashes on his thinking. It was these painful experiences that drove him and his associates to cling to a vision of a truly multicultural society capable of guaranteeing and enforcing equal rights for all citizens, irrespective of their race, language, or religion. This resolute creed has shaped the very fabric of Singapore's national self-image. In the course of Lee's lifetime, Singapore's diverse population became a source of its strength and infused the nation with a richness and resilience that propelled it forwards.

The Indian concept of "unity in diversity" and the American motto of "*E Pluribus Unum*" offer intriguing alternatives to older models of nationalism and separatism. They envision the creation of a single nation composed of various ethnic, racial, and religious groups—all bound by a shared history and future. In the case of Singapore, building a cohesive nation meant steering clear of closed ethnic and religious enclaves.

In this new nation, community was no longer defined by ethnicity, but by citizenship. And to enforce this, the government embarked on a concerted effort to dismantle segregated settlements of different ethno-religious groups. Starting from 1965, the state housing programme proactively promoted cohabitation of the three primary ethnic groups within each neighbourhood, in line with the country's ethnic composition. This deliberate policy aimed to prevent the emergence of isolated diasporas and replaced ethnic enclaves with new integrated housing and by promoting a multiracial environment in schools, shops and playgrounds.

While Singapore achieved remarkable success in nation-building, the process has not been without challenges. One such challenge, according to Lee, was the isolation of the Muslim population. This acknowledgment reflects a commitment to addressing any issues hindering the full integration and inclusion of all communities within Singaporean society. Prior to the revival of Islamist movements, this progressed smoothly and in a positive direction. With the advent of the religious wave, however, signs of opposition started to emerge. These included the steady decline of interfaith marriages between Muslims and non-Muslims, distinct clothing choices, and the separation of food into Halal and non-Halal categories. Recognising the potential for isolation among Muslims, the government took measures to address the issue. Authorities imposed restrictions on the entry of Wahhabi Islamic preachers from Saudi Arabia and emphasised the importance of adhering to traditional Islam and the construction of mosques aligned with this approach. Clothing in certain jobs was regulated and headscarves were prohibited in educational institutions.

On migration, Singapore followed the path of America since the late twentieth century by not granting preferences based on nationality or religious affiliation. Its focus instead was on attracting talented individuals willing to embrace Singaporean identity. Looking back, at the time of Singapore's independence, its multinational and multi-religious society lacked a shared identity beyond the state itself. Lee's vision of a united nation, which had been rejected while Singapore was part of Malaysia, was realised in independent Singapore.

While challenges to the final unification of the Singaporean nation remain, by the time of Lee's passing in 2015, an overwhelming 95 per cent of the country's residents identified themselves primarily as Singaporeans. The path to forging a unified nation in Singapore has required careful planning, social engineering and an unflinching commitment to the creation of an inclusive society. By deliberately designing neighbourhoods and public spaces to reflect the country's diverse makeup, Singapore sought to ensure that the civic idea of citizenship, rather than ethnicity, served as the basis of belonging. Singapore's national policy was aimed not at erasing ethnic identities but rather at forging a unified nation that celebrated cultural diversity. The goal was to unite the population under a common Singaporean identity while preserving and cherishing the rich canvas of different cultures within the country. In striving to realise it, Singapore fostered an environment where different communities can coexist, learn from one another and play their part in collective progress of the nation.

Lee also recognised that the multi-ethnic nature of Singapore could be made to work to the island's advantage. He shrewdly deployed Singapore's ethnic communities as a bridge to the larger countries and regions from which their forebears originated. He saw the global potential and capitalised on it, cultivating strong relationships with China, India and Malaysia by leveraging Singapore's diverse ethnic makeup as a way to build deep connections with those countries. Lee was able to convince Beijing of Singapore's unique ability to serve as a link between China and the rest of South East Asia and develop close ties with Chinese leaders, including Deng Xiaoping, while positioning Singapore as a potential hub for Chinese investment and trade in the region. He recognised, ahead of others, China as a rising power in the world.

In India, Lee saw an opportunity to deepen Singapore's relationship with an ancient civilisation, a multicultural democracy, a liberalised economy with tremendous prospects for growth and a market with an extraordinary buying power. He toiled hard to strengthen ties with India through cultural and educational exchanges and encouraged the study of Indian languages and culture in Singapore. He also promoted Singapore as a destination for Indian tourism, investment and trade.

Malaysia presented a more complex challenge and relations between it and Singapore were often strained. Lee, however, recognised the importance of maintaining strong ties with Malaysia for Singapore's security and economic development. He established agreements with Malaysia in areas such as transportation and trade, while also advocating for greater understanding and cooperation between the two countries' ethnic communities.

Lee recognised early on that, alongside national identity, investing in human capital was crucial to overcoming Singapore's demographic challenges and building a prosperous nation. He made the creation of a robust education system to equip Singaporeans with the skills and knowledge needed to thrive in the global economy an urgent priority of his government.

Established in 1959, the Ministry of Education took on the critical responsibility of formulating and executing a national education policy. Lee's commitment to education was unwavering, as evidenced by the substantial portion of the national budget he allocated to this sector. Drawing from his own experiences as a graduate of Cambridge, Lee understood that education went beyond the mere transfer of knowledge and skills; it was a means to instil values and shape attitudes. Lee saw the linguistic heterogeneity of Singapore as a great advantage. It became mandatory for students to learn English—the neutral "national" language—alongside their mother tongue.

A network of outstanding universities and research institutions was created as a matter of policy. In the 1980s, Lee spearheaded the launch of the National University of Singapore (NUS) and the Nanyang Technological University (NTU). Today, NUS and NTU consistently secure top rankings among universities in Asia and worldwide. Their alumni, including Nobel laureates and influential business leaders, testify to the quality of the education. NUS has also earned recognition for its exceptional research contributions, with several of its institutes ranking among the best globally. In 2021, during a working visit to Singapore, I interacted extensively with the faculty and student body of the prestigious School of Medicine and the Centre for Quantum Technologies at the NUS. The work they are doing is not only cutting-edge, drawing Nobel laureates to the island, but also on par with, if not ahead of, anything being done in the West. The International Council of NUS Medicine is an illustrious network of leaders, scientists and experts dedicated to public healthcare, population research and treatment of various diseases, in particular cancer and diabetes. As I said in a speech I gave at the time, small states can revolutionise their science, technology and healthcare fields by collaborating with Singapore.

Research institutes such as the Institute of Molecular and Cell Biology and the Institute of Microelectronics have encouraged Singaporeans to think beyond traditional roles while bolstering the nation's reputation as an innovation hub over the course of a generation. A rigorous system of meritocracy, which rewards academic excellence and diligence, has ensured that the country's education system consistently ranks among the world's best. Singapore has become an attractive destination for foreign talent, with its universities and research institutions drawing researchers and students from all corners of the globe. And Singaporean students consistently outshine their global peers in assessments like the Programme for International Student Assessment (PISA), while the island boasts one of the highest proportions of university graduates worldwide.

* * *

Despite the limitations of geography, diversity of population and scarcity of natural resources, Singapore has emerged as one of the world's most advanced city-states. Over the course of five decades it has advanced to the vanguard of global development. With foreign reserves and gold holdings hovering in the region of $300 billion, and per capita GDP exceeding $70,000, Singapore ranks as the sixth wealthiest nation in the world. In 2019, the World Economic Forum named it the most competitive economy on earth. Its score of 84.8 on the Global Competitiveness Index (GCI) meant that it outperformed even the United States, which earned a score of 83.7. This achievement is the outcome of Singapore's excellent infrastructure, exceptional healthcare system, dynamic labour market and robust financial sector.

None of this was pre-ordained. Indeed Singapore's early years suggested a bleak and stagnant future. The separation from Malaysia in 1963 abruptly terminated its privileged access to a unified market. That loss was compounded five years later by Britain's decision to withdraw its troops from the island. The ramifications of this decision transcended matters of security. The British military presence in Singapore provided livelihoods not only to military personnel but also to the local enterprises that supported them. As a fledgling nation in the throes of development, the sudden withdrawal of this vital pillar of the economy posed a formidable challenge to the Singaporean government. The repercussions reverberated throughout the economy. Even as it sought to contain the immediate economic consequences, Singapore had to find and allocate substantial resources to bolster its own armed forces. This placed even greater strain on an already fragile financial system.

What sustained Singapore was the resolve of its leadership. Rather than seek consolation in ideology, Lee and his team acted to diversify Singapore's economic foundations; Singapore, they decided, would have to be adaptable, its workforce disciplined and hard-working, if it was to draw foreign investment and, in the long run, stimulate innovation and emerge as a thriving global hub of commerce, finance and technological advancement.

The confidence in Singapore's future radiated by Lee became a crucial factor in luring foreign investment to the country. Historically, the government had maintained an indirect involvement in the economy. The turning point came in 1968 when industrial development took on newfound importance. Singapore's economic evolution since 1959 can be divided into distinct periods, each characterised by specific strategies and objectives.

First, from 1959 to 1965, the emphasis was on industrialisation and creating an attractive environment for foreign investors. The Ministry of Finance crafted and implemented the State Development Plan for 1961-1964, which aimed to generate more employment opportunities and stimulate economic growth. A notable allocation of funds, amounting to $100 million, was dedicated to establishing the Economic Development Council in 1961. This state body played a pivotal role in driving industrialisation efforts, exploring new production avenues, providing financial support and attracting foreign expertise. Goh Keng Swee, the minister of Finance at the time, viewed industrialisation as the key to rapid economic growth and a solution to prevailing challenges.

Next, from 1966 to 1977, Singapore pursued export-oriented industrialisation and actively courted transnational corporations (TNCs). The government adopted a liberalised foreign trade policy and established free trade zones in 1966. The PAP spearheaded this export-oriented approach, relying heavily on foreign investments to finance industrialisation. To create an appealing investment climate, the government introduced financial incentives, including significant tax benefits, and positioned Singapore as a low-risk environment with peaceful labour relations. In addition to creating favourable conditions for foreign capital, the government played a role in supporting investment through the New Development Bank of Singapore, which forged partnerships and mitigated risks.

The period from 1978 to 1985 witnessed the creation and development of high-tech industries, alongside the growth of new service sectors. The already substantial influx of foreign investments doubled during this time. The expansion of offshore banking bolstered the financial sector and elevated Singapore's status as a global financial hub. These developments further diversified the economy, a key priority for the government to ensure sustained growth. The Economic Development Council opened offices in the United States, Japan, and Europe to attract investment, touting Singapore's skilled English-speaking workforce, robust infrastructure, favourable business climate, political stability and government commitment to investment security.

From 1986 to 1998, the focus shifted to completing the reconstruction of the economy by developing the national research and development (R&D) sector. R&D programmes, launched in the late 1980s, culminated in a strategic plan in 1991. The objective was to transition to a knowledge-intensive economy from what was a capital-intensive one. Singapore aspired to increase production in high-tech industries such as electronics and chemicals, and the government facilitated the transfer of labour-intensive production to neighbouring countries, including Malaysia, China, Indonesia and India.

During this period, Singapore also initiated efforts to stimulate investments abroad. The country embarked on a path towards an innovative economy, sparking development in new industries such as medicine and education. In the industrial sector, the focus shifted to aerospace, biotechnology, pharmaceuticals, electronics, petrochemicals and shipbuilding. The government implemented various initiatives to support small and medium-sized businesses engaged in innovative development.

Five notable characteristics leap out when examining Singapore's economic transformation: sustained rapid growth, a growing emphasis on exports, exceptional levels of savings and investments, low inflation and fundamental structural changes. The late 1960s marked the emergence of a coherent and well-defined development strategy. The political leadership recognised the potential of new trade flows and foreign investments in the global economy. And the government, harnessing control over key domestic markets and institutions to capitalise on emerging global opportunities, positioned itself as a planner and catalyst, overseeing a carefully managed free enterprise system as a potent and versatile instrument for driving economic progress.

Interventionism, backed by strong governmental guidelines that carried more weight than mere indicative planning, took centre stage. Unlike traditional advisory approaches, Singapore's interventionist model wielded significant power.

While market dynamics may encounter obstacles, the government's proactive intervention helped address such shortcomings. By assuming a central role in shaping trade policies, fostering meritocracy and strategically guiding Singapore's economic apparatus, the government became the linchpin of the nation's development. Singapore's leaders steered the course of the monetary system, fiscal policies and other critical aspects that underpin the nation's economic vitality. The government mined the intelligence gathered by its Economic Development

Council's foreign offices, which closely monitored global market trends. This detail and data driven approach gave Singapore an edge over its competitors. Between 1960 and 1992, Singapore underwent an astounding economic transformation. Its real gross national product skyrocketed thirteenfold, and the island's per capita income—outgrowing Spain, New Zealand and Ireland—was the seventeenth highest on earth by the early 1990s. At the same time, it built up an outstanding healthcare system and its infant mortality rates were among the lowest in the world while life expectancy steadily shot up. Employment remained at full capacity since 1973, while absolute poverty became virtually non-existent.

Singapore's economic model is exceptional. Its success rests on a combination of seemingly contradictory elements: government control, transparency, outward looking market-oriented principles, strategic investments and competent public administration. The role of the government in driving Singapore's transformation cannot be overstated. A government marred by corruption and incompetence would have sunk the country. The integrity, agility and adeptness of Singapore's administration gave wings to the high hopes of a post-colonial nation state that few believed could survive. For generations, Singapore has been blessed with a capable and stable government that is resolutely committed to development. But today it is not just the government that makes Singapore shine—it is also the people themselves. Singaporeans are now renowned globally for their diligent work ethic, pragmatism and unwavering dedication to achieving the seemingly impossible.

* * *

Singapore's foreign policy, similarly, is driven by pragmatism. A judicious balance in its international engagements has helped it evolve from a regional industrial powerhouse and a bustling port to a major financial centre and a global leader. Recognising early on the potential threats posed by its neighbouring Asian countries, Lee Kuan Yew deftly pursued collaboration with the West, especially the United States, with which he forged a close alliance. This not only bolstered Singapore's security but also served as a catalyst for its economic growth. Lee coupled his proactive outreach to the West with energetic regional diplomacy; he acquired an early reputation as a champion of regional cooperation and played a leading role in the establishment of the Association of South East Asian Nations (ASEAN). Singapore's partnerships with the West and relationships within the ASEAN framework helped position it as a key international player.

In a world where collaboration and interconnectedness are paramount, Singapore's balanced foreign policy offers a compelling model for nations seeking to navigate the complexities of an ever-changing geopolitical landscape. Singapore's track record of steering clear of internal strife and external conflicts since the end of the Second World War is a testament to its rational policymaking. The rigorous management style employed by Lee was driven by one overarching goal: fostering a dynamic and competitive economy while attracting investment. The upshot: a country that began with virtually nothing in terms of resources emerged as a powerhouse in multiple sectors. Today, Singapore is a regional heavyweight in the production of petroleum products and electronics and a global hub for shipbuilding. It has also carved out for itself a leading role in the service industries within the region.

Singapore's engagement extends to various regional and interregional forums, where it actively advocates for its interests. These platforms include the ASEAN Regional Forum, Asian Pacific Economic Community (APEC), Asia-Europe Summit, British Commonwealth, Non-Aligned Movement, East Asian and Latin American Forums, as well as the Group-77. The

United Nations (UN) and the World Trade Organization (WTO) also serve as vital arenas for Singapore's foreign policy pursuits. Singapore unabashedly advocates for principles of fairness, cooperation and global governance within these international bodies; its guiding belief is that an international stage where such principles are upheld will always favour Singapore.

But that is seldom true of international relations. Lee, who recognised this, was the first to float the idea of an international forum designed to preserve and advance the interests of small states and even took the proposal to the United Nations, where he naturally encountered a great deal of resistance. My first and only interaction with Lee occurred in Yerevan in 2009, when he visited Armenia as a state guest. The organisation was not to Singaporean standards, to put it mildly, but Lee, despite his monumental accomplishments, was generous and kind and betrayed no hint of self-importance. He impressed me with his genuinely deep knowledge of Armenia's history—from its church and language to its vast diaspora, some of which, he said with pride, had enriched Singapore by making that island their home. For instance, Singapore's national flower, a hybrid orchid known as Vanda Miss Joaquim, had been bred by Ashkhen Hovakimian, an Armenian-Singaporean. He saw in Armenia a kindred state—a small country struggling with seemingly insuperable problems—but unlike Singapore, he told me, Armenia had certain advantages: it had a long national history to draw upon, a highly educated population, a cohesive national identity and an incredibly successful diaspora. I got the impression that he was rousing his guests to quit deliberating and get marching. Much had changed a decade later, when I hosted Lee Hsien Loong, Lee's eldest son, in Yerevan. Lee had died nearly half a decade before, Lee Hsien Loong was nearing the end of his fourth term as prime minister and I was Armenia's president. Lee Hsien Loong was as bright as his father. He had served as a young man in Singapore's army before studying mathematics at Cambridge University. He obtained a first before returning home and working his way up the government. Lee Hsien Loong's background in mathematics of course made me view him favourably, but he was also indisputably a man of action and achievement. As prime minister, he had reduced the working week to five days (most Singaporeans used to work Saturdays) and supervised Singapore's swift economic recovery following the global downturn of 2008; the Marina Bay Sands development, a highly lucrative tourist attraction and a symbol of Singapore, had been his idea. But Lee Hsien Loong recognised that the international climate was darkening in dangerous ways. The escalating confrontation between the United States and China—giving rise to a new Cold War—is creating an intractable challenge for Singapore.

What began as a clash between two superpowers is now no longer a matter between the antagonists; it is affecting all the countries enmeshed in the global economic network. The reverberations hit Singapore's economy during the first quarter of 2019, coinciding with the onset of the "trade war" between Beijing and Washington. Not only did growth fall below expectations, but the island's economy also registered its slowest pace in almost a decade. The imposition of tariffs on billions of dollars' worth of goods by both sides, coupled with Washington's ban on Chinese tech giant Huawei, inflicted collateral damage on the complex global production chains in which Singapore is intricately involved.

As the political dynamic between the United States and China deteriorates, its indirect effects, rippling through the global economy, will have significant consequences for Singapore. In this sea of uncertainties, Singapore's lifeline lies in diversifying its trade and economic ties. Only by broadening its network of partners can the country navigate the stormy waters and safeguard its economic well-being.

SINGAPORE

It is hardly a secret that trade and technological restrictions are tools in the geopolitical rivalry between the United States and China. In 2019, Lee Hsien Loong delivered a thought-provoking speech at the Shangri-La Dialogue in which he astutely noted that the future of peaceful international trade hinges on the ability of the two great powers to find a resolution to their deepening conflict. Singapore, true to its adherence to pragmatism, firmly believes that there is no insurmountable ideological chasm between the United States and China. For, while China's political structure is rooted in communism, Beijing has embraced market principles. Beijing has reaped extraordinary benefits from existing multilateral institutions, by operating within their framework and refraining from imposing its communist ideology on other nations. In fact, China engages in business with countries and leaders irrespective of their reputation or position, underscoring its commitment to non-interference in the internal affairs of other nations. It ought, however, to be recognised that China is also the largest trading partner of almost all of Washington's allies in Asia, including Japan, South Korea, the Philippines, Thailand, Australia, and numerous friends and partners such as Singapore. This is why an escalation of the US-China conflict serves no one's interests.

According to Singapore, one hurdle impeding the normalisation of US-China relations lies in the shortcomings of existing multilateral institutions, particularly the World Trade Organisation. The United States, for instance, often acts unilaterally, imposing tariffs and trade sanctions that go beyond the boundaries outlined by the WTO regulations. Washington favours bilateral agreements, prioritising its own gains while paying little heed to the preservation of the multilateral system. Such a disposition understandably raises concerns among other participants in the global economic system, as the viability and fairness of this system are called into question.

Singapore, as a small state, cannot afford to overlook the interests of other nations. In bilateral negotiations, it finds itself in a relatively disadvantaged position. Singapore's leadership therefore emphasises the need to reform and bolster multilateral institutions rather than hinder their functioning. Singapore's focus now is on constructing a broader framework of regional and international cooperation—an architecture that promotes deeper economic collaboration and, in turn, not only enhances overall prosperity but also collective security.

When nations have a greater stake in each other's success, it creates the necessity to uphold a favourable and peaceful international order. This arrangement benefits both large and small nations alike. The task, then, is to cultivate a system of regional and multilateral cooperation. Such an approach would ensure that the benefits of economic cooperation go beyond mere material prosperity; they would also give rise to a more secure and harmonious global environment. Large states are evidently failing us. Small smart states, such as Singapore, give us reason for hope.

3

QATAR

FATHER AND SON

On the map, Qatar juts into the Persian Gulf like the prow of a ship. Its position can give the impression of enduring strategic significance. And yet until the eighteenth century, it barely drew the attention of the world beyond the region. Even naval maps showed a blank space. The *Sunday Times* once called it "the land God forgot". Doha was a somnolent fishing village, and pearling was the principal occupation for the peninsula's people, who were organised into networks of tribes which, over time, gave rise to prominent families.

The story of Qatar and its improbable emergence as a highly affluent and hugely influential geopolitical force is inseparable from one such family—Al Thani, or the House of Thani—and two Emirs within it: Hamad bin Khalifa Al Thani, who reigned from 1995 to 2013, and his son and successor, Tamim bin Hamad Al Thani. Long before father and son remade their country, the Al Thanis were members of the Bani Tamim tribal confederation that originated in Nejd in modern-day Saudi Arabia. They settled in Zubarah, on Qatar's north-western coast, in the early eighteenth century. Though they prospered on pearling, they remained for a period spectators to the birth and the rapid ascent of the other great dynasties that rule the Middle East to this day.

It is from Zubarah that the powerful Al Khalifa family, members of the Utub tribe that also traced its origins to Nejd, led the successful conquest of Bahrain in 1782. They consolidated their authority over Bahrain but continued to govern Qatar as a dependency. The Al Thanis flourished in Qatar and emerged as a notable family that rivalled the Al Khalifa rule, which, weakening over time by conflict and uprisings, collapsed after Bahrain and Abu Dhabi dispatched a joint naval fleet to bombard Doha in 1867.

Their joint venture—staged in violation of Bahrain's 1861 treaty with Britain,[1] which had extended British protection in exchange for guarantees that Bahrain would not forge relations with other foreign governments—had the opposite effect. In September 1868, the British Political Resident Lewis Pelly sailed to Bahrain and deposed Bahrain's ruler, Muhammad bin Khalifa Al Khalifa, and replaced him with his brother, Ali. Days later, on 12 September, Pelly entered into a treaty with Muhammad bin Thani, the leader of the Al Thani family.

The birth of Qatar as a distinct political entity was thus interwoven with the formal acknowledgement of Al Thani as its ruler by the era's pre-eminent power. It was not until 1912, and only after a period of Ottoman rule, that Qatar became a British dependency. London managed Qatar's foreign policy; domestic affairs were the Al Thanis' domain. Pearling continued to be a major driver of Qatar's economy until the mid-twentieth century. Although oil was first struck at Dukhan in 1940, war postponed its exploitation. But once they started flowing, revenues from petroleum ignited a swift transformation—social, economic and

---

[1] Treaty of Perpetual Truce of Peace and Friendship

political—that would have been difficult to contemplate only decades before.

In 1971, after exhaustive discussions to form a union with Bahrain and the constituent emirates that make up today's United Arab Emirates went nowhere, Qatar declared independence from Britain. The same year, exploration engineers off the peninsula's north-east coast made a momentous discovery: Qatar, they found, was sitting atop recoverable reserves of 900 trillion standard cubic feet—or 10 per cent of the world's known reserves—of natural gas. Many were disappointed that it wasn't oil, and hardly anyone at the time realised its importance, but it would be natural gas, and not oil, that would boost the wealth and fuel the breakneck rise of this new-born nation of 130,000 people into a wielder of influence and power vastly disproportionate to its small size.

The early decades of independence were replete with challenges as Qatar, led by Sheikh Khalifa bin Hamad Al Thani (r. 1972–1995), embarked on a mission to fortify the nation's statehood. The deluge of new wealth facilitated by fossil fuels was not an uncomplicated boon. It incubated novel problems and intractable challenges that called for a creative and visionary leadership. Qatar's transition from a society dependent on pearling into an economy thriving on oil engendered a social tumult. As old ways of life gave way to new, Qataris felt vulnerable and resentful at the growth of contract workers brought from overseas to work on the oil fields. There had been strikes by Qatari workers about this issue as early the 1950s.

This crisis led the government to enshrine a policy designed to reassure the locals by prioritising them for the employment opportunities spawned by the oil industry. A reckless government or leader (think Idi Amin of Uganda) might have attempted to achieve closure by peremptorily expelling the outsiders altogether. Rather than taking the low road of allaying Qatari fears by victimising non-Qataris, the Al Thanis elected to take the high road of fostering and strengthening the Qatari national identity with stories and symbols of the land's culture and history.

Qatar's ability to weather storms in the initial years of its independence was greatly helped by the surge in world oil prices between 1974 and 1982. The country had been well placed to meet demand ever since the peninsula's largest offshore field, Bul Hanine, became operational in 1972. The government began nationalising its relatively developed oil industry over several stages from 1973 to 1977, leading ultimately to the creation of the Qatar National Oil Company (Qatar Petroleum) in the mid-1970s. Nationalisation allowed for greater control over the industry and helped boost Qatar's standing as a major player in the global oil market.

Following the Arab-Israeli war of 1973 and the subsequent Arab oil embargo, the revenues pouring into the Persian Gulf countries' treasuries skyrocketed. The average price of crude oil leapt from $2.04 per barrel in 1971 to $32.5 in the early 1980s. The Islamic Revolution in Iran and the outbreak of war between Iran and Iraq brought a second price spike between 1979 and 1980. At the same time, the six Persian Gulf countries' combined crude oil production surged by around 80 per cent, leading to massive revenues from oil production that soared from $5.2 billion to $158 billion in that single decade.

The wealth from oil rents made it possible for Qatar to kickstart ambitious projects aimed at creating a comprehensive social welfare system. Excess oil profits were deployed to finance social services, including education, healthcare and affordable housing. The Qatari working class was guaranteed employment as labourers in the construction and maintenance of national infrastructure. New roads and ports were built, fresh water was for the first time piped into people's homes, and housing, hospitals and schools proliferated in the desert. The Emir also provided land grants, interest-free loans and government scholarships to citizens, particularly to those married to Qatari women. Since all this largesse was distributed via the Amiri Diwan, a council led by the Emir, it established a patronage system that reinforced the Emir's power both symbolically and practically.

The generosity and shrewdness of the state pacified the citizenry and the backlash against foreign workers gradually dissipated. Qatar even proceeded to grapple, slowly but sincerely, with the ignoble side of its history, becoming one of the few countries—if not the only country—in the region to acknowledge its complicity in slavery and the slave trade from Africa.

The boom of the 1970s gave way to the downturn of the 1980s as a sharp drop in oil prices resulted in a steep loss of revenues for oil-producing countries. The Cooperation Council for the Arab States of the Gulf (GCC), established in 1981, was hit particularly hard by the downturn. Qatar, heavily reliant on oil exports for government revenue, was badly affected. By 1985, its budget was in deficit and Qatar's Planning Council projected only one profitable fiscal year in the fifteen years ahead.

The economic crisis imperilled the social contract that had underpinned Qatar's wealth redistribution and job creation policies. Austerity measures—rationing of water and electricity, cuts to healthcare and other subsidies—were reluctantly implemented. Real GDP per capita in Qatar dropped by over 50 per cent—from $31,000 in 1984 to $15,000 in 1994. The severe decline provoked something approaching a political opposition for the first time.

Beset by problems, the Emir delegated more and more authority to his second son and eventual successor, the Crown Prince Sheikh Hamad bin Khalifa Al Thani. And it is to his vision that we can trace the beginning of Qatar's evolution into the formidable force that it is on today's global stage. Trained at Sandhurst, Sheikh Hamad already held several key positions in the military and government when he was promoted in the summer of 1989 to the chairmanship of the powerful Planning Council. The impression of stability sought to be conveyed by the reshuffle was, however, frustrated by regional events.

Iraq's invasion of Kuwait in 1990, plunging the region into instability just as it was emerging from a decade of war between Iraq and Iran, dashed Qatari hopes of developing its significant gas reserves. It also demonstrated to Doha the severe vulnerability of small states to larger neighbours. Qatar participated in the multinational military coalition that liberated Kuwait in 1991. But any confidence it gained from its performance in that mission was upended the following year when Saudi forces killed two Qatari soldiers and seized its border post in al-Khofous, 80 miles south of Doha. Qatar was in no position to retaliate in any meaningful way against or escape from the shade of the Saudi giant—186 times the size of Qatar. From this sequence of events, Crown Prince Sheikh Hamad absorbed his most important lesson: Qatar, by virtue of being a small state, faced a permanent security threat, and to survive, it would have to attain parity with its neighbour.

The agglomeration of crises and challenges, emphasising the urgent need to reboot the country's policies, created a climate ripe for Sheikh Hamad's ascent to power. Tensions had begun surfacing between the Emir and his heir as early as 1992, when the Crown Prince had attempted to consolidate his authority by replacing some of his father's loyal supporters with his own allies. The strained relationship between father and son came to a head on 27 June 1995, when Sheikh Hamad, taking advantage of his father's absence from the country, seized power in a bloodless coup. While this was the fourth succession dispute in the history of the Al Thani clan, the ousted ruler and his successor succeeded eventually in repairing their relationship. Sheikh Khalifa Al Thani returned to Qatar in 2004 and was decorated with the honorary title of "Father Emir".

QATAR

Under Sheikh Hamad's relatively youthful leadership, Qatar would go on to leverage its significant energy resources and strategic location to project its influence on the world stage and establish itself as a major player in regional and international affairs. But the new Emir did not exactly enjoy a honeymoon period after taking office. Low oil prices and budget deficits, ravaging the economy for years, dipped further, which showed no a sign of a revival for several years after Sheikh Hamad came to power. The grim economic outlook was aggravated by the Gulf states' refusal to recognise Sheikh Hamad's legitimacy as a ruler. His streak of independence, and his singular emphasis on securing autonomy for Qatar from Saudi dominance, naturally did not endear him to his neighbours.

In 1995, rumours of a Saudi Arabian plot to reinstate the deposed Emir Khalifa bin Hamad Al Thani swirled in the region. The Qatari delegation withdrew in protest from the final session of the GCC's annual meeting and launched a partial boycott of the grouping. Rather than back down, the United Arab Emirates and Bahrain reacted by welcoming Khalifa bin Hamad on a regional tour with pomp and ceremony. Bahrain's Crown Prince Hamad bin Isa Al Khalifa further incensed Qatar by escorting Khalifa bin Hamad in a Bahraini naval vessel within sight of the Qatari coastline.

This provocation, deepening regional rifts, was followed in 1996 with the most serious threat to Sheikh Hamad's nascent reign in the form of a countercoup allegedly backed by Saudi Arabia. It was foiled before a single shot was fired—and more than thirty alleged plotters, including Sheikh Hamad's cousin, the minister of Economy Sheikh Hamad bin Jassim bin Jaber Al Thani, were sentenced to prison for life—but its message was unmistakable. To survive, Sheikh Hamad would first have to shore up his authority within the sprawling ruling family.

In the absence of strong political or public opposition, power in Qatar was concentrated in the hands of a small elite made up of members of the ruling family and a select number of technocratic elites who could use their family ties to key state structures. Sheikh Hamad's early recognition of the fact that in Qatar the most consequential opposition to the ruler emanated not out of social pressure from below but arose from within the ruling family was what helped him to cement his reign. What struck me in my interactions with him was his insistence on involving his family. His daughters or sons were always present in some capacity—as notetakers or support staff—in his meetings. It was his way of instituting a tradition of inclusion and encouraging responsibility.

Sheikh Hamad went ahead with a series of liberal reforms in Qatar. He abolished media censorship in 1995, blessed the creation of the Al Jazeera satellite television network in 1996 and, perhaps most significant of all, oversaw the outright dissolution of the Ministry of Information in 1998. In March 1999, the Emir went a step further by promulgating a procedure for electing 21 members to the Central Municipal Council every four years. Then, in April 2003, he called a national referendum to ratify a new constitution that laid down the law of succession—only the ruler's son can be the legitimate heir—and enshrined civil, political and social rights. The charter's most significant achievement was the establishment of an elected parliament, the Advisory Council or Majlis Al-Shura, which represented a major step towards gradual but greater democratisation of Qatar. Approved by 98 per cent of the electorate, the constitution was adopted in 2004. The same year, Sheikh Hamad implemented sweeping reforms to Qatar's judicial and educational systems, as well as labour laws, and began opening up the country's energy sector to foreign direct investment and foreign technology.

The 1996 countercoup attempt underscored the interconnectedness of internal and external political spheres in Qatar and demonstrated the need for dependable external support. Small countries possess a remarkable ability to pursue an autonomous foreign policy that deftly balances influence and independence, all the while avoiding the pitfalls of rigid coalitions or total neutrality. The highest priority for these nations is securing their safety, which can prove challenging given their limited resources. This is typically achieved through flexible alliances or partnerships with other nations. Alternatively, smaller states may choose to follow a regional leader, even if doing so might be perceived as a threat, or opt to balance power by forming coalitions with other players or engaging with international institutions that can counterbalance larger rivals. The challenge for small nations, then, is to strike a delicate balance between neutrality and participation in regional associations, between involvement in alliances and maintaining the level of autonomy that is critical to their national identity.

Sheikh Hamad energetically strengthened relations with the United States, which had extended support to him when he staged the coup in June 1995 and, in contrast to the Gulf leaders, had immediately recognised his power. In 1996 Sheikh Hamad ordered the construction of the sprawling Al Udeid Air Base at a cost of $1bn. Its purpose was not to service Qatar's air force—it did not have one at the time—but to lure Washington to Qatar. In pursuit of this end, Qatar even allowed the US to store equipment earmarked for the invasion of Iraq at its Sayliya military facility. In 2003, the Americans moved their major military operations from Saudi Arabia to Qatar, eventually converting Al Udeid into the largest American military base in the Middle East. It did not please everybody, but it guaranteed Qatar's security. What distinguishes small *smart* states from states that are merely small is their willingness to recognise their vulnerabilities, steal a march on their adversaries and invest in the future. Qatar did all three.

What Qatar did not do is place all its eggs in a single basket. Instead, it perfected the "hedging strategy". A nuanced approach to foreign policy adopted by other small states in the region, it involves building multi-level and multi-format coalitions that can pivot quickly to respond to any number of uncertain challenges and threats. By doing so, small states can maintain a high degree of autonomy in decision-making, even in the face of confrontations with their coalition partners. Qatar, for example, has cultivated relations with Israel and Iran, while forging a close alliance with Turkey to confront Riyadh and Abu Dhabi in several Middle Eastern arenas. Traditionally, small states have tended to *respond* to challenges. Qatar, dispensing with convention, has sought to *influence* international politics to pre-empt its rivals. Qatar's close political relationship with the United States is cautiously balanced with trade and economic ties with Japan, China and India, as well as carefully calibrated flirtations with Russia. It has foreign policy plans that can seem contradictory to outsiders and go beyond cooperation with its immediate neighbours—something that makes it atypical among small countries.

Qatar's unorthodox foreign policy is enabled by its natural gas reserves and its ability to export them to foreign markets. Sheikh Hamad's rise to power in 1995 became the turning point for the country. In order to secure additional sources of income for Qatar and bolster its position in an antagonistic environment, the new Emir supervised the rapid construction of liquefied natural gas (LNG) production facilities. Ignoring the counsel of those who dismissed the utility of gas, he poured $20 billion into the project. In another first, he bypassed traditional partners and lenders and reached out to Japan for help in developing essential infrastructure. Tokyo advanced significant private and state assistance with engineering and marketing and entered into the earliest sales contracts for LNG with Qatar. Another partner was Exxon Mobil. It was a fortuitous association because among the Exxon executives who helped Qatar was Rex W. Tillerson, who would go on to become the US Secretary of State just as Qatar faced the most concerted regional effort to curb its influence. The first shipment of LNG from Qatar to Japan, completed in 1997, laid down the foundation for the peninsula's economic prosperity, domestic stability, autonomy from its neighbours and geopolitical manoeuvrability.

Revenues from natural gas supplied the material basis for—and sustained—Qatar's expanding international influence. In fact, by 2020, Qatar had exported $45.1 billion worth of natural gas, a figure that accounted for 61 per cent of all its exports. Between 2016 and 2019, the export of hydrocarbons generated up to 55 per cent of the government's revenues, a number that soared to a staggering 82 per cent when combined with dividends from Qatar Petroleum. These significant financial resources, coupled with a small population that shares in the earnings from hydrocarbon exports, have given Qatar the means to pursue a costly "hedging" policy by which it retains significant independence even as part of coalition associations.

It would be facile, however, to ascribe Qatar's success purely to the existence of natural resources. There are other large nations with comparable reserves but they are nowhere near as affluent or influential as the tiny Gulf peninsula. Qatar's success is down to its ability to anticipate the value of its resources, find the most suitable partners to exploit them, build the means to turn them into an exportable commodity and then cultivate reliable markets for the commodity.

Natural gas to Qatar has become a tool for ordering various aspects of the country's life. But, against the backdrop of global energy markets, Qatar's determination to dominate the gas sector stems from three key national objectives: sustainable economic growth, political stability and foreign policy independence.

By the mid-2000s, Qatar's significant financial resources established it as a "soft power". It had by then developed a reputation as a regional peacemaker and international mediator—the neutral ground upon which warring parties from Lebanon, Sudan and Somalia could meet and resolve their differences. In 2008, as major states plunged into economic crisis, Qatar brokered a landmark peace deal, called the Doha Agreement, between rival factions in Lebanon. The region erupted with effusive praise for the peninsula, billboards carrying messages of thanks appeared all over Beirut and ice cream shops sold scoops named after the truce. But what distinguished Qatar for me was its hesitation to rest on the laurels it had earned. I had just then returned to the world of diplomacy, having been asked by the Armenian government to oversee its mission in London, and observed closely Qatar's diplomatic push. The joke in diplomatic circles was that the only way to reach Hamad bin Jassim bin Jaber Al Thani (not the same man as the coup-launcher), Qatar's powerful foreign minister and later prime minister, was to call his pilot. HBJ, as he is known, seemed permanently to be jetting between conflict-riddled nations in an effort to make peace and cement Qatar's reputation as a reliable international mediator. In 2010, he achieved a major breakthrough when Qatar brokered a truce between Sudan and the Darfur rebels, bringing respite to the survivors of a conflict that had claimed half a million lives.

Qatar also engaged in what is called "chequebook diplomacy", making investments not only for economic returns but also political gains. At home it raised institutions dedicated to diplomacy and mediation, including the Qatar Fund for Development, which provides funding for humanitarian and development projects around the world, and the Doha Institute for Graduate Studies, which offers a range of courses in diplomacy and conflict resolution. At the same time, it also extended its hospitality to the Palestinian group Hamas, an assortment of Muslim Brotherhood leaders and Taliban representatives on the same soil as the largest American military base in the region.

The push to project influence did not come at the expense of Qataris, who numbered among the citizens of one of the world's richest countries by 2015. Rather, it was complemented by a massive effort to modernise life at home. Without vacating the cultural middle-ground it occupied—more modest, socially, than the UAE, and more tolerant and open, religiously, than Saudi Arabia before Mohammed bin Salman—Qatar experienced something akin to a cultural revolution. The person who oversaw it was Sheikha Moza bint Nasser Al-Missned, the wife of Sheikh Hamad. The Qatar Foundation, which she launched in 1995, has over the years spent billions of dollars on education, science and community programmes. In 2016 Sheikha Moza opened the Sidra Medical and Research Centre, a state-of-the-art women's and children's hospital and research centre with an $8 billion endowment, in Doha. It was a source of pride for me that Sheikha Moza's chief advisor on the project was Lord (Ara) Darzi, a world-renowned academic surgeon, former minister in the Labour-led British government, co-chair of the Institute of Global Health Innovation at Imperial College, London, and a luminary of the Armenian diaspora. Major American universities—among them Georgetown and Carnegie Mellon—have been lured to Qatar by Sheikha Moza, who has overseen the creation of the Education City outside Doha. But her most impressive achievement, to me, is the Qatar National Library, and I don't say this because it was another Armenian—Vartan Gregorian, the "saviour" of the New York Public Library— who helped Sheikha Moza give it shape. As national libraries go, Qatar's is a marvel to behold. The surge of admiration I felt as I browsed its collections, strolled through its great halls and took in its public events after its opening was mixed with a tinge of envy: here, I felt, is a model for all small states. There is hardly a library built in the past decade that can match the ambition, vision or capaciousness of the QNL.

Sheikha Moza's endeavours have been matched by her daughters'. Sheikha Hind, her younger daughter, has distinguished herself as the deputy at the Qatar Foundation. Her older daughter, Sheikha Mayassa, was appointed chairperson of Qatar Museums in 2006. Her annual budget for acquisitions—$1 billion—was an early indication of the seriousness Qatar attached to culture. And in the decade and a half since her appointment, Sheikha Mayassa has presided over Qatar's transformation into a leading centre of art in the Middle East. To motivate young Qatari artists with aspirations to break into the West, she has acquired contemporary works by Andy Warhol, Richard Serra, Damien Hirst and Jeff Koons, among others, for public galleries such as the Arab Museum of Modern Art in Doha. These works, however, constitute merely one facet of a grand vision to build cultural institutions in the region. In 2008, Qatar inaugurated the Museum of Islamic Art, a staggering edifice situated on an artificial peninsula off the Doha Bay. To signal their openness, the Qataris deliberately chose a non-Muslim architect—the late Chinese-American I.M. Pei—for the project. That openness is the basis of such initiatives as the Doha Forum and the WISE summit, two platforms at which I had the pleasure of participating and which have helped establish Qatar as a hub of intellectual deliberation and exchange.

Natural gas has helped Qatar stand apart from other Gulf countries, where oil dominates the economy, and made it a major player in the gas market with geopolitical clout on a par with Saudi Arabia's role in the world oil trade. Qatar is often referred to as "Saudi Arabia with gas"—a comparison that, while flawed, highlights the country's emergence as a significant player in the energy sector. This unique status raises Qatar above the other small countries in the region.

Qatar and Saudi Arabia share a common ability to influence the hydrocarbon market, but their methods differ. While Saudi Arabia alters the volume of supply to affect the market, Qatar changes the export flows, particularly between Europe and Asia. This approach has enabled the country to maintain a degree of autonomy from its neighbours in the GCC, where Saudi Arabia wields significant power as the group's leader. Qatar has been able to pursue a foreign policy focused on building strong relationships with external players and retain a high degree of independence and influence outside of the region.

The perils of this admixture of wealth, clout, an assertive sense of its own distinctness and a restless pursuit of autonomy became apparent with the "Arab Spring" uprisings of 2011-12, which coincided with Qatar's emergence as a confident actor on the global stage. One enduring aspect of Qatar's quest for independence was its patronage of the Muslim Brotherhood, an Islamist movement that originated in Egypt in 1928 and gained a steady following and foothold across the Arab world. The Brotherhood did not advocate theocratic rule, but its emphasis on political Islam *and* democracy made it a target of both secular dictatorships and puritanical monarchies in the Arab world. Qatar, rather than conform to the prevailing elite consensus in the region, followed a different path by supporting the Brotherhood. It granted Muslim Brothers political refuge, financial aid and diplomatic assistance, and even turned the Brotherhood's most charismatic preachers into celebrity televangelists by giving them shows on Al Jazeera.

All of this provoked and perturbed Qatar's neighbours, but Doha was driven by a cold logic that was in perfect harmony with its strategic ambitions. By sponsoring an Islamist movement that enjoyed a significant measure of unstated sympathy across the Arab world, Qatar wagered that it would emerge the pre-eminent player if and when the Brotherhood acquired power via a people's mandate. It was a kind of investment in the future. And that future materialised when Arab masses rose up against their rulers. The mutinies that were labelled the "Arab Spring" by the press were internally disordered, chaotic and messy. What united them was a profound citizenly rage. It was the Brotherhood—and its epigones and acolytes—that converted people's anger into coherent political action. Qatar's bet seemed to pay off. Egypt's indurated military dictatorship bowed out in 2011. And when Egypt held an election in 2012—the first fair vote since 1950—the Muslim Brotherhood emerged victorious. Suddenly, the most powerful country in the Arab world had a popularly elected government that venerated Qatar.

This is the moment that Qatar's neighbours realised just how far the nation they had once dismissed as a minute and insignificant peninsula had travelled. Sponsoring the government in Egypt and backing armed opposition groups in Syria and Libya, Qatar was shaping regional events. Even though their objectives aligned with Qatar's in Syria and Libya, its larger neighbours worried if theirs would be the next regime to be brought down by the forces sustained by Doha. The blowback was swift. Mohammed Morsi was deposed from office and detained by the Egyptian military just over a year after he took the oath of the presidency. Egypt was the physical headquarters and the intellectual fount of the Brotherhood; its removal from power sent a clear message to the region. Qatar's bet had failed.

But the mood within Qatar was far from despondent. If anything, it was optimistic and hopeful. The reason was the country's young leadership. In March 2013, Sheikh Hamad outsmarted his rivals by doing something unprecedented not only in his country but also the region: he voluntarily abdicated and handed the reins to his son and heir, Sheikh Tamim. It was a decision informed no doubt by the lesson he learnt during his own turbulent early years after seizing power in 1995: stability in Qatar is contingent upon stability in the ruling family. The Emir exited with his entire cabinet—including HBJ, the formidable prime minister—and gave his successor a superabundant exchequer, a clean slate and a fresh start. As a politician and businessman, I've seen countless instances where patriarchs "leave" their position without ever actually vacating it. This was perhaps the first authentic voluntary resignation I witnessed. I can attest to the fact it was a wise decision.

Sheikh Tamim, all of thirty-three when he took office, stood out in a region where the rulers tended to be grizzled old men. Educated at Sherborne and Harrow, Tamim was groomed for leadership only after his older brother, Crown Prince Jassim bin Hamad bin Khalifa Al Thani, relinquished the title in 2003. Although he was trained, like his father and brother, at the Royal Military Academy Sandhurst, Sheikh Tamim is more a diplomat than a military man. He is a polished speaker and, even more importantly, a keen listener who subjects all that is spoken around him to minute internal analysis before offering his response, as I found in my extensive interactions with him over the years.

Sheikh Tamim's first trial as Emir came in 2014, when Saudi Arabia, Bahrain and the UAE, in an effort to intensify their pressure on Qatar and test its new ruler, accused it of interference in their internal affairs and withdrew their ambassadors from Doha. The standoff, lasting nine months, was defused when the Emir offered his personal reassurances to investigate their concerns. That predicament, in retrospect, was a preview of the full-blown crisis that erupted three years later, in 2017, when Egypt joined Saudi Arabia, Bahrain and the UAE in a diplomatic boycott of Qatar. Qatar was handed a list of conditions—from shutting down the Al Jazeera television network to ending diplomatic relations with Iran, from terminating military cooperation with Turkey to paying reparations to its neighbours and falling in line with their policies—and given a ten-day deadline to satisfy them.

The sole land crossing into Qatar, from Saudi Arabia, was sealed off and the peninsula was effectively isolated. Qatar's regional ostracisation was accompanied by international condemnation. The quartet's trump card, as it were, was President Donald Trump, who had toured the region weeks before the boycott of Qatar was announced. He not only endorsed the blackballing of Qatar, but even claimed credit for it. Rumours went out in the region that the US was considering closing down its base in Qatar.

Qatar could not comply with its neighbours' demands without surrendering its sovereignty. Given that its offshore gas field is shared with Iran, it cannot snap its relationship with Tehran without jeopardising its most important source of revenue. At the same time, the embargo imposed by the quartet threatened its survival. Besieged and assailed from all directions, its land borders closed and its air and sea links severely curtailed, Qatar's most immediate challenge was keeping up imports of food, medicine and other essentials. It was not unreasonable to expect Qatar to submit.

Sheikh Tamim, however, confounded his observers. Rather than bend or back down, he deepened Qatar's relations with Turkey. Ankara became a major supplier of fresh produce, dairy products and other food items. Qatar turned to Iran and Oman for sea access, importing goods through ports in those countries. Thousands of cattle were airlifted from Europe to Qatar to create, almost from scratch, a dairy industry. In Washington, Rex Tillerson, the old Qatar hand whom Trump had appointed his Secretary of State, argued for keeping Doha in the US fold. Qatar's "chequebook diplomacy" helped. Qatar went out of its way to secure its relationship with Washington. It became the first Gulf country to sign a Memorandum of Understanding with the US on counterterrorism and held a strategic dialogue with Washington on combatting terrorism. Within two years of the blockade, Sheikh Tamim received a warm reception from President Trump in the White House.

Qatar made clever use of its wealth to bypass the blockade. But the blockade also quickened Qatar's diversification of its economy. Having for decades relied heavily on its oil and gas exports, it revised its economic strategy and focused on tourism, finance and technology. It invested heavily in its infrastructure and embarked on a massive expansion of the Hamad International Airport, turning it into one of the largest and most modern airports in the world. This helped to offset the effects of the blockade on Qatar Airways, which had been forced to cancel many of its flights due to the restrictions imposed by the quartet. The airport also served as a hub for other airlines, providing an alternative route for travellers and goods. In yet another sign of "hedging", it also poured significant investment into renewable energy. Its goal is to generate 20 per cent of its electricity from renewable sources by 2030.

Rather than plunge Qatar into chaos, the blockade brought stability to Qatar. Ordinary Qataris—once members of tribes indistinguishable from their neighbours—asserted their national identity by rallying behind their flag and leader. Without any official directive, Sheikh Tamim's portraits proliferated: people put them in their homes, artists painted them on public buildings.

Wealth did not breed complacency in Sheikh Tamim, who led Qatar through the blockade with the same fortitude as his father. But aware of the potential pitfalls of relying solely on gas exports, his government has expended considerable energy on actualising the strategic vision and long-term development goals advanced in 2008 by the Qatar National Vision 2030 (QNV 2030), a comprehensive roadmap for achieving a diversified and sustainable economy through the implementation of the United Nations' Sustainable Development Goals (SDGs). This forward-thinking document has functioned as the conceptual basis for social and economic reform of Qatar.

The QNV 2030 plan is founded on four developmental pillars: economic, social, environmental and human. Resting on these pillars, the plan outlines a variety of objectives and initiatives that are intended to transform the nation in significant ways.

One of the key objectives of the QNV 2030 plan is to diversify the Qatari economy away from reliance on hydrocarbon exports. The plan aims to achieve this by developing new industries, including information technology, renewable energy and tourism. Additionally, it seeks to foster a culture of entrepreneurship, with the creation of a conducive business environment, providing opportunities for Qatari citizens to start and grow businesses. The QNV 2030 also emphasises social development, with a goal of ensuring that all Qatari citizens have access to high-quality education, healthcare and social services. It endorses gender equality and supports the growth and development of Qatari youth through a range of initiatives, including sports and cultural activities.

The QNV 2030 strives to balance economic growth with sustainable resource management. The plan includes initiatives to protect and preserve Qatar's natural resources, including air, water and land, and promote renewable energy and reduce greenhouse gas emissions, with a goal of achieving carbon neutrality by 2050. Finally, the QNV 2030 emphasises human development, with a goal of ensuring that all Qatari citizens have the skills and knowledge necessary to succeed in the twenty-first century economy. It proposes a range of initiatives to promote lifelong learning, including expanded access to higher education and vocational training, as well as supporting research and development in key areas.

Despite challenges and setbacks along the way—the most significant being the blockade—the Qatari government has continued to invest in the plan's initiatives and has successfully diversified its economy away from hydrocarbon exports.

With a well-developed conceptual framework, the Qatari government is paving the way for a more durable economy. And its capacity to adapt was demonstrated by the 2022 FIFA World Cup. After years of anticipation and controversy, the most important event on the footballing calendar proved to be a successful tournament that exceeded expectations. It not only spotlighted Qatar's ability to host a major international sporting event but also its willingness to listen to criticism and address human rights concerns.

From the outset, the World Cup was surrounded by controversy, particularly concerning the treatment of migrant workers who were helping to build the tournament's stadia and other infrastructure. Human rights organisations castigated Qatar for its treatment of these workers, who often experienced poor living conditions and inadequate wages.

In response, the Qatari government launched a series of labour reforms aimed at improving the working conditions of migrant workers. These reforms included the abolition of the kafala system, which had tied workers to their employers, and the introduction of a minimum wage. The government also established an independent commission to investigate labour conditions and ensure that workers' rights were being protected. Workers were granted the right to change employment and leave without informing their employers. Those who never paused to criticise the venue of the World Cup remained blind to the changes it actually brought.

The success of the tournament itself also helped to change perceptions of Qatar. Despite concerns about the weather and the country's lack of experience in hosting major international events, the tournament was widely praised for its organisation and hospitality. The stadia and other infrastructure were completed on schedule and to a high standard, and fans and players with whom I interacted were full of praise for the quality of the facilities, which were vastly superior to anything in Europe. The country's decision to allow alcohol consumption in designated areas around the stadia turned out to be a smart decision because it minimised disruption and maximised the enjoyment of the spectators. People who had travelled long distances were able to watch multiple games during the day and relax with a drink or attend a party in the vicinity of the stadia in the evenings.

Something else that was notable about the tournament was the host nation's openness, contrary to the impression sought to be created in the West, to cultural exchange and dialogue. Qatar's decision to allow female fans to attend matches and the presence of female referees and coaches on the field demonstrated the country's commitment to gender equality—a promise outlined in QNV 2030.

Speaking for myself, a lover of football, I have attended countless tournaments over the decades. But in Qatar, as the final match of the World Cup came to a close, I found myself filled with joy and pride, along with countless others around the world. "The tournament is coming to an end," I told a friend, "but its effect will undoubtedly be felt for years to come." Qatar, as a small state, faced doubt and criticism from the world. Instead of backing down, however, it rose to the occasion and delivered a truly remarkable event.

Throughout the tournament, Qatar demonstrated its expertise in organisation, logistics and hospitality, turning Doha into a global village where people from diverse backgrounds came together to celebrate their love of football. At a time when the world was facing the uncertainties caused by war and economic turmoil, the World Cup, bringing together people from all walks of life, was a miracle to behold. This accomplishment has become a source of national pride for Qatar and is now deeply intertwined with the country's identity and heritage. It has also shown what small states, with smart thinking and perseverance, can do. Going forward, Singapore might offer a useful guide for the utilisation of the impressive infrastructure raised by Qatar for the World Cup.

Over the years, as Qatar underwent a dizzying transformation, I engaged in deep discussions with Sheikh Hamad and Sheikh Tamim about economics, culture, technology and religion. We also debated and explored the contours of a Small States Club. Sheikh Tamim's principal preoccupations throughout were the security of the state, economic prosperity and peace in the Gulf. Today, a long period of regional strife is giving way to an age of cooperation among Arab states. This harmony can only enhance the global influence of the region. And given its remarkable journey so far, Qatar's place in the region as neutral ground that shapes global politics and economy is assured.

4

UNITED ARAB EMIRATES

A DEAL IN THE DESERT

On a crisp autumn evening in 2021, my beloved wife and I decided, after forty-five years of blissful marriage, to have a church wedding. Nouneh and I first met at school. I was fifteen, and she, a year younger than me, was one of my closest friends. I had already won several academic prizes for science and maths, but Nouneh was the person around whom I felt utterly grounded. She had read everything, and yet her luminous intelligence existed alongside an easygoing personality and understated manner. As the years rolled on, and we graduated from school and entered university, our friendship gradually blossomed into love.

Nouneh's family were Armenians from Georgia; her father was a newspaper editor and her mother a distinguished teacher. Persuading our families proved to be relatively easy. The toughest obstacle to realising our romantic dreams was the state. Its position was that we could not have a religious ceremony. The church holds a special place in the hearts of Armenians, members of the oldest Christian state in the world, but the Soviet Union regarded faith with disdain and suspicion. Strictly speaking, we *could* have had a church wedding—but only at the expense of our careers: we would have instantly been blacklisted, and neither of us could have had anything resembling a viable career. Pragmatism is a trait that has served Armenians well. And so, after some discussions with our family and friends, we had a civil wedding, in 1978.

Forty-three years later, I decided to give Nouneh the church wedding of which we—like countless other Armenian couples—had cruelly been deprived. That afternoon, I wrapped up the third Summit of Minds, a forum that drew business leaders, writers, politicians and investors from around the world to Dilijan, the stunningly beautiful town in the Armenian mountains that had once served as a retreat for Soviet leaders. The Summit of Minds was an important element of my overall ambition to restore Armenia's ancient status as a commercial and intellectual hub in Eurasia and convert it into an economic force and a crucible of innovation in the twenty-first century. The third edition of the Summit, held in person following the Covid-induced global lockdowns of the preceding year, had been a remarkable success. Delegates, arriving from every corner of the world, were thrilled to be able to rub elbows and exchange ideas with others in a setting that encouraged discussion. In the final session of the event, which I personally moderated, the Nobel-winning theoretical physicist Kip Thorne spoke arrestingly about space, science and music. We even discussed religion. Kip disclosed that he is an atheist, a fact which prompted me to reminisce about my debates with my late friend Stephen Hawking about the existence of God. I would tell Stephen that I, the citizen of a godless empire, could feel the presence of God in science.

Once the Summit drew to a close, Nouneh and I, accompanied by our children and grandchildren, drove the short distance from Dilijan to Tavush, a veritable paradise on earth. The historic grandeur of Tavush, home to the monastery complex of Haghartsin, is set against the majestic backdrop supplied by the beautiful Armenian mountains. The result is sublime. Haghartsin is an architectural marvel of the Armenian medieval era. Its precise origins are not fully ascertained, but historians agree that it was built over three centuries—from the tenth to the thirteenth—even as Armenia was shaken by invasions and earthquakes. After its completion, Haghartsin became a centre of knowledge and culture in Armenia and the Caucasus.

Haghartsin's splendour lay in its rich historical tapestry and the harmonious union it forges between its architecture and the enchanting landscapes that envelope it. Like so many Armenian monasteries dating from the seventh to the thirteenth centuries, Haghartsin belongs to the esteemed *katoghike* family of dome-shaped structures. These typically rely on four commanding columns as the fulcrum of their design—a centralising force within their architectural symphony. It is not uncommon to find monastic ensembles housing multiple churches and chapels, a tradition upheld by Haghartsin. In this hallowed sanctuary, three churches stand in solemn unity: the Church of the Holy Mother of God, St Gregory's and St Stephan's. The oldest among them, St Gregory's, was established in the tenth century. And beneath the Church of the Holy Mother of God lies a concealed subterranean vault, accessible to none save the monks themselves—an impenetrable sanctuary safeguarding sacred relics. Another secret subterranean passage offers a clandestine escape route for worshippers.

Inside, among its many wonders, is the refectory hall, a paragon of medieval Armenian architecture. Every aspect of it, designed with mathematical precision and economic sensibility, heightens the monastery's magnificence. Dormer-like domes, perched atop the complex, invite sunbeams that illuminate the expanse of the refectory. Standing upon a dozen columns—each symbolising one of the twelve Disciples of Christ—the refectory is a testament to the monastery's multifaceted role as not just a spiritual centre but also a fount of intellectual enlightenment. Once upon a time, a vibrant community of 300 monks found solace within Haghartsin's sacred precincts. Today, its halls are still filled with the hypnotic echoes of prayer. When we arrived that afternoon, the congregants in the halls spontaneously applauded us. As a friend said to me, Nouneh and I, as the First Couple of Armenia, were symbolically undoing a wrong inflicted upon Armenia by the Soviet Union by renewing our vows in the church.

But why *that* particular church? The reason we selected Haghartsin was not purely because it is a symbol of Armenia's cultural sophistication. It is also an emblem of the enduring friendship between Armenia and the United Arab Emirates. Haghartsin's exquisite condition after being in existence for a millennium is a tribute to the generosity of the UAE—specifically of my friend Sheikh Dr Sultan bin Mohammed al-Qasimi, the erudite, literary and enormously large-hearted Emir of Sharjah. Indeed, so deeply devoted is Sheikh Sultan to learning that I have often wondered if he might not, in a different age, have felt perfectly at home among the knowledge-seeking medieval monks who had made Haghartsin their home. When I saw him in 2018 in my capacity as president, Sheikh Sultan's cerebral and inquisitive mind was on powerful display. He quizzed me about Armenia and its culture, food and religion. During the meeting I explained the utility of a direct air-route between Yerevan and Sharjah. He immediately approved the idea. When I returned to Yerevan, I found that he had sent me a boxful of books written by himself. I savoured them in the evening hours during the pandemic.

That afternoon at Haghartsin, after Nouneh and I renewed our vows, I whispered thanks to Sheikh Sultan. How many people had any idea that this antique monument to Christ in the oldest Christian state in the world owed its shipshape appearance to the benefaction of a Muslim Arab?

UNITED ARAB EMIRATES

* * *

It is this fraternal spirit that truly sustains the United Arab Emirates, a state willed into existence against all the odds by a visionary and truly humane leader. Sheikh Zayed bin Sultan Al Nahyan grew up in a land that was poor and undeveloped. Agriculture, fishing and pearl-diving supported the economy, and people wandered the desert in pursuit of pasture. Tribal hierarchy was determined by the number of camels owned by a family. The Al Nahyans, as the leading members of the region and the ruling family of Abu Dhabi, were said to own 180 horses and 400 camels at the time of Zayed's birth, in 1918. Zayed was the fourth son of Sultan Al Nahyan, and his large family, which had status but no real income or wealth, was being winnowed down by fratricidal bloodletting in which several of his uncles had lost their lives. Zayed's mother, Salama bint Butti Al Qubaisi, was a remarkable woman—the kind of behind-the-scenes person who changes the course of history by making a brief appearance. As the elders in the Al Nahyan clan killed each other, Salama decided to act. One day, she assembled her young children in a room and extracted a promise from them: no sibling would harm another. Zayed never wavered from that oath.

When Zayed was about thirty, the British traveller Wilfred Thesiger encountered him in the sands of Abu Dhabi. "He was a powerfully built man," Thesiger later recalled. "He had a strong intelligent face, with steady observant eyes, and his manner was quiet but masterful. He wore a dagger and cartridge belt; his rifle lay on the sand beside him." The weapon was perhaps an ornament. "Zayed is a Bedu," his friends told Thesiger. "He knows about camels, can ride like one of us, and knows how to fight." This seemingly vivid description had the defect of being somewhat reductive. Zayed was also an avid learner. Although his early education was primarily rooted in religious study, he was

71

always curious, and absorbed the minutest details of countries he toured in later life. He was a man of profound depths and an unimpeachable character—something that became apparent in the immediate aftermath of the discovery of oil in Abu Dhabi.

As the fourth son, Zayed never harboured aspirations of succeeding his father or ruling his country. Instead, he loyally served his older brother, Sheikh Shakbut, who in 1946 appointed him governor of Al Ain region, with its capital Al Ain City on the eastern side of Tawam oasis—the subject of intense territorial dispute between Abu Dhabi and its powerful neighbour, Saudi Arabia. Five years into his governorship, Zayed was offered a bribe of £30 million—£700 million in today's money—to allow Aramco to prospect for oil in the contested region. Zayed turned down the money.

In 1955, Zayed travelled to Switzerland to testify before the arbitration tribunal convened to resolve the Buraimi crisis—and returned with plans to recreate in Abu Dhabi the successful educational and medical institutions he had studied in Europe. He had no interest in betraying his brother—he never forgot the promise to his mother—but it became crushingly obvious as petrodollars flowed into Abu Dhabi that Sheikh Shakbut was clearly not cut out for the job. He not only refused to spend the enormous revenues from oil exports on essential projects, but, distrustful of banks, he proceeded to stash vast amounts of cash in boxes under his bed, where they were reportedly devoured by rats. This habit eventually became untenable; Abu Dhabi, despite becoming rich on paper, had none of the fruits of wealth. In August 1966, the ruling family, with British encouragement, deposed Sheikh Shakbut and anointed Zayed the new ruler. It was a peaceful—almost a civil—transfer of power, and Zayed lost no time in winning the confidence and affection of his dethroned brother.

What truly distinguished Zayed, however, was his political genius. Prior to the formation of the UAE, the region, on the south-eastern tip of the Arabian Peninsula along the Persian Gulf, consisted of seven independent sheikhdoms: Abu Dhabi, Dubai, Sharjah, Ajman, Umm Al Quwain, Fujairah and Ras Al Khaimah. In the early nineteenth century, the British established treaties with some of the coastal emirates, including the "Trucial States", a term that owes its origin to the collective truce at which they arrived. The British extended their protection to the Trucial States in exchange for control over their foreign affairs. By the 1960s, the sheikhdoms of Abu Dhabi and Dubai emerged as the dominant powers—the former had significant oil reserves, while the latter established itself as a prosperous trading port.

In the late 1960s, Britain, undergoing its own diminution from an Empire into a junior partner of the United States, announced its decision to withdraw from the region and floated the parting idea of a federation as a means to preserve the security and prosperity of the sheikhdoms. It was by no means an easy sell. The obstacles were many, and the complications myriad. Would the union have one military force, and if so, who would command it? What would its currency be? Would it be a centralised state with federal taxes? Where would the capital be located? Qatar and Bahrain, envisaged as members of the proposed union, decided to go their own way. And the remaining sheikhdoms weren't so certain, either. Luckily for the unborn generations who are today citizens of one of the wealthiest states in the world, Zayed was around. And helping him was Sheikh Rashid bin Saeed Al Maktoum, the ruler of Dubai. The two sheikhdoms had a history of rivalry. But their rulers also knew that if they came together, the others would follow suit. Zayed and Maktoum, combining the force of their personality and their political skill, together willed the UAE into being.

In February 1971, the two rulers met in a pair of tents erected on the once-disputed borders between their two sheikhdoms. The ruler of Dubai brought along his son to the negotiations. Sheikh Rashid, the current vice president of the UAE and ruler of Dubai, was then a nineteen-year-old man fresh from military training in the United Kingdom. His job was to serve coffee. In 2019, I was flown on a chopper from Dubai to meet Rashid at a tent he had pitched up in the desert. Even though Dubai is today one of the most prosperous city states in the world, Sheikh Rashid feels at home in the sands. It grants him the time to concentrate, away from the bustle of the city his family have helped to build from scratch. He meditates on the past and develops ideas for the future. He remembers vividly the birth of the UAE.

Britain was poised to leave by the end of 1971. Adversaries looked covetously at a region that was rapidly accumulating riches. Could it unite? Zayed and Maktoum held a series of fateful meetings in the desert. As the summit came to an end, Sheikh Zayed asked the ruler of Dubai: "Rashid, what do you think? Shall we create a union?" "Give me your hand, Zayed," Sheikh Rashid, the older of the two men, answered. "Let us shake upon the agreement. You will be president." They issued a joint statement: "The Union of Arab Emirates comprises one people, and has one policy, one diplomatic representation, one army, and one economic and social structure." In the months following the handshake, Sharjah, Ajman, Umm Al Quwain and Fujairah offered to join. And thus was born the most enduring Arab union of the modern era. On 2 December 1971, the rulers of the six states hoisted the flag of the United Arab Emirates outside the Union House in Dubai. Ras Al Khaimah, the sole holdout in the early negotiations, joined the UAE in February 1972.

The UAE's federation, an extraordinary and bold decision for an Arab country in the Middle East, has been vindicated over the past half century. The socio-economic success or failure of a country can be attributed to its underlying state structure. In the UAE, a distinctive blend of Eastern and Western traditions has been tailored to the specific needs of a small and nascent political nation. The constitution, which initially held temporary status, earned its permanent standing only after being tested for a quarter of a century. It bestowed upon seven distinct emirates the authority to independently address local matters, regulate economic and social policies, and most significantly, control their own oil resources. The establishment of a federal union thus gained legitimacy as it proved to be profitable. In 1997, with the dissolution of the individual emirates' local armies, the federal structure became even more advantageous in terms of security and overall prosperity.

The amalgamation of the federal framework and adherence to Islamic jurisprudence is not the sole example of combining European and traditional elements. Faith ensures stability, while the European influence allows for adaptability to changing circumstances. In this context, the coexistence of traditional legitimacy, as per Weber's theory, does not impede the existence of an efficient bureaucracy operating on rational-legal principles. This is partially because the UAE does not solely rely on an individual's traditional legitimacy, but rather emphasises a systemic approach that garners public consensus regarding the right to govern the state and manage its resources effectively.

Besides, despite eschewing comprehensive political reforms and the adoption of Western-style multiparty systems and democracy, the state has endeavoured in earnest to engage its citizens in its decision-making process. Its goal has been to instil a sense of responsibility within each individual for the country's future and collective well-being.

In 2006, the UAE held the maiden elections to its Federal National Council. It was a significant political milestone in the country's history, and came about not by pressure from below but from a directive from above in the form a resolution issued by the late Sheikh Khalifa bin Zayed Al Nahyan, the president of the UAE. The electoral college consisted of 6,595 members nationwide, with 456 individuals vying for FNC membership. Campaigns for the elections revolved around crucial community concerns, including national identity, employment opportunities, education, healthcare, women's and children's rights, and improving the living conditions for UAE citizens. Electronic machines were deployed at ballot booths, incorporating computer technologies to register and store candidate and voter data while ensuring secure identity verification. More than 22 per cent of the total seats were won by women—one of the highest rates of female representation.

At the second FNC election, which took place in 2011, the electorate expanded to 135,308 voters and there were 469 candidates, including 85 women. The voters comprised 54 per cent men and 46 per cent women. Candidates used social media networks to canvass voters. By the third FNC elections, held in 2015, the size of the electoral college rose to 224,279 voters, with women accounting for 48 per cent of the number. The fourth cycle of elections, in 2019, allowed voters to cast their ballots from abroad. Members from the Arab parliament, the General Secretariat of the Arab League, the International Centre for Parliamentary Studies, and delegates from Saudi Arabia, Bahrain, Kuwait and Egypt were invited as observers and returned with vital insights into the UAE's experience in organising elections and implementing state-of-the-art electronic voting systems. Women's representation in the FNC was raised to 50 per cent.

To be sure, only a fraction of Emiratis have been granted passive suffrage, and the elected parliament possesses limited authority. Electoral practices have not been welcomed with great enthusiasm by the local populace—voter turnout has never exceeded 49 per cent—but their very introduction reflects both the government's willingness to implement reforms and its careful approach to avoid any destabilising shocks. The state is cautiously embarking on the path of liberalisation, primarily in the pursuit of social progress and stability. In 2020, the UAE announced a comprehensive revision of its legislation based on Sharia, which led to significant changes. For instance, unmarried couples were permitted to reside together from 2022 onwards, and restrictions on alcohol consumption were eased. Additionally, honour killings were banned, and foreign residents were granted the option to avoid Sharia courts when dealing with matters concerning marriage, divorce and inheritance. These incremental and well-managed concessions serve to preserve the foundation of the system while attracting fresh talent to the country, thereby strengthening the nation and fortifying the system itself.

* * *

The UAE's remarkable socio-economic development cannot be attributed solely to its substantial oil reserves and small population of fewer than 1.5 million citizens. While oil exports have played a significant role in the country's global standing for over three decades, the 2008-2009 global economic crisis revealed the dangers of relying heavily on oil. Plummeting oil prices, the housing market collapse and the international banking crisis had devastating consequences for the UAE's economy. Western commentators were quick to pronounce the end of the UAE's economic rise. Prudent governance across all sectors, however, not only facilitated economic recovery but also prevented the Arab Spring uprisings that raged through the Middle East in 2010-2011 from setting off instability at home. The government's focus on investing in infrastructure in the less affluent northern emirates and addressing dissent helped maintain stability. The UAE's leadership not only responded promptly to regional events but also actively engaged in the internal affairs of neighbouring countries. They allocated significant funds to aid Egypt's economic recovery and joined the coalition against the Islamic State.

In the development of the state, oil became a valuable resource but not the primary resource. In fact, oil revenues now account for about 30 per cent of the UAE's GDP, as the sustained decline in oil prices since 2014 has had a minimal impact on the country's economic health. The UAE's leaders made calculated investments in their people, guided by rational motives rather than mere altruism. Recognising the significance of human resources, they attracted the best talent from around the world while also prioritising their citizens' well-being.

As of 2022, the UAE's population stood at just over 10 million people, of which immigrants comprised approximately 88 per cent. The UAE's migration policy exemplifies how diligently the state safeguards the privileges of its citizens. The criteria for national belonging are well-defined: citizenship cannot be acquired by birth alone; one's father (or mother, if the father is unknown) must be a UAE citizen. Naturalisation takes around thirty years, but there is no official mechanism to achieve it and the state prohibits dual citizenship.

And yet, despite such policies, the UAE ranks thirteenth globally as one of the best places to work, according to a survey conducted by the Boston Consulting Group among foreign citizens. The UAE offers a range of visa options tailored to different categories of individuals. "Golden" visas, valid for ten years, are granted to investors, entrepreneurs, highly skilled professionals, exceptional talents and scientists. Professionals receive a green visa with a validity of five years. In October 2022, the UAE introduced a "digital nomad" resident visa, allowing employees of foreign companies to work remotely in the country for up to one year. A number of other visa programmes are also available for current and potential investors.

According to the Global Talent Competitiveness Index 2022, the UAE ranks fourth in the world in its ability to attract talent. The UAE's development strategy for 2031 aims to significantly enhance its competitiveness in other areas as well. Reducing dependence on foreign specialists by cultivating local resources remains a priority, and the government is investing heavily in programmes to educate citizens in skills relevant to the national economy and organising competitions to encourage innovative solutions.

Over the past five decades, this Arab federation has not only survived; it has also emerged as a confident regional leader and a vaunted player on the international stage. Consider the achievements of a country born in uncertain circumstances only fifty years ago:

- The UAE passport holds the distinction of being recognised as the world's finest, according to the Passport Index of Arton Capital. This speaks volumes about the country's global reputation.
- Surpassing even China, the UAE achieved a remarkable feat by becoming the fifth nation to reach Mars. Their mission, named al-Amal or hope, conducted a comprehensive study of the Martian atmosphere, shedding light on the climate dynamics of the enigmatic red planet.
- Breaking new ground, the UAE became the inaugural Arab country to host the World Expo in 2021. This grand event served as a platform for formulating their development ideology and showcasing their remarkable technological advancements. Over 24 million visitors from around the world flocked to the exhibition over six months, and 80 per cent of all the constructed infrastructure is to be repurposed.
- Abu Dhabi garnered acclaim as the most pandemic-resistant city worldwide. The government's adept crisis management

during the challenging times of the Covid-19 pandemic, leveraging strategic public-private partnerships and a highly skilled workforce, demonstrated its effectiveness. The increase of hospital beds by 200 per cent and intensive care units by 300 per cent, along with successful policies on citizen repatriation, migration legislation adjustments, food security, testing and vaccination, exemplified the Federation's united approach.

- The UAE has become a global frontrunner in digitalisation. Their National Digital Government Strategy goes beyond conventional digitalisation initiatives commonly seen in other countries. The innovative platform, *Basher*, streamlines business registration, completing the process in a mere fifteen minutes. By adopting a non-bureaucratic approach to governance, Dubai alone has saved approximately $350 million and 14 million work hours.

- The UAE has emerged as a trailblazer in combating climate change and stands proudly among the world's top three solar energy producers. Pioneering efforts in the city of Sharjah have transformed waste into a valuable energy source, with over three-quarters of urban landfill waste already successfully eliminated—an unprecedented achievement in the region.

These examples only scratch the surface. I witnessed first-hand the streamlined decision-making process that has served the UAE so well during my presidential visit in 2022. Ordinarily, it takes years for ideas to be realised by governments. Often, they get stuck in committee and governments change. The UAE learnt from the failures of others. I was struck by the impressive speed with which Sultan Al Jaber, the minister of Industry and Advanced Technology, and Mariam Almheiri, the brilliant minister for Climate Change and Environment, metabolised complex ideas. Khaldoon Al Mubarak of Mubadala, who runs the Mubadala

Investment Company, was equally hands-on with my proposal to collaborate on solar energy. Masdar, the sustainable development pillar of Mubadala, was immediately brought on board and we signed an agreement for a 200-megawatt photovoltaic power plant to be built in Armenia with Emirati investment.

The state's efficiency is the result of a meticulous process of matching skills and duties. Consider Sarah Al Amiri, a young, US-trained scientist who was appointed the head of the United Arab Emirates Space Agency in 2020. Within months of her appointment, Amiri told me, she and her team were working on the design of a 1,380 kilogram spacecraft to map the atmosphere of Mars in the course of a single Martian year. The mission required relentless dedication, which Amiri possessed. The probe was successfully launched just six months after her appointment—catapulting the UAE into the exclusive club of space-explorers dominated by big powers. Education had been something of an obsession with Sheikh Zayed and his son, the current president of the UAE Mohammed bin Zayed Al Nahyan. He wanted every Emirati to be educated, and he toiled especially hard to convince families to educate their daughters. Amiri and Almheiri and Jaber, who represent the UAE's future, are products of that endeavour.

Looking ahead to the future, the UAE's national development strategy outlines specific economic growth objectives that include further diversification of exports, increased foreign trade and the development of the tourism industry to contribute around 15 per cent of its GDP. The UAE's ambition to be numbered among the most economically competitive and socially attractive countries in the world reflects its unique philosophy. It seeks not only absolute well-being but also relative prosperity compared to its competitors. In addition to proactive economic policies, the UAE prioritises health and human development, emphasising security at both the national and city levels, as well as focusing on food and cybersecurity.

An unconventional approach to novel challenges has become something of a hallmark of this aspirationally progressive state seeking prosperity. A prime example in this regard is the UAE's establishment, in 2019, of the Ministry of Possibilities, a department that embodies the state's commitment to embracing innovation within the political and business spheres. Another notable manifestation of this approach is the creation of Palm Jumeirah, an artificial island shaped like a palm tree, along with the rest of the captivating Palm Islands archipelago. These structures, connected to the mainland by a monorail, bridge and tunnel, not only expanded the UAE's coastline by 78 kilometres but also became a symbol of architectural ingenuity. The development of a driverless urban metro system known as the Dubai Metro is an instance of another astute investment in the future. Setting a world record for its extensive length, this visionary project not only facilitates efficient transportation but is projected to generate a staggering $49 billion in revenue by 2030, significantly surpassing operating costs.

The rational use of resources has become a top priority for the UAE, and digitalisation plays a key role in achieving this goal. While many parts of the world interpret digitalisation as merely moving services online, the UAE has taken up a digital lifestyle and mindset. It boasts the fastest mobile internet speed, exceeding the global average by a significant margin, and ranks among the top twenty countries measured by per capita consumption of digital content. The result: it has the most vibrant e-commerce sector, with per capita spending nearly twice the global average.

The UAE has also established itself as a prominent hub for data storage in the Middle East, hosting Microsoft Azure's first cloud regions. The growth of cloud computing between 2017 and 2022 has resulted in the creation of over 30,000 local jobs.

Besides economic benefits, the creation of data storage facilities in the country has compelled the government to update its regulations to meet exacting data storage requirements while maintaining a degree of digital sovereignty. This, in turn, has boosted the UAE's ability to exert significant political influence regionally. For, by prioritising digitalisation and leveraging its technological prowess, the UAE has not only demonstrated its commitment to resource efficiency—it has also put down the foundations for its own role in a digital-first future.

The UAE has positioned itself as a global pioneer in the rapidly emerging field of Artificial Intelligence by formulating its own strategy and establishing a dedicated ministry for AI. It is currently training 100 civil servants in AI technologies, as well as training teachers who will instruct students in AI throughout the country's school networks. In 2020, the prestigious Mohammed bin Zayed University of Artificial Intelligence was granted a research university licence. Situated in the eco-city of Masdar, it serves as a strategic think tank, bolstering the UAE's capabilities in AI and drawing top research talent from around the world. Currently ranked twenty-fourth globally, it is, as of now, the world's only specialised university in AI, machine learning and natural language processing.

The energy sector represents another vital arena of innovation in the UAE. Since 2010, the country has been implementing stringent standards for constructing environmentally-friendly and sustainable buildings. By 2030, these measures are projected to save the government approximately $10 billion and reduce carbon emissions by around 30 per cent. The adoption of these new construction standards reduces energy consumption while upholding the state's commitment to enhance the well-being and health of residents. The Emirate of Ras al Khaimah, which has implemented separate construction standards since 2020, has seen a remarkable 30 per cent reduction in electricity and water consumption. In 2014, Dubai launched a visionary smart city strategy, emphasising efficient electricity usage, urban zoning and robust public transportation systems. Through digital innovation and sustainable practices, the UAE is charting a future that encourages the embrace of cutting-edge technologies without despoiling the environment.

Small states, as I have mentioned before, are endowed with a survival instinct. The UAE, faced with a looming water crisis, is aggressively employing a range of smart measures to mitigate it. Adjustments to tariffs and subsidies are being made, and the construction of specialised groundwater monitoring stations—over 1,300 in Abu Dhabi alone—is underway. Residents are being encouraged to monitor their water consumption through the introduction of usage indicators. Solar desalination plants, which convert saline groundwater into drinking water, are also being established, alongside experimental methods involving algae to separate salt from water. As a scientist, I am conscious that these advances are not risk free: desalination technologies, for instance, can harm marine life and algae populations.

To address such risks, the UAE government is collaborating with research institutions and farmers to implement greenhouse construction, hydroponics and vertical farming. These advancements aim to optimise water usage, in alignment with the UAE's Water Strategy, by 2036. Since the UAE could potentially lose up to 6 per cent of its land area by 2100, it is also equipping the agricultural sector for the gradual reduction of available arable land.

One impressive achievement here is the construction of the world's largest vertical farm spanning an area of 1.2 hectares. This ground-breaking facility will be capable of cultivating crops that would typically require 360 hectares of land. The water consumption of this vertical farm is 99 per cent less compared to traditional farming methods. Alongside these innovative solutions, the UAE is also placing significant emphasis on tackling food waste and enhancing the efficiency of food production. The country has set ambitious goals to cut its food waste in half by 2030.

The UAE's determination to address climate concerns, apparent in its political decisions and actions, is driven by a balance of both long-term environmental and economic considerations. By prioritising renewable resources, the country aims to diversify its economy while promoting sustainability. The Emirates has set a precedent in the region by joining the Paris Agreement and committing to achieving net zero carbon emissions by 2050. It has also made significant advancements in hydrogen production and undertaken a large-scale effort of planting 100 million mangrove trees. The city of Masdar, which utilises technology and solar energy to minimise water and energy consumption, stands as a shimmering example of sustainable development in the Middle East. Environmental education has even been integrated into school curricula across the Emirates.

* * *

While the UAE remains strongly united as a federation, there exist certain contradictions among its emirates, particularly between those with greater resources, like Abu Dhabi and Dubai, and those with fewer resources. On one side, the less resource-rich emirates receive substantial support from the federal budget. On the other side, the wealth and influence of Abu Dhabi and Dubai translate into significant political weight, shaping national policies. Tensions do occasionally arise, such as when Dubai perceived the decision to boycott Qatar as detrimental to its business interests. Given Abu Dhabi's greater wealth and size, it often wields influence over federal policies, while seeking to strike a balance with Dubai's openness on matters of national security. These contradictions, including minor territorial disputes between the emirates, are not, however, sufficiently severe and pose no significant threat to the country's unity, unless compounded by other risks, the most important being water scarcity.

One of the foremost challenges to the stability of the UAE lies in the composition of its population—less than 15 per cent of whom are citizens—and the gradual, albeit regulated, opening up of the nation. The government is striving to define the boundaries of the national community and reduce its reliance on foreign labour in the future through its "Emiratisation" initiative. As of yet, however, this has not led to any decline in the influx of migrant workers. The UAE faces significant socio-demographic challenges. Currently, the elderly population constitutes a mere 2 per cent—a stark contrast to the higher percentages seen in developed Western nations—but this advantage is certain to shift dramatically in the decades ahead. While the relatively small number of citizens might not present a major threat, when combined with other societal transformations, it has the potential to trigger a social and even a political crisis. The government, moving quickly, has established a Ministry of Youth Affairs to address this gathering problem.

With its robust diplomacy and skilful leveraging of personal relationships, the UAE follows a remarkably self-assured foreign policy. While publicly eschewing democratisation and the emulation of institutional models like political parties, it has adeptly integrated itself into the prevailing liberal world order. It has even tailored this order to suit its internal and external requirements, forging diverse and multilateral connections, and ultimately amassing significant soft power capital. Regional rivalries and tensions can still test it, as they did during the diplomatic spat with Qatar. It was apparent from the beginning that the falling out would not yield benefits and could in fact harm all sides. Given my long friendly relationship with the Al

Thani family in Qatar and my friendship with the leadership of the UAE, it was personally distressing for me to witness these rationally-driven fraternal states that had emerged against all the odds engaged in such a mutually detrimental standoff.

The UAE's international image is built upon its identity, heritage, culture and contributions to global development. Its diplomatic efforts in the cause of combating climate change around the world, and its record of successfully managing the pandemic at home, have only enhanced its status. It has used its growing clout to even make efforts to mediate between Russia and Ukraine. It is hardly surprising that the UAE occupies an impressive tenth place globally, and the first spot in the region, in the Global Soft Power Index. The UAE's record of giving—Sheikh Zayed supported charities in fifty-one countries while never advertising it, and his sons continue the tradition—ranks it among the most generous in the world. International investment, particularly in the UK, is as an additional lever for the UAE's evolving foreign policy.

As a strategic ally of the United States in the region, the UAE has deployed its special forces alongside the Americans in Kosovo, Somalia, Afghanistan and Libya. It joined the coalition led by the US to combat the Islamic State in Iraq and Syria and has provoked Iran's fury for siding with Washington against Tehran. All of this demonstrates the country's strong military and political commitment to the US. At the same time, the UAE has progressively deepened its cooperation on all fronts with China, India and Russia. While China is the sole strategic rival to the United States on this list, Washington's reaction to China's growing involvement in the region has been relatively tempered. If the United States is primarily visible in its military presence, Chinese engagement is unmissable on the economic front. Both powers, however, accord the Middle East a lower priority when compared to their rivalry in the Indo-Pacific region. Their interests in the Middle East—prioritising peace and stability—actually are in alignment. The United States appeared to believe until recently that partnering with China in the region was more productive than outright restricting Chinese investment and technology.

* * *

In conclusion, I should reiterate that the UAE's success was not predestined. It is by avoiding easy solutions, prioritising people and employing comprehensive planning and innovative utilisation of limited resources that the UAE has emerged as a nation synonymous with opportunity on the global stage.

Stability and sustainability in the UAE are achieved through a unique blend of Arab and Muslim traditions and Western practices. This combination underlies the flexibility and adaptability of the system, allowing it to not only endure but also prepare for an uncertain future better than many modern nation-states. Unlike the Western-centric ideal of state structure, the UAE's federal principle prevents the formation of a sense of historical injustice that could threaten unity. While economic and political influence may be unevenly distributed, it currently facilitates centralised decision-making, especially in foreign policy matters.

Effective and rational planning is by now deeply ingrained in the UAE's political tradition. Reforms are substantive and intricate, prioritising originality over imitation. The UAE has achieved remarkable advancements in digitalising public administration, fostering business innovation and developing Artificial Intelligence, cloud computing and more.

Throughout its existence, the UAE has faced persistent threats that have only grown more relevant. For all its prosperity and relative stability, ecological and environmental challenges—particularly water shortages—have worsened, and the population has become ethnically and age-diverse. Despite narrowing room for manoeuvre and mounting external pressures, however, the UAE's proactive approach and timely actions have positioned the country to be heard by major global players. Its connections, leverage and appeal to citizens make it an influential small state that punches well above its weight. Its internal legitimacy and stability render it less vulnerable to external forces. The UAE's flexibility and realistic assessment of available resources will continue to maintain the current balance.

5

ISRAEL

"IF YOU WILL IT, IT IS NO DREAM"

I nearly went to prison for Israel long before I ever set foot in the country. As a Soviet theoretical physicist in the 1980s, I had published articles on the bi-metric theory of gravitation. These papers, circulating through the academic world, somehow landed on the desk of Professor Nathan Rosen, the fabled Israeli-American physicist who had worked with Albert Einstein on entangled wave functions. Professor Rosen was sufficiently impressed to share my work with a promising student of his called Mark Israelit. After discussing the paper between themselves, the two men wrote me a letter, replete with equations and drawings, and dispatched it to my university. The missive was intercepted, as all correspondence was in the Soviet Union. And I was summoned by the KGB.

"Comrade Sarkissian," the humourless officer opposite me said gravely, "can you give us an explanation of what these letters mean?" Since I had not seen the letter and had no idea who had sent it or what was in it, I told them that I could not. They suspected that the equations were secret codes and that I was up to no good. Finally, when they showed me the paper, I smiled with relief. I was also touched. Einstein was my hero, and here I was, decades after his passing, holding a letter praising my work and urging further discussion by a living link with that great man.

I put down the letter and tried my best to explain to the perplexed KGB official that there was nothing subversive about the letter. Ultimately, it took the rector of the Yerevan State University, Professor Hambartsumian, to convince the KGB to leave me alone. I was let go, but the letter was impounded. I wrote an admiring note to Professor Rosen and resolved that I would one day visit him in Israel. When that day finally arrived, after the collapse of the Soviet Union, Professor Rosen was no longer alive. My first visit to Israel was a mixture of frustration, sadness, admiration and a touch of envy. Here was a country that had so much in common with Armenia—an ancient nation, a tiny dot on the map, determined to survive, to thrive, and punching so high above its weight.

Modern Israel belongs in a unique group of nations whose statehood is rooted in an ancient national ideology. This historical backdrop is intimately entwined with the metaphysical notion of a divine bond with God, who specifically chose the Jewish people and granted them the land as a sanctuary for their existence and progress. The privilege to construct their homeland in the territory of Canaan was bestowed upon the Jews by God Himself, who assumed the role of the singular sovereign and the ultimate guarantor of its protection. The concept of an everlasting covenant with God thus emerged as an inherent facet of Jewish identity and supplied the philosophical underpinning for the Jewish people's return to the sacred land and the establishment of the State of Israel. To gain a proper understanding of Israel today, let us delve into the principal phases of its historical formation.

The united Kingdom of Israel had a brief existence, shorter than a century. Following the passing of King Solomon in 928 BCE, it underwent a partition, giving rise to the Northern Kingdom of Israel and the Southern Kingdom of Judah. The two states found themselves locked in a protracted conflict, and the resultant fraternal strife weakened the Jewish people and set the stage for external conquest. Thanks to the civil discord, the Kingdom of Israel was conquered by Assyria, while the Kingdom of Judah fell under the vassalage, initially, of Egypt, before falling under the dominion of Babylon. The Babylonians invaded Jerusalem, razed the sacred Temple and forcibly exiled the majority of the Jewish population. With the conquest of Babylonia, the Persian king Cyrus permitted the Jews to return to their city and undertake the reconstruction of the Temple. Judea, however, endured a long period as a Persian colony, marked by constant hostilities within the Jewish aristocracy, which hindered their ability to unite in the cause of reclaiming independence. Eventually, Judea was conquered by Alexander the Great, who implemented a policy of injecting Hellenistic culture into the Jewish way of life through the appointment of loyal governors.

In due course, Judea experienced a temporary resurgence of independence under the Hasmonean dynasty. After about eighty years, it was once again subjected to subjugation, becoming a province within the vast expanse of the Roman Empire. The prolonged period of autonomy, however, rekindled a sense of national character and revived the conviction that preserving Jewish sovereignty was a divine decree. Rome faced a formidable challenge in suppressing this awakened self-awareness, which steadily fortified the Jewish people's unwavering resolve for self-determination. But despite their organised uprisings, their efforts paradoxically yielded contrasting outcomes. Following Rome's quelling of two rebellions during the first and second centuries CE, the year 70 CE witnessed the catastrophic annihilation of the second Jerusalem Temple, accompanied by the mass expulsion of Jews from the Palestinian territories, with the exception of Galilee. These momentous events served as catalysts for the formation of the Jewish Diaspora.

The era following the destruction of the Second Temple is commonly referred to as the "Talmudic period" within Jewish history. During this significant epoch, the intellectual and spiritual elite of the Jewish community meticulously catalogued the essence of Jewry, methodically organising the rich tapestry of Jewish heritage and its indispensable legal principles, including the sacred right bestowed upon them by God to return to their Promised Land. It is impossible for Armenians not to find echoes of their own past in the Jewish story of dispossession and their striving to preserve their identity. Armenians too chose to abandon their gold and jewellery and carry with them the manuscripts and other artefacts that are the bases of their national identity.

The fruits of Jewish endeavours find expression in two distinct versions of the Talmud: the Jerusalem Talmud compiled in Galilee, and its Babylonian counterpart. Through these seminal works, the groundwork was established for the preservation of Jewish identity in the diaspora, anchoring their profound connection with God (faith). These foundations served, moreover, as a springboard for the progressive development of a comprehensive national ethos.

During the medieval era, the idea of a gradual physical return to Palestine gained prominence. This idea primarily resonated among religiously devout Jews, who considered it crucial to pray to God in the sacred land and eagerly await the arrival of the Messiah. While the minimal objective of preserving their cultural identity had been accomplished, the transition to constructing a secular national elite within the Jewish community remained unfulfilled. This was due to the reluctance of radical religious factions to relinquish their exclusive influence over Jewry, coupled with the widespread infringement upon the rights of Jews in their countries of residence. Only in the nineteenth century, when more than 70 per cent of the world's Jewish population resided in Europe, did the situation undergo a change. The advent of bourgeois-democratic revolutions and the Enlightenment era facilitated the emergence of marginalised groups from the shadows, enabling their integration into the burgeoning European nations.

The period spanning 1815 to 1914 stands as a testament to the profound social and educational revolution experienced by European Jewry, characterised by emancipation and the attainment of equal rights and enlightenment, which opened the doors to European education and culture. These transformative processes engendered both partial assimilation and the erosion of traditional foundations among European Jews, while simultaneously fostering the emergence of a new, dogmatic and *national* self-awareness. It was these currents that gave rise to the formation of national elites, namely the Zionists, who outlined a roadmap for the eventual restoration of Israeli statehood in Palestine. But due to their limited exposure to high politics and state affairs, Jewish nationalism became susceptible to manipulation by the prevailing powers of the era. France and Russia, for instance, viewed the idea of establishing a Jewish national homeland in Palestine as an opportunity to advance their own interests, strategically leveraging the "Eastern question", which gained importance following the disintegration of the Ottoman Empire.

But, blessed with wise leadership, the Zionist movement skilfully navigated away from self-enervating entanglements in geopolitical ventures. They discerned early on the importance of acquiring expertise in and enhancing their lobbying capabilities. A strategic decision was made to unite Jewry through the establishment of a philanthropic movement. This initiative aimed to generate national capital by rallying financial support from prosperous Jews to aid their less fortunate brethren residing in Palestine. Since this very community would serve as the driving force behind the eventual creation of the Jewish State, its fortification came to be seen as an indispensable prerequisite for success. The funds collected were primarily directed towards the advancement of general education, vocational training, and the establishment and equipping of agricultural settlements, artisanal workshops and manufacturing facilities. The social responsibility borne by affluent Jews in the preservation and empowerment of Jewish communities assumed a wider scope, becoming an integral facet of their systemic approach to attaining statehood. This discipline is what brought people together and paved their way to their historic homeland.

* * *

The ascent of Jewish national consciousness and the socio-economic empowerment of European Jewry occurred concurrently with the decline in living standards experienced by other European nations. This precipitated a fervent surge of radical nationalism across Europe, with anti-Semitism emerging as an inseparable component. Recognising these trends, the Zionist movement grasped the genuine perils threatening the physical survival of the Jewish people. Discussions ensued regarding the urgent establishment of a sovereign state, causing a division within the intellectual elite. One faction advocated for seizing any available proposal, even considering territories in Africa or Latin America. The second camp staunchly believed that Eretz Israel, the historical land of Israel, stood as the sole suitable site for the construction of a Jewish state. Meanwhile, the religious elite formed a third group, vehemently opposing the notion of creating a Jewish state. They maintained that the Jews ought to return to the Promised Land solely upon the arrival of the Messiah, and until then, they must engage in prayerful anticipation.

The Basel Congress of 1897 conferred upon the Jewish national-state concept the status of a political agenda. The State of Israel slowly acquired shape, with the creation of a flag and an anthem. Theodor Herzl, the paladin of the Zionist movement, devoted particular attention to the secular character of the state, championing the principles of a novel, diverse and inclusive society. Herzl envisioned a "new open society" capable of integrating the Arab populace of Palestine. "If you will it," he said, "it is no dream." Within a state founded upon the most progressive ideals, the Jewish people would liberate themselves not only from discrimination and oppression, but also from the yoke of archaic traditions, and would secure in it a worthy position at the forefront of progressive humanity.

Zionism was not a monolith. It gave rise to various interpretations of the national idea and produced divergent models for the Jewish national state. A multitude of political tendencies emerged within the World Zionist Organisation. These encompassed the Social Zionist Poale Zion, the religious-Zionist Mizrachi and the impartially progressive faction of the General Zionists. Each political and ideological stream engaged in endless debates regarding the essence of the future state and deliberated upon its structure and model. And yet, despite their differing perspectives—be they socialist, liberal, conservative, or centrist—all factions unanimously recognised that the establishment of the State of Israel derived from the eternal covenant between the Jewish people and God. The historical entitlement of the Jewish people to reclaim the land, with Jerusalem as its capital, never encountered serious dissent from the movement's intellectual elite.

It is important, however, to emphasise that in the 1920s and 1930s, a split emerged between moderate Zionists, who advocated for the realisation of Herzl's vision, and radical Zionists led by Ze'ev Jabotinsky, who placed their faith solely in a power-oriented approach to establishing Israel. This conflict served as a convenient tool in the hands of the major powers, who used it to revisit their commitments to aiding the creation of Israel. The eruption of the Second World War, accompanied by the mass extermination of Jews in the Holocaust, put an end to internal disputes and Jewish elites resolved to embark on concrete actions to forge a state in the pursuit of national salvation.

* * *

The establishment of the State of Israel stands as a remarkable testament to the pursuit of a national vision. The Zionist movement gave it wings. This extraordinary endeavour also invited a fresh set of challenges. In its early years, Israel was beset by a substantial influx of immigrants hailing from both Europe and Afro-Asian regions, predominantly Arab and Muslim nations. Within the first three years of Israel's founding, the proportion of Sephardic Jews surged from 15 per cent to 33 per cent, and by 1967, Sephardim constituted over half of the nation's Jewish population. Derived from the European nationalism of the nineteenth century, which assimilated other continental concepts, the Zionist ideal initially appeared foreign to the Sephardim, who for centuries had been exposed to a distinct civilisation. The result was a collision between the progressive social Zionism embraced by European Jews and the traditional bedrock of the religious Sephardim.

Such conflicts have the potential not only to fragment societies but also to ignite full-scale civil wars. For small nations like Israel, with all their inherent weaknesses, civil strife can be a recipe for imminent demise. The Israeli state devised a path forward by embracing the principle of "differences fostering survival and fortification". A great deal of effort was exerted to disseminate the notion that amidst all the inhabitants of Israel, one constant prevails—survival—and that all ideological, cultural and traditional distinctions should melt away in the cause of strengthening the state and its institutions.

At the core of this consolidation lay two pivotal establishments: education and the armed forces (the Israel Defence Forces, IDF). The contemporary Israeli education system is renowned as one of the most cutting-edge and well-endowed worldwide. At the same time, military conscription ensures that every Jew understands the imperative nature of safeguarding the state. It became an accepted fact of Israeli life that the state would always take care of its soldiers. As a result, individual Jewish ideological and religious communities began to coalesce into a singular Israeli nation.

This overarching sense of unity struck me when I first visited Israel in the 1990s as a callow diplomat. Though I did not have the good fortune to see Professor Rosen, I was lucky enough to be granted an audience with Yitzhak Rabin and Shimon Peres. Rabin was a formidable figure, a man who inspired affection, admiration, reverence (and even loathing) in his people. But the person who received me was an avuncular teacher. He displayed a surprisingly deep knowledge of Armenia's past and was curious to know about events in the country. How was Armenia coping after its recent independence from the Soviet Union? He reminded me that we were both members of ancient civilisations that had survived every attempt to wipe them out. Like the Jews, the Armenians had endured religious persecution, genocide and exile from their homeland.

"We are survivors," Rabin said. "We should never forget that." The generosity of the great man was as surprising as it was moving. But he wasn't done. He offered me any and all assistance. Since survival and state-building were also Armenia's primary goals at the time, I asked if I could meet leaders of the IDF, the United Jewish Agency, and other government and non-governmental organisations. Without wincing or wasting a moment, Rabin picked up the phone and made all the arrangements. He was assassinated not long after we met.

A few years later, I returned to Israel with my family as a private citizen and toured the entire country and visited ancient Armenian sites. Israel is home to the oldest Armenian diaspora in the world. Armenian monks made their way to Jerusalem in the years following Armenia's conversion to Christianity in 301 CE, but there was an Armenian presence in Jerusalem as early as 55 BCE, during the reign of Tigranes, the great Armenian ruler whose kingdom stretched from the Caspian Sea to the Mediterranean. In the twelfth century, the Armenian Patriarchate of Jerusalem made its home in the Cathedral of St James in the city's Armenian Quarter. The second wave of Armenians came as refugees from the genocide in the Ottoman Empire. They not only enlarged the ancient Armenian community but also enriched the crafts of Israel by resuming in Israel the skilled ceramics works that had been decimated by the Ottomans. The finest "Kuthaya ceramics", named after the Armenian city in Anatolia, were thereafter to be found in Israel. Ceramic tiles crafted by Armenian refugees went on to decorate some of Israel's most illustrious buildings, including the Rockefeller Museum, the American Colony Hotel and Beit HaNassi, the residence of the Israeli president. The most recent Armenians to settle in Israel are economic migrants. The Armenian church, with its fabulous treasure of antiquities, owns a third of Christian holy places in Jerusalem, while the city's Armenian Quarter has a millennia-long history.

Given Armenia's history with the Holy Land, it is striking that there was almost no high-level contact between the two countries. In 2020, I became the first Armenian head of state to make an official visit to Israel. This fact made it, to borrow the word used by the press in both countries, an "historic" visit. Of course, I had visited Israel several times before and counted Israelis among my friends and confidants. But travelling as the head of state to Israel, I sensed that I would not have found the place unfamiliar had I never been there before. I sensed the same warmth there I had encountered when the late, great Rabin had welcomed me as a young diplomat.

The occasion that took me to Israel was the seventy-fifth anniversary of the liberation of Auschwitz. Almost fifty other heads of state, including the presidents of France and Russia, and the vice president of the United States had come to the Yad Vashem Holocaust memorial museum. But as a senior Israeli official reminded me, Armenians could relate to the place and all that it memorialised in a "different" way. It was the Armenian Genocide that had inspired Hitler to proceed with his plan to deport and liquidate Europe's Jews. "Who remembers the Armenians?" Hitler had asked. My decision to visit Israel was partly an answer to that question. I wanted, as the head of the Armenian nation, to say on behalf of my people that we would never forget the suffering of the Jews—and we would never let it recur. As I wrote in the visitors' book at Yad Vashem:

"Armenians and Jews are connected by history and destiny, by the will to survive and to preserve their identities."

There was, as the Israelis themselves recognised and acknowledged, an element of bitter irony here because, despite the camaraderie and sense of solidary shared by our two peoples, Israel never formally recognised the Armenian Genocide. This fact was invoked by a few who felt I should not go to Israel. I of course brushed them aside. And yet—and yet. Facts were facts, and Israel's failure to acknowledge the Armenian Genocide could not be swept under the carpet. At the same time, I felt, it could not be made the condition of deepening relations between our two countries. Israel's choices were dictated by delicate geopolitical considerations: a nation surrounded by adversaries and shaped by war did not always have the luxury of making the correct choices. The reluctance to recognise the Armenian Genocide must not be equated with *denial* of the Armenian Genocide. Indeed, as I made it a point to say in the presence of President Reuven Rivlin, the recognition of the Armenian Genocide by the US Senate could not have happened without the support of the Jewish community in the United States. But there was another awkward fact that needed to be confronted: Israel supplied arms to Azerbaijan. The government of Azerbaijan has echoed the racist sentiments of the Ottomans, and the fact that Israel gave it weapons—which were deployed to lethal effect in the 44-day war waged by Azerbaijan months after I toured Israel—was something that could not be ignored. This reality, however difficult or painful, was dictated by the cold logic of international relations: no nation is automatically entitled to the support of another; it has to work to gain it. And Armenia and Israel, sadly, had squandered decades that could have been used to cultivate mutual ties in every field, including defence.

I tried to make a beginning in this direction. Other leaders departed, but I was extended an invitation to stay on a while longer and accepted it. I met the leadership—President Rivlin and leaders of the Knesset were as hospitable as Rabin had been a quarter century before—and spoke at length about the recognition of the Armenian Genocide and deepening our economic, scientific and economic ties.

What I most cherished were the opportunities to interact with Israeli businesses, students, academics and ordinary citizens. At Technion, the pre-eminent Israeli institute of technology that numbers at least three Nobel laureates in its faculty, I gave a lecture on the quantum challenges of the twenty-first century. Since Technion was the institution with which the late Professor Nathan Rosen was associated, it was a distinct honour for me to speak there and interact with the professors and the student body. I also visited the Tel Aviv Technological University, which is doing cutting-edge work on Artificial Intelligence, and hammered out an agreement for joint research on AI between the university and Armenia.

* * *

Israel's great advantage is that it is a parliamentary republic that upholds the tenets of liberal democracy. On the one hand, it resembles numerous liberal democratic nations; on the other hand, it exhibits several distinctive attributes. From the onset, Israel was envisioned as a Jewish democratic state—an idea that embodied the consensus of various Zionist ideologies. Surprisingly, there is little contradiction between these two defining characteristics. The right to self-determination for peoples, manifested in the form of an independent national entity, is regarded as an inherent civil right, making the concepts of a "Jewish state" and "democracy" interchangeable. Nevertheless, the establishment of Israel in accordance with the Jewish national idea and the Zionist movement has significantly shaped its ideological and political character and exerted considerable influence on its democracy.

A distinctive attribute of Israeli society is the absence of a predominant political force, which necessitates rule by coalition governments. The proportional representation of a faction within the Knesset, Israel's parliament, typically determines the allocation of ministerial portfolios to said faction. The law does not explicitly specify the permissible ministries within the government; rather, it is the prerogative of the prime minister to determine their composition. Functioning as a collegial body, the government reaches decisions through majority voting, ensuring collective participation in the decision-making process.

Israel is also distinguished by the prominent legal standing it accords to deputy ministers, who occupy a fully-fledged political position in government. The law specifies that deputy ministers must be members of the Knesset. The appointment and dismissal of deputy ministers do not fall under the purview of individual ministers, but are collective decisions made by the government as a whole. The elevated status of deputy ministers is also a product of a political system populated by numerous influential political parties. This practice facilitates the prime minister's task of forming a coalition government by allowing for the appointment of a minister from one party and a deputy minister from another. The system thus mitigates the likelihood of strategic crises that could precipitate chaos and anarchy, a vital criterion for a nation confronting heightened internal and external threats. In other words, it cleverly maintains a balance of power.

In examining the structure of Israel's state power, one cannot overlook its legal framework, deeply rooted in history. This framework draws upon four primary sources: "Jewish law", encompassing the Talmud and Jewish religious legislation; "Ottoman law", referring to the legal code of the former Ottoman Empire; "English law", which has influenced the system since the era of the British Mandate; and "Israeli law", comprising legislation passed by the Knesset, municipal ordinances and Supreme Court judgments.

The jurisdictions in which these systems are applied are not rigidly confined. Nevertheless, when it comes to personal status matters, Jewish law takes precedence over the others, while Ottoman laws predominantly govern disputes related to land ownership.

* * *

Israel's economic trajectory has always been heavily influenced by ideological and political factors. Situated in a tumultuous region, the nation's economic partnerships were restricted to select military and political allies, resulting in reduced interactions with

Eastern Europe, which initially fuelled Jewish immigration. The persistent military conflicts in the Middle East have also led to a heightened level of militarisation within Israel's economy. Unlike other settlement nations, Israel's economic foundation was established in a dynamic and expedited manner, deviating from conventional stages of development. Factors such as accelerated borrowing, production and management practices driven by foreign policy and ideological considerations, the country's small size, and the rapid pace of global civilisation following the scientific and technological revolution contributed to this phenomenon.

In addition to these factors, the Jewish diaspora played a significant role in the development of Israel's economy. Jewish communities from around the world provided financial support, investments, and expertise, which contributed to the growth and modernisation of the Israeli economy. The influx of skilled professionals and entrepreneurs from the diaspora brought new ideas, innovation, and business networks to the country, fostering economic development and technological advancements.

Israel's distinct budgetary framework borrowed from the British model, comprised of the amalgamation of the consolidated fund and the national loan fund. However, the concept of segregating current and capital long-term revenues and expenditures, predicated on such a structure, proved highly compatible with Israel's circumstances. As a nation in economic transition, characterised by a remarkably elevated level of government expenditure and a significant proportion of foreign capital in its overall financial resources, it was deemed preferable for the state apparatus and primary expenditures to be funded, whenever possible, through internal, relatively dependable, and low-inflationary means like taxes and service sales. Simultaneously, loans, particularly of a long-term nature, could also be utilised to facilitate economic development.

Since its inception, one of the primary objectives of the state has been to alleviate the trade deficit. Following the establishment of the State of Israel, the country adopted a prolonged stance of stringent protectionism. Initially, the emphasis was on import substitution as the principal guideline for developing domestic production in relation to foreign economic interactions. In the 1950s, many developing nations pursued a policy aimed at replacing foreign goods in the local market through measures like customs protectionism, import quotas, exchange rate controls, and comprehensive support for domestic entrepreneurship. In the case of Israel, the early stages of import substitution were shaped not by deliberate national interests and a comprehensive approach to economic development, but rather by the prevailing, at times specific, needs of the country.

The establishment and growth of large-scale industry were primarily driven by the state and trade union sectors of the economy assuming a leading role. The state employed various administrative mechanisms to steer economic affairs, exemplified by the utilisation of a "little black book" of Pinchas Sapir, a prominent figure who held the positions of minister of Finance and minister of Trade and Industry at different times. This renowned government official wielded sole decision-making authority in determining the location of specific enterprises, their ownership structure and the extent of state subsidies. He meticulously recorded all these particulars in a dark little notebook, effectively guiding the trajectory of the Israeli economy.

Israel had a noteworthy advantage, as we have noted—a substantial Jewish diaspora spanning numerous countries worldwide, alongside the international relationships of the country's Arab population. As economic activities became increasingly globalized, the significance of connections with the diaspora intensified. Despite internal trade restrictions, Jewish and Arab communities managed to maintain commercial links on an international scale. In the present era, with nation-states assuming a diminished role in the global economy and the ascendance of groups sharing common ethnic heritage and cultural values, Israel actively leverages its diaspora connections to expand the involvement of its companies in overseas production. This phenomenon of diaspora engagement also characterizes other ethnic segments within the global diaspora (such as the Chinese, Indians, Japanese and others), constituting a vital and dynamic component of the world economy.

By the twenty-first century, government agencies had made considerable efforts to establish a sufficiently efficient system of an innovative economy in Israel. One notable example of an outstanding cooperation model is the collaborative R&D programme between Israeli start-ups and leading transnational corporations (TNCs), meticulously developed by the Office of the Chief Scientist (OCS). Participation requirements for TNCs entail a minimum annual income of $2 billion and global reach, while Israeli start-ups should have an annual income not exceeding $70 million, abstain from engagement with TNCs and focus primarily on R&D activities. Currently thirty-seven prominent companies, including Cisco, Alcatel, HP, IBM, Intel, NEC and others, participate in this programme. The OCS provides half of the necessary funding for joint R&D, while the remaining portion is contributed by the partnering TNC.

What is striking is that the involvement of TNCs in this programme does not solely involve direct financial contributions. It can also include the provision of essential infrastructure, licenses for necessary software and other support measures. In such instances, the ownership of intellectual property rights may be shared between the research partners or entirely held by the Israeli start-up. This programme has the potential to yield significant success in addressing the challenge of preserving Israel's innovative capacity domestically, while simultaneously promoting Israeli innovation prospects worldwide. This is achieved by enabling TNCs to implement the technologies resulting from their collaboration with Israeli start-ups across their diverse branches, thereby showcasing the prowess of Israeli innovation on a global scale.

* * *

Since its foundation, Israel has been engaged in a constant struggle for its survival. This has underscored the utmost significance of safeguarding the security and integrity of the state against both external and internal threats, leading to the prominence of law enforcement agencies over civilian matters. As a result, the formulation of defence strategy was significantly influenced by these agencies. Notably, this trend was established during the tenure of David Ben-Gurion, who served as both prime minister and minister of Defence. His perception of Israel's position in the Middle East and the indispensable nature of the security apparatus laid the groundwork for subsequent defence plans.

The Jewish community refers to the very concept of security as *bitachon*, a term that encompasses notions of security, assurance and guarantees in Hebrew. Prior to the establishment of the State of Israel, this term was primarily used within the context of Judaism, symbolising a sense of faith-based identity and security, accompanied by self-assurance. After 1948, *bitachon* assumed a predominantly military and political connotation. The historical persecution endured by the Jewish people, including the haunting memories of the Holocaust, intertwined with life in a hostile environment and a perpetual state of preparedness for mobilisation, gave rise to an atmosphere of what I would call "subdued unease" in Israeli society.

The distinct sense of security experienced by the Jewish people sets it apart from the way other nations perceive this concept. It is characterised by heightened sensitivity. Former

Israeli Foreign Minister Abba Eban eloquently highlighted this cognitive paradox, which arises from the disparity between Israeli strength and the psychology of vulnerability. Even a thrown stone, let alone a bomb, is perceived by Israelis as a direct threat to the very existence of the entire nation. Hence a more accurate translation of *bitachon* would not simply be "security" but rather "an absolute state of security". It encompasses not only a feeling of security but also the absence of potential threats.

In 2016, the Israel Defence Forces (IDF) published their official strategy. Examining the objectives and principles of the IDF doctrine reveals their diverse nature. The actions of the IDF are directed towards safeguarding Israel's security from both external and internal adversaries, while concurrently bolstering its standing in the regional and global arena. This implies a close intertwining of security and foreign policy. The IDF is expected to be versatile, prepared to undertake any tasks assigned by the Supreme High Command that go beyond conventional military operations. Nevertheless, the IDF strategy bears a certain degree of inconsistency. The core element of the doctrine revolves around the principle of deterring potential adversaries. In the event of war, the swiftest triumph over the enemy with minimal casualties becomes crucial. The paradox lies in the fact that achieving this objective necessitates a pre-emptive offensive operation aimed at neutralising the enemy's armed forces even before they attain full combat readiness. In simple terms, for a rapid triumph with minimal losses, Israel is always compelled to strike first.

The issue of nuclear weapons has held a significant position in the Israeli Concept of National Security since the 1980s. The origins of the Israeli nuclear programme go back to the 1950s, aided by French experts. David Ben-Gurion believed that Israel's mere possession of nuclear weapons would have a calming influence on its Arab neighbours, potentially fostering enduring peace. However, reality has revealed that it is more advantageous for Israel to maintain secrecy around its nuclear capabilities, preserving the option to accumulate, modernise and potentially employ them. Israel harboured concerns over the prospect of other Middle Eastern nations acquiring nuclear weapons. "The Begin Doctrine" emerged as a result, stipulating that a hostile country would be prevented from obtaining or developing nuclear weapons that could pose a threat to the Jewish state.

In conclusion, it is important to highlight that the State of Israel stands as an example of small nations that have successfully accomplished the formidable undertaking of establishing their independence. Clearly, an independent state extends beyond superficial symbols (such as flag, anthem and coat of arms) to embody a purposeful coherence driven by a national ideology. In broad terms, Israel fulfils various significant roles, elevating it to the status of an advanced power whose interests must be taken into account by both regional and global stakeholders: safeguarding its historical and cultural legacy, Israel presents itself as an entity deeply rooted in ancient history; Israeli citizens confront daily threats; however, they stand ready to make personal sacrifices in order to fortify their country and its institutions; despite its ideological designation as the "Jewish state", Israel remains a secular nation with independent executive, legislative, and judicial branches; Israel has consistently demonstrated its resolve as an active participant in international relations; and the Jewish diaspora, one of the most influential worldwide, is deeply integrated into the socio-political and economic fabric of various countries. Israel is regarded by the global Jewish elite as a focal point that organises and reinforces the influence of the Jewish factor in international political and economic spheres. This factor automatically grants Israel the status of one of the two transnational states (alongside Ireland) whose strength is not derived solely from conventional factors of Realpolitik, such as size, geography, population, or natural resources.

It is crucial to understand the potential risks and threats inherent in the current landscape. With the escalating confrontation between the United States, China and Russia, extricating itself from the necessity of making a definitive choice will prove increasingly arduous for Israel. Neutrality now presents a formidable challenge, necessitating a comprehensive restructuring of its international political strategy. Israel must now strike a delicate balance between adaptability and steadfastness, practising astute foreign policy that eschews unwarranted machismo and populism from the equation. This is a challenge for all small states.

6

ESTONIA

GLIMPSE OF A FUTURE

Estonia is one of the most striking examples of a country that has changed beyond recognition. I first went there as a seventeen-year-old, the head of a student delegation. We pictured Estonia as a microcosm of the West inside Soviet Union—it had that reputation—and its capital Tallinn was said to grant a window into the world beyond our sealed frontiers. It delivered more than I had imagined. You could practically see Helsinki from the rooftops of its buildings. The USSR's great and good—and their children, grandchildren, and relatives—all holidayed there. Among others, I met and befriended the grandchild of a politburo member in Tallinn. Young Estonians, for their part, preferred to travel to Armenia: that is where they could barter for Western denims with members of the Armenian diaspora visiting home. Tallinn holds a special place in my heart for another reason. Unless sponsored by their parents, newlyweds in the Soviet Union seldom honeymooned and generally returned to work soon after the marriage ceremony. Since Nouneh and I could not have a church wedding—and I knew how much she had wanted a religious ceremony—I decided that I would take my wife away. As the recipient of the Lenin scholarship award for my academic performance, I earned a princely stipend that was roughly equal to the monthly salary of a professor. By organising my expenses carefully, I could afford the trip. But where would we go? Nouneh and I blurted out the same answer: Estonia. The memory of the visit that followed in the winter of 1978—long morning walks on the pavements of Tallinn, touring the libraries, attending concerts—is lodged vividly in my memory.

The beauty of Tallinn concealed a great deal of agony, which would become apparent thirteen years later. A visitor to Tallinn in 1992 would have seen a bleak picture: apartment blocks without heating, bare shelves at supermarkets, a serious shortage of medicine and oil, and a fractured government. Half a century of communist rule had culminated in the loss of Estonia's former economic ties, its currency and a significant part of its own production. Inflation was at 1,000 per cent and the capital's population was evacuated to the countryside to cope with scarcity of food. Three decades on, Estonia is a prosperous and developed state, a member of NATO and the European Union. That isn't all: Estonia also has the lowest public debt to GDP ratio in the EU and is now firmly ensconced in a league of politically and economically free nations. Tallinn, its capital, has been repeatedly recognised as one of the most innovative cities in the world. The state hasn't retreated: it provides the population with services whose quality is comparable, if not superior, to what is on offer in the most developed countries.

Estonia's transition to its current state was riddled with seemingly insurmountable impediments. In addition to the hardships arising from the USSR's rapid collapse, Estonia had to overcome the many vulnerabilities seeded over long decades of Soviet statehood. There was no private business in the country; the food market, designed to function in accordance with top-

1. At my desk in Yerevan, Soviet Armenia, with the IBM PC XT machine on which we perfected Wordtris 1980s.

2. Meeting Mrs Thatcher, who as Prime Minister had put me on the spot, in her retirement. Early 1990s.

3. En-route to Armenia with Shirlene Sarkissian, better known as Cher, with a humanitarian mission in the winter of 1994.

4.With Bill Clinton in London. Late 1990s.

5. Presenting credentials to Her Majesty Queen Elizabeth II
following my recovery. October 1998. PA Images / Fiona Hanson.

6. His Royal Highness Charles III, one of the most humane
monarchs in the world, visited Armenia in 2013 as my guest.

7. Being inaugurated as the Fourth President of Armenia.
April 2018.

8. Pushing for peace and dialogue in the midst of protest and
agitation. Republic Square, Yerevan, Armenia. April 2018.
Photographer Asatur Esayan.

9. Nouneh and I at a concert with Emmanuel Macron of France and the charming First Lady Brigitte Macron. October 2018.

10. Catching up with my old friend Henry Kissinger in New York. October 2018.

11. Visiting Sergio Mattarella, a long-standing friend and President of Italy. November 2018.

12. Conversing with Chancellor Angela Merkel of Germany, who had earlier reminded me that she had attended my lectures on Quantum Physics. November 2018.

13. With my beloved wife Nouneh, and our grandchildren Armen Jr, Gabriel and Savannah. December 2018.

14. A conversation with Sheikh Hamad bin Khalifa Al Thani, the wise leader of Qatar, is always a learning experience. December 2021

15. Sultan bin Mohamed Al-Qasimi, the ruler of Sharjah and the benefactor of a historic church in Armenia, is one of the most erudite world leaders I have met. January 2019.

16. With Joe Biden in February 2019. I asked him if he was planning to run for the US Presidency.

17. Addressing the Armenian General Benevolent Union in Paris in February 2019.

18. Exchanging views with Secretary General of the United Nations António Guterres. April 2019.

19. With Prime Minister Lee Hsien Loong of Singapore during his visit to Armenia in September 2019.

20. Taking the Kardashian sisters to dinner in Yerevan during their visit to Armenia in October 2019. Kim is an untiring champion of Armenia.

21. The world is a poorer place without Shinzo Abe of Japan.
October 2019.

22. Sheikha Moza bint Nasser, a transformative figure in Qatar's
history. November 2019.

23. There is never a dull moment with Sheikh Tamim bin Hamad Al Thani, the young, promising Emir of Qatar. November 2019.

24. With President Mahmoud Abbas. I made it a point to visit him in Ramallah during my trip to Israel in January 2020.

25. Being received by President Emmanuel Macron, a strong friend of Armenia, at the Elysee Palace in Paris in October 2020.

26. Being received by my good friend King Abdullah II bin Al-Hussein during my state visit to Jordan in November 2020.

27. With His Holiness at the Vatican. October 2021.

28. Meeting Mario Draghi, Prime Minister of Italy,
in October 2021.

29. Exchanging vows with my beloved wife of 45 years at the ancient Haghartsin Monastery. Among its patrons is the ruler of Sharjah. October 2021.

30. Sharing my views with Naftali Bennet, Prime Minister of Israel, in November 2021.

31. With my friend Narendra Modi, the prime minister of India, a country with which Armenia has had cordial relations for millennia. November 2021.

32. Mohamed bin Zayed Al Nahyan, the President of the UAE and the ruler of Abu Dhabi, is realising the dream of Sheikh Zayed, the founder of the United Arab Emirates. December 2021.

down directives, had effectively crumbled; goods and services were scarce; money had no real value; and savings were worthless. Perhaps the biggest barrier of all to success was the Soviet legacy of unproductive job security, which, in the grim economic atmosphere, snuffed out citizen initiative and motivation.

Estonia dealt with this basket of problems, as the European Commission's Signe Ratso has noted, by embarking on rapid reforms: price liberalisation, the introduction of its own currency and the implementation of a tight fiscal policy. These measures were augmented swiftly by privatisation, liberalisation of foreign direct investment (FDI) and trade, and other structural reforms. Tallinn supervised its transition from a centrally planned economy to an entrepot of free trade through a combination of macroeconomic stabilisation (monetary, exchange rate and fiscal policies) and structural reforms such as price, trade, FDI liberalisation, banking sector reform, enterprise reform and competition policy. In 1992, it adopted the kroon as its currency. Pegged to the German mark, the kroon was fully convertible for current account transactions, with no restrictions on capital account convertibility.

The result? By 2005, Estonia had brought the structure of its economy in line with developed Western countries. And two decades on, it stands out as an acknowledged world leader in digitalisation and a pioneer of online voting, which it launched in 2005. Estonia is the only democracy that fully implements online voting in elections at the national level. Given the risks associated with online voting and the mixed experience of other democracies (most notably, of course, the United States of America), Estonia's willingness to persist with digital balloting is a measure of the system's stress-resistance, the credibility of political institutions and the electorate's faith in them. Governmental efficiency and political stability are underwritten by coalition governments, which, despite changes in their composition, maintain consistency in upholding long-term goals by not deviating from priorities such as a prudent tax policy and a knowledge-based economy.

Certainly, it would be inaccurate to say that *all* the circumstances were against Estonia at its independence from the USSR. Its position in the north of Europe, giving it access to the sea, and proximity to Finland were among the favourable factors that helped in the success of the development trajectory it chose. But this geographical advantage came with a critical downside: physical proximity to Russia—a reality that threatened to doom Estonia to the fate of a buffer state invested in survival and unable to devote its talents to generating lasting prosperity. Latvia and Lithuania supply examples of the alternative scenario (although, in all fairness, in comparison to several other post-communist states, they too have turned out to be relatively more stable and successful).

What made Estonia stand apart was a combination of factors: the political will of its first leaders, the belief reposed in the state's ability by society, the country's discipline and its willingness to face as a united nation hardships on the path to an affluent European future, and a competent financial policy as well as commitment to innovation, which optimised the management of limited human capital. Balanced budgets, starting off as a painful decision, have gone on to become not only a component of the country's brand, but also the key to an almost constant surplus.

Few individuals are better equipped to demystify the Estonian "miracle" than Mart Laar. Estonia's prime minister from 1992-1994 and then 1999-2002, Laar held the reins at two crucial periods: the end of the Soviet empire and the turn of the century. He has ascribed Estonia's runaway success to successive governments' adeptness at converting crisis into opportunity. The gravity of the situation at Estonia's independence called for rapid decision-making, but politicians had to be mindful that the public trust and tolerance had limits. If Laar and his young team of reformers went too far too fast, they risked inviting a backlash, potentially spawning an unbridgeable national divide and jeopardising any prospect of giving radical, alternative solutions a chance. At the same time, a gradualist approach to, and slow implementation of, unpopular and painful yet necessary measures not only risked failure but would also prolong the crisis. This tension created a period known as "extraordinary politics", the banner under which Estonia's leadership rationalised the imperative to rapidly enact bold initiatives.

The Estonian leadership learned two crucial lessons from their reforms: prioritise political change over economic transformations and take decisive decisions despite the challenges and sacrifices involved. While the success of their chosen path vindicated them, these lessons were not absorbed or applied rigidly. Political consensus was vital in implementing significant reforms whose legitimacy, particularly among ethnic Estonians, was underwritten by a genuine appreciation of the dire state of affairs and a collective aspiration to reintegrate into Europe. Thus, the overhaul that followed was accepted as a bitter yet necessary remedy—to be embraced if Estonia were to secure a place among prosperous European nations. The Estonian leadership, to its credit, recognised the indispensability of consensus in the democratic process, and promoted accountable institutions and fair elections as the means to achieving it. Democratisation was deemed crucial in breaking away from the past and everything it represented. The bottom-up demand for change was complemented and bolstered top-down proposals.

Mart Laar, recounting the Estonian miracle, frequently highlights the youthfulness of his cabinet. In his first stint as prime minister, which he began when thirty-two, many of his ministers were younger than him. Their youth endowed them with an impatience that blurred the line between what was feasible and what was impossible. Ultimately, Laar and his comrades accomplished extraordinary feats. And the reason for this wasn't just their impatience; they were also wise. To ensure stability within the coalition government, the parties entered into an agreement to smooth out the implementation process of essential reforms without straying from the path of reform. This approach enabled the ruling party to prevail against populist obstacles and execute sound policies, irrespective of opposition discontent. Thus, the determination of the young to achieve what may have been dismissed as impossible by seasoned politicians became a key source of Estonia's modern success.

Reform wasn't a closed-off process. When devising policy, the government sought external input. It engaged various think tanks—The Heritage Foundation, the International Republican Institute, the Adam Smith Institute and Sweden's Timbro. Estonian think tanks also played a part. Collectively, they not only provided expertise but also facilitated public discussions, helping to make the programme transparent. However, unlike some other post-Soviet states, the government did not blindly follow international expertise. From the outset, Estonian leaders rejected assistance and loans from global economic institutions they feared would pave the way for structural reforms designed by outsiders. This decision came from a representative elite with long-term goals who had no desire to sugarcoat the pill for their own population, which, they believed, would eventually face the consequences as the Estonian leadership embraced unpopular measures like spending cuts and benefit reductions to balance the budget.

Transparency cemented the public's faith in the state. Still, recognising that resistance to change would inevitably arise at some point, the government maximised the available resources. A short while into the reforms, it achieved a balanced budget and solidified its importance through legislation. Subsequent budget adoptions became smoother as only balanced budgets were presented to parliament. Additionally, the government recognised the need to prepare the population for its institutional design. Decades of state paternalism had resulted in the decay, if not death, of economic individualism, initiative and risk-taking. Tallinn, in pressing for a national revitalisation, stressed that it could only assist those willing to help themselves. Despite the unpopularity of this stance, the government did not change course. Instead, it strove to change attitudes. And slowly but surely, the principles of open trade, the removal of restrictions on entrepreneurship, privatisation of state-owned companies, and the promulgation of plain and comprehensible rules fostered competition and increased citizen participation in economic activities. By relinquishing regulatory powers and eliminating subsidies and selective privileges, the state eradicated the sources of potential corruption.

Mart Laar has said that Estonia's dire financial situation actually simplified the choices before him and his team. Their top priority was achieving macroeconomic stability, which required monetary reform and a balanced budget. Subsidies to state-owned companies were revoked not only because of funding constraints but also to stimulate new businesses and drive structural changes in the economy. Although building consensus within the government posed challenges, ministers were united by common objectives: curbing inflation and inflationary pressures from the east, establishing a stable exchange rate and overcoming the cash crisis. Pegging the Estonian kroon to the German mark instilled confidence in the Estonian economy. But balancing the budget proved much more difficult initially because the underlying ambition, though appealing in theory, faced significant opposition in practice. Enterprises no longer receiving state funding faced the choice of adapting to survive or dissolving under bankruptcy. Ultimately, many attuned themselves to the new reality. As mentioned earlier, a balanced budget became an essential pillar of the Estonian financial system, consistently providing the state with surpluses.

Another remarkable feature of Estonia—one of its smartest economic decisions—was the implementation of a flat tax. This instantly addressed multiple issues. Tax collection became much simpler, and the system became clearer, making life significantly easier for both taxpayers and fiscal officials. The latter, freed from excessive paperwork and complex calculations, were able to focus on combating tax evasion. The upshot: the tax system's efficiency improved, compliance with tax laws increased, the shadow economy took a severe hit and tax revenues began to surge. The numbers speak for themselves: in 1992, Estonia had around 2,000 registered businesses; by the of 1994, that figure had soared to 70,000. Estonia, reborn in 1991 as a country of the working class, had transformed in a matter of a few years into a nation of entrepreneurs. Naturally, this transformation also drastically cut down the unemployment rate.

Estonia's tax system, a catalyst for steady economic growth, fuels entrepreneurialism by exempting income reinvested in enterprise development. Personal income tax matches the corporate tax rate (20 per cent) and doesn't apply to dividends. Property tax is solely imposed on land, not real estate or capital. With small exceptions, domestic corporations registered in Estonia enjoy full exemption from double taxation. Its bold (and sometimes unpopular) measures have not only helped the Estonian government quickly achieve macroeconomic stability and sustained long-term economic growth. They have helped Estonia dominate the global Tax Competitiveness Index for nine consecutive years.

Estonia's developmental journey clearly demonstrates that digitalisation was more than just a passing fad; it was a vital need for the newly independent nation. By digitising public administration, time and effort were sublimated into fostering innovation, encouraging entrepreneurs and fashioning a favourable technological landscape. "E-Estonia", representing the nation's most ambitious technological undertaking, has become an integral part of every citizen's identity. This all-encompassing initiative seamlessly interconnects every facet of the nation, including its politics, and permeates every aspect of life, from local affairs to matters of utmost state importance.

The success of Estonia's e-government implementation rests on the "X-Road" platform. Introduced in 2001, it is a secure layer for sending and receiving data between both private and public sector organisations and facilitates stable interaction and data exchange between the state and businesses. More than 2,300 public and private services utilise it, while nearly all of Estonia's population possesses a digital ID and digital signature. The Estonian government estimates that this electronic system saves the state around 2 per cent of GDP and more than 800 years of working time annually. Since 2016, X-Road's open-source code has been published under licence from MIT, and it has been integrated with Finland's data exchange system since 2018.

The advantages of early digitalisation became apparent during the Covid-19 pandemic. Estonia was fully prepared to deliver educational and medical services online. This was especially useful in the face of demographic challenges, such as the ageing of schoolteachers; declining school and university sizes due to urbanisation and migration; and a decrease in the corresponding age group. These challenges have led to the closure of many rural schools and consolidation of university departments.

Small, closely connected networks of motivated civil servants and entrepreneurs are believed to have played a pivotal role in Estonia's success, something that might have proved challenging for nations with lower levels of trust. Estonia's "luck" arose from its near-bankrupt starting point, which compelled it to avoid large centralised systems. Instead, a distributed IT infrastructure emerged as a more viable solution to meet the government's and citizens' needs. As it refused to settle for less and embarked on its unique path, other factors also contributed to Estonia's triumph in digital transformation. First, credit must go to the technological foundation inherited from the Soviet era. Estonia gained independence with a talented pool of researchers and IT experts trained in advanced specialised institutes. Second, these talents swiftly integrated into the rapidly expanding Scandinavian telecommunications companies and the burgeoning domestic private enterprises, capitalising on favourable conditions for their development. The telecommunications sector in neighbouring Scandinavia experienced unparalleled growth in the 1990s, precipitating an environment that nurtured innovation in Estonia. Third, decentralisation in the implementation of digitalisation enhanced trust in the systems and increased efficiency. Fourth, a strong commitment to continuous technological updates ensured that solutions remained current within a thirteen-year timeframe. Fifth, priority was given to in-house development from scratch, rather than relying on off-the-shelf software. This approach kindled innovation while minimising technological vulnerabilities. Finally, the system was designed to streamline processes and eliminate redundancy by requiring businesses and citizens to provide data only once.

The effectiveness of these conditions was bolstered by the unwavering commitment of the government and skilled workforce. However, it is important to acknowledge that not all principles have been fully executed. Still, digitalisation has liberated valuable resources for development and propelled social modernisation in a small population enthusiastic about reclaiming its independent statehood. As a vital component of public administration, it has played a central role in Estonia's economic expansion, producing distinctive ties between the state and its citizens.

Beyond its frontiers, Estonia, unlike many European countries and even some fellow NATO members, continues to evince an unwavering commitment to the US-led world order. The US State Department recognises Estonia as a reliable and effective transatlantic partner. Despite its challenging neighbourhood, Tallinn chooses not to diversify its partnerships but rather sends clear signals of its intentions, expecting reciprocity in return. This confidence in Estonia's positioning is no doubt influenced by its limited engagement with China. Despite China's significant presence in Estonia's science-intensive and technological sectors, Tallinn has consistently resisted growing Chinese influence without being deterred. In 2011, when the Dalai Lama visited Tallinn, Beijing retaliated by placing a ban on the import of Estonian dairy products into China. This had minimal effect on Estonia's budget revenues, however, due to the relatively low level of trade and interconnectedness between the two countries.

From its expertise (and significant role) in Arctic research to hosting NATO cyber units and the renowned Silmet rare metal factory, Estonia holds obvious importance for China. Notably, it ranks second in the world for neodymium production, trailing only behind China itself. Beijing extends its influence primarily through Huawei, which invests in science and telecommunications. The ramifications of this engagement are occasionally visible in acts of self-censorship, such as the University of Tartu's refusal to publish, in 2020, an article critical of its agreement with Huawei. The University of Tallinn houses a Confucius Institute, and Mandarin courses are offered at some public universities funded by China.

The deregulation and open trade policies that have helped raise Estonia economically have also rendered it susceptible to potential infringements on its telecommunications sovereignty and even surveillance, spanning from airports to the fibre optic networks beneath the Baltic Sea. The Estonian government, always a quick adaptor, has clearly learned from this experience—a fact it demonstrated by requiring operators to remove Huawei equipment by 2023. The situation surrounding the acquisition of Estonian technology companies' assets by Chinese state-owned enterprises, however, presents a more complex scenario.

But despite such challenges, Estonian leaders exhibit a generally consistent approach in pursuing their chosen course, remaining focused and undeterred by situational factors. In the summer of 2022, Estonia, along with Latvia, followed Lithuania in withdrawing from the China-Central and Eastern European Countries Cooperation format. This decision highlights the strong alignment of policies among the Baltic nations, prioritising the European Union, shaped by their unique circumstances, including their proximity to Russia. While stepping away from the format, Estonian representatives stressed their commitment to continued cooperation with China within the framework of a rules-based world order and their own values, particularly human rights.

It is in this spirit that, in 2021, the Estonian prime minister Kaja Kallas declined to participate in a virtual summit hosted by Chinese president Xi Jinping, instead delegating her foreign minister to attend. Simultaneously, Estonia's major publications ceased running advertisements funded by the Chinese government. In 2020, Estonia even signed a petition denouncing China's policies towards Hong Kong and the Uyghurs of Xinjiang. That same year, employees of the Estonian Information System Authority (RIHA) were prohibited from installing TikTok due to security concerns regarding their data.

Estonia, after initially signing a Memorandum of Understanding with China for the New Silk Road project in 2017, has adopted a different stance in recent years. In 2021, Prime Minister Kallas delivered a speech emphasising the need to counter the Silk Road project by integrating Western countries' infrastructure.

The aim of the speech was to capture the attention of major Western leaders and underline the potential of small states like Estonia that could still be "saved". This proactive approach very clearly showcases Tallinn's determination to go beyond mere adaptation to the changing world order and actively position itself as a beneficiary in the future configuration of international relations, in which Estonia will seek to reassess and strengthen the dominance of the West.

* * *

Knowledge, the willingness to tackle issues head-on, and the non-partisan approach to certain political and economic fundamentals: these have been the pillars of Estonia's success. There is, however, one area of concern that casts a shadow over this success, and that is Estonia's shrinking population. While positive trends in immigration exist, the small population size calls for more drastic measures if Estonia is to ensure that the sacrifices made by a generation in the 1990s bear long-lasting fruits.

With their unwavering commitment to innovation, economic discipline and responsible government, Estonia's elite and society exemplify the essence of a thriving state: constant, efficient and creative work. The Estonian elite, upholding the continuity of national interests and the trusting society, epitomise the triumph of human agency over history's hardships, even if those hardships played a role in shaping Estonian society. By rejecting populism on matters of national importance, particularly in implementing challenging and seemingly unfair financial measures, Estonia has created a system in which citizens have greater freedom to pursue their own happiness while contributing to the prosperity of the nation.

Estonia's foreign policy demonstrates that small states are not necessarily compelled to cooperate with everyone to survive; they can instead reach a level where they have the luxury of choosing reliable allies independently. In the 1990s, pragmatism and idealism converged, resulting in sound and effective decision-making. While such fortunate coincidences are rare in world politics, there is every reason to believe that, should the need arise, Estonian elites and society will pragmatically safeguard their ability to pursue their interests and ideals in the future.

7

SWITZERLAND
ALPINE ASCENT

Post-war Europe envied Switzerland. In a continent devastated by war, the mountainous confederation enveloped by the Alps came to epitomise beauty, sophistication and perfection. The late historian Tony Judt memorably described his elation, as a schoolboy in the 1950s, when he crossed from "poor and run-down" France into Switzerland: "a land of neat, flower-bedecked chalets, air-brushed streets, prosperous-looking shops, and smart, satisfied citizens." He might have added high culture. To attend the Lucerne Festival, for instance, is to be transported to a higher spiritual realm. Immersed in classical music, one can forget that, among comparable small states, only Singapore began with fewer natural resources than Switzerland. But federated Switzerland's political history, which dates back to the thirteenth century, is quite unlike centralised Singapore's.

It all began, if legend is to be believed, on 1 August 1291, when representatives of Uri, Schwyz and Unterwalden—the three autonomous small states known as 'cantons'—convened on a meadow called Rutli on the shores of Lake Lucerne to forge an alliance against the Habsburg dynasty. Historians dispute the details, but Switzerland's national myth is forged in the belief that this gathering of emissaries—which is said to have included the Swiss folk hero William Tell—made a solemn oath to support each other in the cause of preserving from external threats their freedom, independence and special status as highly independent members of the Holy Roman Empire.

What is indisputable is that the roots of modern Switzerland can be traced to the defensive alliance formed in the thirteenth century called the Swiss Confederation. The Habsburg threat prompted other cantons to join the grouping. In 1497, the first parliament of the cantons (the Tagsatzung) convened in Stans to codify and coordinate the actions of the confederation's members. Organised as a representative assembly, the Tagsatzung granted each canton, regardless of its size or population, an equal vote. The assembly convened periodically, usually in different locations, and the presidency rotated among the cantons on a fixed schedule. With responsibility for making decisions on matters of common interest, such as foreign relations, defence, taxation and the resolution of disputes between cantons, the Tagsatzung effectively functioned as a (relatively weak) central governing authority of the Old Swiss Confederation. Its members had the power to negotiate treaties, alliances and trade agreements, and to declare war and settle internal conflicts. And its utility became apparent whenever the cohesion of the confederation was tested—as it was during the Thirty Years' War, the Toggenburg War (1712-1718) and the Sonderbund War (1847)—and it was called upon to resolve conflict and maintain stability within the confederation.

The position of the Tagsatzung as a legitimate governing body was consecrated by the Peace of Westphalia, signed in 1648, which officially recognised the Swiss Confederation as a politically independent entity and gave legal status to the confederation's neutrality and autonomy. The Protestant Reformation, led by key figures such as Ulrich Zwingli and John Calvin, had altered the Swiss religious landscape, and the resulting conflict between Protestant and Catholic cantons culminated in religious factionalism and the ruinous Thirty Years' War (1618-48.) Fractured from within, Switzerland's hard-won independence fell apart with the French invasion of 1798 and the subsequent replacement of the confederation—which had grown to include thirteen cantons—with the rigidly unitary Helvetic Republic.

The cantons of Uri, Schwyz, and Nidwalden raised a force of 10,000 to fight the French but were forced to submit to the superior arms of the adversary. What ultimately brought down the Helvetic Republic was the endless squabbling, conflict, debt, and civil discord aggravated by unitary cast of the Helvetic state. "Switzerland is not like any other state," Napoleon Bonaparte finally conceded to Swiss representatives in 1802. "Nature has made your state a federal one, and no wise man would want to flout her." With the demise of the Helvetic Republic, the restored Old Swiss Confederation made way for the modern Swiss federal state. The 1815 Treaty of Paris, following the Napoleonic era, reaffirmed the legal standing of the perpetual neutrality of Switzerland, which by then was recognised to be constituted from twenty-two cantons enjoying, in theory at least, equal rights.

Beneath the surface, however, there was a deep division in Switzerland between Catholic and Protestant cantons. In 1845, the Catholics formed a secessionist alliance, the Sonderbund. This sparked a brief but decisive civil war (*Sonderbundskrieg*) in which the liberals prevailed. The French Revolution—or, more accurately, the ideas of equality and democracy emanating from that revolution—had profoundly affected Swiss liberals. And in 1848, led by such remarkable figures as Jonas Furrer, Switzerland formally transitioned from a loose confederacy of cantons into a relatively centralised federal state. The Federal Constitution, promulgated in 1848, made way for a stronger federal government with powers over defence, foreign affairs, trade and transportation. With its emphasis on democratic principles, it established separation of powers, enshrined individual rights and instituted a system of direct democracy.

It wasn't just the fervour for political reform that had ended the old confederation; the technological advances of the nineteenth century had also demonstrated its unsustainability. A measure of political autonomy was one thing, but Switzerland could not compete, develop and prosper while maintaining multiple internal borders, citizenships, currencies, weights and measurements. The Federal Constitution rationalised this bureaucratic convolution by introducing a single currency, measures, weights and citizenship. The old Tagsatzung was reinvented as a bicameral parliament: the *Ständerat*, or Council of States, representing the cantons, and the *Nationalrat*, or National Council, representing the citizens. The Oath of Rutli, having faded into oblivion, was vigorously revived during this period as an aid to the process of nation-state-building and consolidation. The result is that the Tagsatzung commands reverence to this day—a symbol of the early efforts of the Swiss cantons to address common challenges by laying the foundation for the principles of cooperation, decentralisation and direct democracy by which contemporary Switzerland is ordered— while 1 August, the date of the meeting at Rutli, is memorialised as Switzerland's National Day.

The centralisation of 1848 heralded the most significant shift in Switzerland's political structure and governance and incubated the most extraordinary (and, in Switzerland's experience, successful) experiment in direct democracy. The centralising impulse crystallised a political culture that was sufficiently secure in itself to nourish one of the most *decentralised* administrative systems in the world: local governance, taxation and public spending are cantonal—and thus *very* local—affairs in Switzerland; and the individual—invested with the power to mobilise public opinion and granted genuine means to shape, shore up, or abort laws—is truly sovereign.

Cultivating democratic habits and proclaiming neutrality was one thing; becoming prosperous within and shielding its neutrality in a volatile continent riven by repeated wars were challenges of a different magnitude. Switzerland's disadvantages were many: it was landlocked and cut off from sea routes, had few resources and no empire, and its Alpine terrain was a hindrance to communication and travel. So what turned Switzerland's fortunes around and gave rise to what came to be known as the "Swiss miracle"? Was it Weber's "Protestant ethic", manifested in the much-lauded work ethic and entrepreneurial spirit of the Swiss? Or, as some critics complained, was it Switzerland's adeptness at freeriding on the backs of others—appropriating technology by bypassing patents, as Eric Schiff documented in his landmark 1971 study *Industrialisation Without National Patents*, and competing with high-quality goods in markets opened by an unequivocally non-neutral process of globalisation by imperialism—that powered Switzerland's economic ascent? Or was Switzerland's entry into the topmost tiers of affluence, as Roman Studer has painstakingly demonstrated, a twentieth century phenomenon: a dividend of the morally stolid secrecy laws that governed its banking?

It is a combination of the three. The Swiss work ethic helped Switzerland develop a successful agricultural sector between the eighteenth and nineteenth centuries; the willingness to appropriate the patented technology of others—castigated by German businesses as "a system of parasitism"—supported by hydropower spawned a second industrialisation: by the close of the nineteenth century Switzerland was home to some of the leading companies in textiles, food-processing, and chemicals. Switzerland's fabled banking houses, devolved from prominent trading firms or titans in the textiles industry, had been enjoined to secrecy as early as 1713 by the Council of Geneva. And they played a pioneering role in their nation's domestic progress in the nineteenth century. Credit Suisse, for instance, was founded in 1856 by Alfred Escher, a prominent politician and industrialist, to finance the country's railways—a feat of engineering that finally linked landlocked Switzerland to Europe's trading ports—and went on to help create a single currency. The code of secrecy, enshrined in law in 1934, swiftly turned Switzerland into an international centre of wealth management in the twentieth century. Indeed, Swiss banks tended to prosper during periods of economic turmoil elsewhere because capital always seeks a safe haven.

Switzerland's economic transformation would not have been possible without Swiss neutrality. The country's long tradition of granting asylum to political refugees provoked a current of fury and resentment in the mid-nineteenth century because, in the eyes of its detractors, it could not claim be neutral while sheltering renegades from other regimes. But Swiss diplomats fiercely guarded their state's neutrality, which, when the world wars came around, acquired a new importance: Switzerland, by virtue of its detachment, could function as an impartial conduit between the belligerents. It did, to a great extent, perform this role. During the Second World War, however, Swiss neutrality effectively served as scaffolding for what can reasonably be called wartime profiteering. Swiss banks, the financial pillars of a nation that proclaimed to be dispassionately detached, arguably kept the Nazi boat afloat. In the words of the Swiss parliamentarian Jean Ziegler, they:

> fenced and laundered the gold stolen from the central banks of Belgium, Poland, Czechoslovakia, Holland, Luxembourg, Lithuania, Albania,

Norway, Italy, and elsewhere. It was they who financed Hitler's wars of conquest. Switzerland, the world's only neutral financial centre of truly international standing, accepted Hitler's looted gold throughout the war years in payment for industrial goods or as bullion that was fenced and laundered and exchanged for foreign currency or traded off in other financial centres under new, 'Swiss' identity.

Switzerland could reason that it was upholding, not undermining, its doctrine of neutrality by transacting business with Hitler. But as its neutrality made it an attractive destination for continental cash and bullion, Switzerland's political establishment, in an early example of what has become a commonplace phenomenon since, subordinated itself to the financial establishment. A nation that prided itself on providing sanctuary to the persecuted went out of its way to erect barricades against Jews fleeing the Nazi exterminations. The Third Reich began stamping "J" on the passports of Jewish citizens in 1938 on the advice of Switzerland, which wanted to identify and filter out Jewish arrivals from the rest.

Swiss conduct during the Second World War is explained away by some as a form of necessary appeasement—a pre-emptive insurance policy against the constant threat of invasion of Switzerland by Hitler, who in fact had a plan, Operation Tannenbaum, to do just that. But how could such reasoning be reconciled with the fact that Switzerland had accepted Nazi gold weeks before Germany's unconditional surrender to the Allies? In the immediate aftermath of the war, Swiss diplomats, led by Walter Stucki, forcefully pushed back against the imputation that their country had helped the Nazis—or compounded the harm caused to the victims of Nazism—and rejected the call to open their wartime profits to claims for compensation and settlement.

Part of the reason I have meditated on this ugly aspect of Switzerland's recent economic history is because it would be neglectful of me, as an Armenian, to sidestep it. For the same reason, I also recognise the healing power of acknowledging a wrong, which the Swiss actually did in the late 1990s, when a consortium of the top banks belatedly accepted that they had indeed profited from Nazi gold. That acknowledgement was followed, a year later, by a historic speech by Switzerland's then president, Arnold Koller, announcing the creation of a $4.7 billion fund to help "those who endured unspeakable sufferings" during the Holocaust. In 1998, Swiss lenders paid $1.25 billion to settle a class action on this subject. (I should note here that Switzerland holds a special place for me because it was the country that gave shelter—and, later, citizenship—to Albert Einstein after he relinquished his German nationality and moved to Zurich in 1895. I first went to Switzerland with the reverence of a pilgrim visiting a holy place.)

A quarter century on from that reckoning with history, Switzerland's economy is characterised by the dominance of market laws, unrestricted competition, minimal government intervention. These principles shape the Swiss National Innovation System (NIS) and the roles of key actors within it. The federal government's involvement in innovation is limited; it concentrates its energies, instead, on creating and sustaining a favourable climate for innovation. It assumes the majority of costs for infrastructure, education, training and fundamental science, indirectly supporting researchers and their teams with grants and through state funding agencies.

Federal funds primarily support research and development at universities, public research institutes, non-profit research organisations and EU framework programmes. Private sector research and innovative projects, in keeping with the Swiss emphasis on free competition and minimum government intervention, do not receive direct funding from the federal budget. State ownership is limited to a few nationwide entities.

The private sector can receive indirect support through co-financing research projects carried out by universities in collaboration with private companies.

Cantonal budgets principally finance university education, university research, and a small portion of research and development partnerships between universities and private businesses. The cantonal authorities have significant autonomy in distributing budgetary funds for regional development. The Swiss National Science Foundation (NSF) and the Swiss Innovation Agency InnoSuisse play pivotal roles in Switzerland's scientific, technical and innovation policy. These federal agencies provide financial support through competitive selection processes. The NSF backs basic research across academic disciplines, prioritising areas that expand scientific knowledge but may have limited commercial potential. It pays special attention to helping young researchers and fostering Swiss participation in international scientific projects.

InnoSuisse, on the other hand, focuses on applied research projects aimed at commercialisation, supporting start-ups, renewable energy, environmental technologies and technology transfer. InnoSuisse's project support requires participation from private sector enterprises interested in commercialising project results and willing to co-finance at least 50 per cent of the project. This approach encourages collaboration between science and industry and contributes to Switzerland's top-ranking global innovation index in terms of scientific and technical partnerships between universities and businesses.

Switzerland's tax system is simple, transparent, business-friendly—and without specific tools to stimulate innovation. Bern believes that market laws, free competition and little government intervention are sufficiently excellent incentives for innovative activity. Switzerland's corporate income tax rates, consistently among the lowest in developed countries, have enabled entrepreneurs to make optimal decisions regarding investment, research and innovation.

The Swiss NIS revolves around the business sector. The majority of Swiss enterprises (99.7 per cent) are small and medium-sized, with a constant renewal of small businesses demonstrating their flexibility and responsiveness to market changes. Private businesses are the primary source of funding for R&D in Switzerland, and their focus is on industries such as pharmaceuticals, mechanical engineering, electrical equipment, electronics, optics, high-tech tools and the food industry. Swiss entrepreneurs also make substantial investments in fixed assets, exceeding the EU average. Armed with modern machinery, high-tech equipment and skilled workers, Swiss production unsurprisingly achieves high labour productivity in sectors such as pharmaceuticals, food, electricity, electronics and chemicals. Swiss businesses actively engage in international research, investing abroad as well as at home. Large companies, including Roche, Novartis, Nestlé, and others allocate a significant portion of their research and innovation investments to subsidiaries outside Switzerland. Additionally, foreign sources contribute significantly to Switzerland's domestic research and innovation spending, surpassing both the OECD and EU average.

Socially, Switzerland is a repudiation of the far-right fixation with homogeneity. Its success is a story also of harmonious human coexistence—of what I would call the beauty of balance. Many of the most iconic Swiss brands—from Nestlé and Patek Philippe to Maggi and Roche—were in fact spawned by migrants to Switzerland. Switzerland's achievement is especially striking given that its human cast is composed predominantly of descendants from nations—Germany, Italy, France—with a tragic history of mutual antagonism and war. In Switzerland, speakers of German, Italian and French have, through their joint endeavour to create a shared nationhood, willed into existence a model of successful heterogeneity. Switzerland's diversity is, in fact, a feature that distinguishes it from other small states. Singapore is another small state that has turned its diversity into strength. But while Singapore's rise was facilitated by the authority wielded by one party and one visionary leader, Switzerland reached the zenith of its prosperity via a bewilderingly democratic path.

Switzerland is the only country apart from Bosnia and Herzegovina, Andorra, and San Marino to be run by a collective executive. The Federal Council, Switzerland's national cabinet, functions as the joint head of state and government and is responsible as a whole for federal government. Its seven elected members, called Federal Councillors, exercise executive authority in areas of federal competence such as foreign affairs, defence, economy, finance, internal security and justice, and environment, communication and transportation. The Swiss president, a rotating position, acts as the nominal chair of the Federal Council but lacks any special powers in what is essentially and effectively a cabinet of equals. Major political parties are represented proportionally, and decision-making on federal affairs is a collegial process driven by consensus, collaboration and compromise. The Federal Council works closely with the Federal Assembly, composed of the National Council and the Council of States, on proposals, drafting legislation, and providing reports for deliberation and approval. This parliamentary oversight acts as a check on the Federal Council and ensures that policies are aligned with the Federal Constitution and the collective will of the Swiss people, as expressed in referenda.

From 1959 to 2003, a so-called "magic formula" of seat allocation ensured that the same set of major parties governed Switzerland: Free Democratic Party (FDP), Social Democratic Party (SP), Christian Democratic People's Party (CVP) and the populist Swiss People's Party (SVP). This consensus-building mechanism, by including all the big parties, prevented political polarisation. The distribution of seats was based on party strength in the Federal Assembly. The FDP, CVP and SP received two seats each, while the SVP received one seat. In 2003, the SVP achieved a significant victory by defeating Ruth Metzler, a CVP member, in Federal Council election—the first victory against an incumbent since the 1870s. This success broke the long-standing four-party consensus and led to the modification, for the first time in forty-four years, of the Federal Council's composition. But what is more remarkable is that this unvarying set-up at the top of the government existed alongside one of the most vibrant forms of direct democracy in the world.

Switzerland's political system is singular in its adherence to and enactment of direct democracy in the form of mandatory plebiscites, optional referenda and popular initiatives—a practice that originated in the medieval open balloting system called *Landsgemeinde*. Today, constitutional amendments warrant compulsory plebiscites, while a vote is optional when laws and regulations are subjected to change. The requirements for popular initiatives vary from canton to canton, but advocates of federal popular initiatives or constitutional changes wishing to trigger a national referendum must garner between 50,000 and 100,000 signatures. Any proposition that procures sufficient backers is then placed before the electorate, though the constitution is additionally safeguarded by the requirement of a double majority to amend it.

While direct democracy has worked well for Switzerland, its majoritarian dangers are obvious enough. If the dominance of the majority in direct popular votes carries the risk of undermining equality and individual protections, the lack of expertise among the general population in the minutiae of complex policy questions can oversimplify issues and produce nominally democratic outcomes that are detrimental to the health of Swiss democracy. Manipulation and populism are additional concerns:

charismatic leaders have demonstrated elsewhere their ability to incite public opinion for short-term gains and jeopardise long-term societal harmony. Frequent referenda and initiatives can lead also to policy instability, hindering effective governance and planning. Determined, well-financed groups can skew policies towards specific interests rather than the broader good of the society. Low voter engagement and limited access to accurate information can impair the moral legitimacy of decisions directed by direct democracy processes.

The best argument against the fearful possibilities of direct democracy in Switzerland is the Swiss record of direct democracy itself. Defenders of this tradition can cite a number of propositions—from approving tighter gun controls (2011) to rejecting increased holiday entitlement (2012), from condemning homophobia (2020) to rebuffing attempts to curb free movement of people from the EU (2021), from endorsing a global minimum tax on businesses and a plan to cut fossil fuels and reach zero emissions by 2050 (2023)—in which the electorate voted responsibly rather than reactionarily. But these instances do not necessarily nullify the inbuilt hazards of direct democracy, which can, in the absence of institutional guardrails, just as equally produce a benighted outcome, as indeed it did on the question of women's suffrage: a referendum to enfranchise women was defeated in 1959, and Swiss women obtained the right to vote only in 1971, well after small states such as Israel and Sri Lanka had elected female heads of government.

There is an institutional recognition of the perils of direct democracy in our toxically populist era—in 2019, the Supreme Court of Switzerland made an unprecedented intervention to overturn the result of a national referendum on tax laws on the grounds that lack of transparency had violated the freedom of the vote—and an increasing public recognition that striking a balance between direct and representative democracy with safeguards that protect minority rights, ensure informed decision-making, prevent manipulation or abuse of the system and expedite decision-making (particularly in the realm of foreign policy) is critical. As Dieter Ruloff and Thomas Bernauer, among other scholars, have argued, "a sword of Damocles hangs over [the Swiss government's] head in the form of referenda on foreign policy issues".

Switzerland has often been exposed to the tension arising from reconciling its passive foreign policy, anchored in political neutrality, with its hyperactive commercial engagements. Efforts by the economic affairs department of the Federal Council—the Swiss executive—to achieve deeper integration with Europe have frequently been stymied at the ballot box. But Switzerland's conception of its neutrality has sufficiently evolved since 1992, when voters narrowly rejected the proposition to join the European Economic Area (EEA), and 2002, when Switzerland became the 190th member of the United Nations following a referendum in which 54 per cent of the Swiss electorate voted in favour of membership.

In 1993, the Federal Council set out Switzerland's revised approach to maintaining neutrality in a transformed geopolitical landscape. Recognising that neutrality as it was commonly understood alone could not safeguard the nation against emerging threats like terrorism, organised crime and environmental destruction, Switzerland, it said, would henceforth "exercise its neutrality in a way that allows it to take the necessary military precautions for its own defence, also with respect to new threats. Depending on the threat, this could also entail international cooperation in the preparation of defensive measures". This approach was described as an "active" foreign policy capable of transcending traditional notions of neutrality.

Micheline Calmy-Rey, appointed Switzerland's foreign minister in 2003, reinterpreted this to mean a return to

Switzerland's "humanitarian tradition". A native of Sion in the south-western canton of Valais, Calmy-Rey studied international relations at the prestigious Graduate Institute of International Studies in Geneva, before launching her political career there in the 1980s. Two decades later, as the first female head of Switzerland's Department of Foreign Affairs, she advanced the concept of "active neutrality". She did not repudiate neutrality but redefined it to mean active political engagement. Two months into her job, she gave an illustration of this by becoming the first holder of her job to cross the demarcation line between the two Koreas and hold talks with North Korea's leadership.

I got to know Calmy-Rey well. As president, I received her in Armenia—she received the Armenian Medal of Honour a year after leaving the presidency—and worked closely with her on a number of initiatives. Her "active diplomacy" was not a play on words. Calmy-Rey pushed hard to find a settlement to the intractable conflict between Israel and Palestine. She expanded Switzerland's presence in Asia and Africa, vocally championed peace and human rights, and established the Human Rights Council in Geneva. Her fervour sometimes had limits: in 2003, when the Swiss parliament voted to recognise the Armenian Genocide, Calmy-Rey spoke against it out of fear of alienating Turkey, which cancelled a proposed visit by her. But she recovered quickly: her hesitation on the question of the Armenian Genocide, for instance, vanished fairly fast, and by 2005 she was urging Turkey, in the interests of long-term peace, "to conduct an in-depth historical research of its own past". Discussion, even with those with whom we disagree, is the essence of diplomacy and often the best solution to problems. On the eve of the centennial anniversary of the First World War—the period during which Ottoman Turks perpetrated the Armenian Genocide—I was asked by Swiss media if I would engage with the Turkish president Recep Tayyip Erdogan, and if so how I might broach the subject of our difficult past. My answer, informed by history but looking to the future, was clear:

> First, I would say, 'Good morning, Mr President, I think we have an issue to discuss together. You are the president of Turkey and I am the president of Armenia. My family, my grandparents, are from Erzurum, Van and Bitlis, and there is a history behind my own family. Let's speak about our individual stories.'

Calmy-Rey, who believed in stern dialogue, drew the ire of her colleagues, particularly on the right, for what seemed to them like an unusually activist foreign policy—but she proceeded nonetheless to place Switzerland front and centre on thorny international issues during her tenure as foreign minister (2003-11), before moving to the presidency in 2011.

The transformation of Swiss neutrality initiated in 1993 and intensified by Calmy-Rey a decade later was in evidence in 2022, when Switzerland reacted to the conflict in Ukraine by adopting EU sanctions against Russia. "We are in an extraordinary situation where extraordinary measures could be decided," Swiss president Ignazio Cassis told a news conference in Bern. Switzerland was not finally shedding its neutrality; but its conception of what it means to be neutral has been changing to keep pace with the altering geopolitical landscape. The advantages of neutrality are many—for the world, the utility of a neutral territory where conflicting parties can convene cannot be overstated. At the same time, the Swiss belief that neutrality will guarantee its security is fading. One indication of this are the consequences of the growing strategic rivalry between the United States and China for Switzerland, which are the subject of heated debate within the country.

China's significance to Switzerland, particularly in the economic sphere, has been steadily growing—although the United States remains its second-largest business partner overall. In 2007, Switzerland officially recognised China as a market economy, and in 2014, it became the first continental European country to establish a free trade agreement with China. This relationship further deepened when Switzerland joined the Asian Infrastructure Investment Bank in early 2016. Johann N. Schneider-Ammann, Switzerland's then president, forged an innovative strategic partnership with China in April of the same year. Currently, China ranks as Switzerland's third most important trading partner, trailing behind the EU and the United States. This trend is expected to intensify in the years ahead. In 2020, Switzerland exported goods worth 16.4 billion Swiss francs to China and imported goods valued at 16.6 billion Swiss francs. In comparison, Switzerland exported goods worth 68.8 billion Swiss francs to the United States and imported goods amounting to 19.8 billion Swiss francs in the same year.

There is currently a vigorous debate in Switzerland's domestic political discourse about the feasibility of maintaining a stance of neutrality in relation to both Washington and Beijing. Switzerland faces the challenge of resisting pressure from both the US and the EU to align itself with one side or the other. Switzerland has traditionally wielded considerable diplomatic influence, notably through its "good offices" role in mediating between Washington and Iran, as well as hosting high-level meetings between major powers, but its record of neutrality has instances of non-neutrality. During the early Cold War, Switzerland aligned itself with Washington in various ways. For instance, the Hotz-Linder Agreement signed in 1951 obligated Switzerland to refrain from supplying military materiel and dual-use goods to Eastern Bloc countries. By acquiescing in American demands, Switzerland gained access to modern weaponry. But its "neutral" status was compromised in the eyes of the Soviet Union, the United States and its allies. The direction of arms supplied from Switzerland during the Cold War further illustrates Bern's position at the time. At one point during the Vietnam War, around 90 per cent of Switzerland's gear exports were destined for the US military industry. From an economic perspective, between 1946 and 1989, around 95 per cent of Switzerland's foreign trade was conducted with non-communist Western countries, primarily NATO members.

On the non-governmental front, Switzerland has become the home of the most powerful annual gathering of thinkers, business titans and politicians at Davos. The World Economic Forum has transformed an Alpine resort town of 10,000 into one of the most important global centres of deliberation. It was at Davos that F.W. de Klerk shook hands with Nelson Mandela. It was also there Greece and Turkey signed a declaration that averted war in 1988. The WEF was also the first non-governmental institution to partner with Beijing's economic development commissions that helped spur rapid reforms in China. Where the WEF has fared less well—and I say this as someone who served as the first chairman of its Global Council on Energy Security and introduced my ideas of rapid evolution ("R-Evolution") and Quantum Politics at Davos—is in helping small states. Although located in a small state, it has become a playground for big powers. The political caution that governs what the attendees air can stifle unorthodox thinking.

For a small country like Switzerland, attempting to balance concerns of security, economic prosperity and a commitment to liberal democratic values poses complex dilemmas. Today, Switzerland is heading to a point where it must again consider its options and weigh the advantages and disadvantages of aligning itself with one power or maintaining a position of neutrality. As such, it is a classic example of a successful small state that, having thrived against the odds, is now racing to a position of having explicitly to take sides—an illustration of the quandary faced by small states for centuries and an urgent reminder, as Singapore's Lee Kuan Yew phrased it, that small states have a duty to group and "seek a maximum number of friends".

8

IRELAND
A DREAM FULFILLED

In 1845, Frederick Douglass, a former slave turned passionate social reformer and influential abolitionist, toured Ireland. The shock he registered upon arriving in Dublin remains to this day a haunting measure of Ireland's degradation under British colonial rule. Douglass had endured the horrors of the slave plantations in the United States, among the most harrowingly wretched sites on earth, but the squalor of Dublin was of a different magnitude: "of all the places to witness human misery, ignorance, degradation, filth and wretchedness," he recorded in his diary, "an Irish hut is pre-eminent." His trip coincided with the beginning of the greatest calamity to strike the Irish nation: *an gorta mór*, or "the great hunger", which claimed a million Irish lives and resulted in the dispersal of many millions more from their homeland.

The cause of the Irish Potato Famine originated, in June 1845, in Belgium in the form of a fungus called *phytophtera infestens*. By August it reached Ireland. Within a year, it destroyed Ireland's potato crop. Ireland wasn't the sole casualty of the disease caused by the fungus, but no other nation was as wholly reliant on the potato crop for its nutrition as the Irish. Before the arrival of the potato, the Irish diet had relied mainly upon dairy ("whitemeats"), and cattle were central to Irish life. Indeed, one of the most important and celebrated epics of ancient Ireland, the *Táin Bó Cúailnge*, is centred on kine (cows). By the eighteenth century, the potato, having first been imported to Ireland as a garden crop, had displaced dairy, particularly among the poor, and a third of the island's arable land was given over to its cultivation.

At least a million Irish perished from starvation and disease. Equally tragic was the concentrated mass exodus of people from Ireland to other parts of the world. In 1841, Ireland's population stood at 8.2 million. By 1851, that number had dropped to 6.5 million. Outward migration, principally to the United States, was a fact of Irish life throughout the nineteenth century, but the leavers tended, before the Great Famine, to be young workers. After 1845, people of all ages began to exit Ireland with the support of the burgeoning Irish diaspora.

The colonial administration, despite the presence of some sympathetic officials, behaved as colonial administrations do: callously. English rule of Ireland, beginning with the arrival of an Anglo-Norman force led by Richard de Clare in 1169, had become consolidated in the sixteenth century with the creation of extractive economic institutions that, while failing to contribute to building basic infrastructural necessities in Ireland, amply served the needs and interests of the metropolis. The English Crown saw Ireland as a potential source of wealth, and successive English kings sought to assert their authority and expand their influence on the island. London's attitude to Ireland was summed up by the fulminations of the treasury official Charles Trevelyan, who described the famine as a lesson from God. The well-being of the Irish was a secondary concern; maintaining control was the Crown's main objective. This is one reason why, as the historian

John Gibney has noted, at the peak of the tragedy London's expenditure on famine relief (£9 million) was significantly less than its outlay on security (£14 million).

Thanks to British imperial rule, the processes of industrialisation bypassed Ireland, which looked even more primitive in the 1850s than it had in 1800. In the second half of the nineteenth century, when Western Europe and North America experienced unprecedented socio-economic growth, Ireland, having lost a substantial chunk of its population, continued to be dependent on agriculture. However, there was not enough arable land for agrarian development, so further emigration became the only available alternative to high taxes (for landowners), unemployment and hunger, intensifying and reproducing vicious cycles of permanent economic decline. By the end of the nineteenth century, Ireland recorded the lowest natural population growth and the highest rate of late marriages in Europe. It is estimated that some eight million Irish people settled overseas between 1801 and 1921, a large proportion of them after the famine. Many of them succeeded in the favourable conditions in North America and found opportunities for their compatriots to emigrate before laying the foundation of the Irish transnational nation.

At home, the Great Famine, shaking the Irish to their core, opened their eyes to the unjust rule under which they were forced to live and kindled a belief in the possibility of change. A nationalist ferment swept through the country and its people felt that their fate rested in their own hands—that only the Irish could rescue Ireland. The Irish came to appreciate that the cause of their hardships was the conditions imposed on them by the colonisers, rather than any inherent flaws within their own nature, as the ruling dispensation suggested. Although the transition to statehood and a broader national identity was not immediate, a proactive minority emerged in Ireland, drawing inspiration from other nations fighting for self-determination. It is this awakening which began the long and arduous struggle that yielded statehood for Ireland seventy years after the famine.

* * *

Today, a century after its partition and independence, Ireland is a model small state that punches well above its diplomatic weight and manages to secure a seat at every important table and advance its own interests on the international stage. Its transformation from one of the poorest countries in Europe into one of the richest in the world—from an agricultural economy into an exceptionally stable and democratic European nation—has few parallels. Ireland's political institutions, virtually unchanged, have maintained their legitimacy for more than 85 years. And yet it would be difficult, if not impossible, for a visitor from the 1920s to believe that this post-industrial economy was not so long ago the scene of seemingly insoluble religious strife and the source of mass emigration.

Ireland began to fully emancipate itself from the twin curses of underdevelopment and economic stagnation only in the 1980s. From 1989 on, the country's gross national output grew annually by 7.5 per cent in real terms, surpassing the expectations even of the most optimistic economists. In 1994, as growth reached an impressive 8.6 per cent, Ireland earned the sobriquet "Celtic Tiger" and was clubbed with the economic success of Asian nations. Its most significant economic strides were made at the turn of the new millennium. By the early twenty-first century, Ireland had successfully attained European living standards. Its GDP per capita was the second highest in Europe in 2003. Unemployment was nearing extinction. And its fertility rates were among the highest in the continent. In the 2002 and 2007 elections, issues such as healthcare and education took centre stage, reflecting the nation's elevated living standards.

Ireland's economic transformation was the result of a combination of factors, chief among them its openness to investment and trade, a skilled labour force, the economic boom in the United States, subsidies from the European Union, tax cuts, price controls to enhance competitiveness and wage growth. Each of these measures was part of a comprehensive strategy to revitalise the economy. For instance, alongside tax cuts, Dublin saw the task of fostering trust and confidence between businesses, consumers and the state as crucial to enhancing Ireland's attractiveness as a destination for foreign direct investment. The successful execution of these measures was facilitated by closer ties with the EU and the United States, as well as the presence of competent personnel and a responsible opposition that prioritised long-term gains over short-term benefits.

There were challenges along the way. Ireland's economy, dipping in 2001, experienced a resurgence three years later with the arrival of a new influx of workers from countries that joined the European Union in 2004. This inward migration, reversing the country's historic trend of outward flight, was one indication of the country's affluence. Unfortunately, this surge in prosperity proved short-lived as the Irish economy began to feel the initial pinch of the escalating international financial crisis by mid-2007. Confronted with a global problem, the Irish government made the fateful decision to provide financial assistance to the major banks buried under losses. Subsequent investigations into the banking crisis have shed light on several contributing factors, including failures within the banking sector, the imprudent actions of developers, inadequate oversight by state institutions, and flawed tax policies.

In Ireland, the fallout from the financial crash was compounded by political choices made by Fianna Fáil, the ruling party, which reacted to the crisis by implementing a series of stringent austerity measures. In 2008, it introduced an austerity budget, proposed revoking medical cards for elderly citizens and reinstating university fees. Pensioners and students poured into the streets of Dublin to protest these measures. Two years later, child benefits and social welfare payments became the casualties of budgetary cuts, and a controversial decision was made to terminate a cervical cancer vaccination programme directed at young women. This step culminated in a social and economic disaster.

In 2009, a significant (and, for those with a national memory, embarrassing) turning point occurred as, for the first time since 1995, more individuals departed Ireland than entered it. The era of the "Celtic Tiger" boom was over. But Ireland, determined to reinvent itself, embarked on a period of introspection and self-improvement. Recognising the urgent need to reconfigure the dynamic between the government and the business sector, it moved towards a more liberalised economic model. This momentous shift had political consequences: the 2011 parliamentary elections witnessed a notable decline in the ruling party's parliamentary representation, which plummeted from 78 to a mere 20 deputies, and gave rise to a new ruling coalition between the liberal-conservative Fine Gael party and the Labour Party. Nearly a decade later, in 2020, the relatively populist Sinn Féin party won a quarter of the votes by moving to the centre. Fine Gael scrambled to join forces with Fianna Fáil and the environmentally conscious Greens to form a coalition to stop Sinn Féin from taking power.

Irish democracy, undergirded by the constitution of 1937, not only survived the tests to which it was subjected. It even upheld the stability of the system by ensuring that political elites adhered to certain unspoken ground rules—chief among them the total rejection of populism—that require them to subordinate narrow political ideology to overarching national interest. The elections of 2020, in which Sinn Féin emerged as a serious contender for power, offered a striking illustration of politicians rising above partisan priorities. Sinn Fein ("We ourselves") had been founded by Arthur Griffith, an Irish journalist, in 1905. Its political vision—a form of independence for Ireland from British rule under an overarching British monarchy—barely enjoyed any support and the organisation would likely have withered away had advocates of Irish Home Rule not appropriated its name. More than a century after its establishment, Sinn Féin was deemed, despite moving to the centre, too much of a departure from the centre-ground. The alliance between the liberal Fianna Fáil and the conservative Fine Gael parties was not forged easily, but it was a necessary partnership that preserved their promise to the electorate to keep Sinn Féin from taking power.

* * *

Ireland is home to no more than 10 per cent of the global population of those who identify as Irish. For more than a century, emigration from Ireland was a gauge of its failure as a nation. But a smart state is one which converts its weakness into strengths. And Ireland grasped the value of its diaspora even before it attained statehood. Eamon de Valera, one of the founders of Ireland, visited the United States in 1919 to drum up support for the cause of Irish independence. Although de Valera fell short of his goal of obtaining recognition—Washington was too close to London to confer its blessings on a cause reviled by the British political establishment—he furnished his peers and successors back home with a lesson in the potential, indispensability and importance of the Irish diaspora, which he considered, correctly, to be Ireland's greatest asset.

The constitution of Ireland grants a special place to the Irish diaspora, recognising their significance and connection to the Irish nation and acknowledging a sense of shared identity, and offers a foundation for fostering ties with Irish communities abroad. It also affirms the aspiration to unite all people of Irish heritage, regardless of their location, and recognises the Irish nation's duty to cherish its traditions, language and culture, which extends to the Irish diaspora around the world. The Irish government has constitutional authority to extend voting rights in presidential elections to Irish citizens residing outside the country. This provision admits the diaspora's right to participate in choosing the country's leadership and shaping its future and reinforces their connection to Ireland's democratic processes. It also recognises the president as not merely the head of the Irish state, but as an ambassador of Irish peoples and their culture. In addition to constitutional provisions, the Irish government has engaged with the diaspora through initiatives such as the Global Irish Network and programmes aimed at strengthening its links with diaspora communities.

Some nations fear their diaspora. Ireland has reaped the benefits of embracing its diaspora, which provides it with an extensive network of connections worldwide. The professional networks, friendships, and business relationships established over more than a century by Irish emigrants offer invaluable opportunities for collaboration and trade. And these connections are often mined by Irish businesses, entrepreneurs, and government officials to expand their global reach and influence. They have also helped transform Ireland, in the words of the *Economist*, into a "diplomatic superpower". Irish leaders visiting Washington are guaranteed to receive lengthy audiences with the US president, the vice president and the speaker of the Congress. For a country with a population of fewer than 6 million, this is quite extraordinary. But that is not all. Some of the most important institutions and groupings in Europe—from the Eurogroup to the European Central Bank—are headed by Irish representatives. Ireland even defeated Canada (140 times its size) to take a non-permanent seat on the UN Security Council, Irish officials have twice held the position of secretary general of the European Commission, and Dublin more or less set Brussels's tone on Britain's exit from the European Union. Once again, for a truncated island the size of North Dakota to thwart big powers on the diplomatic front is truly exceptional.

Ireland's most potent resource remains its diaspora in the US. The immigrant Irish community's integration into American political life occurred over long decades. From supporting the American struggle for independence from a common coloniser to participating in the country's territorial expansion and fighting for the North in the Civil War, the Irish were instrumental in moulding the modern character of the United States. Active in the advocacy for human rights, they also played a crucial role in the economic development of the United States. They established large farms and constructed essential infrastructure, laying the foundation for American economic prosperity. Ireland is a bipartisan priority in the USA. This is not only because the Democrats and the Republicans court the Irish-American vote, but because the cause of Ireland was elevated, by generations of Irish-Americans, into an *American* cause. Irish emigres (and their descendants) such as the Kennedys, the Thompsons, the Fitzpatricks, the Feeneys and the Donovans—having left Ireland to be spared the harshness of British rule—became the principal donors of the armed struggle for independence from Britain and later lobbyists for the interests of independent Ireland. In addition to their contributions on a national level, the Irish acted as representatives of American Catholicism—intermediaries between the United States and the Vatican. This connection not only brought the two states closer together but also bridged two distinct worlds: American Protestantism and European Catholicism. The fusion of these worlds found expression in two presidents of Irish origin: John F. Kennedy and Joseph Biden.

The impeccable citizenly reputation of Irish-Americans, augmented by the luminaries their community bequeathed to the US, ensured that their cause always received sympathy from all quarters. During the Troubles in Northern Ireland, the Republic of Ireland succeeded in obtaining solidarity from a Republican president (Ronald Reagan) and a Democratic president (Bill Clinton). It was the effort of the Irish diaspora that produced a commitment from Clinton, even before he became president, to push for settlement in Ireland. As president, Clinton, defying the counsel of his advisors, signed a decree granting a 48-hour visa to the Sinn Féin leader Gerry Adams to take part in an official conference on Northern Ireland in the United States. Clinton even shocked the British by appointing George Mitchell, of Irish descent, as his special advisor on Ireland. Dublin's role in the peace process in Northern Ireland, which culminated in 1998's Good Friday Agreement, put on clear display the value of its diaspora, the skills of its diplomatic corps and its talent for brokering agreements. The island, garnering international recognition, has since been viewed as a credible and trusted mediator in conflict resolution efforts, boosting its influence in international diplomacy.

Ireland's energetic diplomacy exists alongside a longstanding policy of military neutrality. Ireland was one of the few neutral states during the Second World War, and its bureaucracy at the time elevated this stance into such a sacred belief that when news of Hitler's death filtered out from Germany, Dublin issued a standard note of condolence. It was an untypical misjudgement on the part of Eamon de Valera, and it was justly castigated. But the Irish leader rose to defend the principle of neutrality when Winston Churchill, in his victory address, hurled gratuitous insults at Ireland and congratulated himself for not violating its sovereignty because he had not felt the need for it. "Mr Churchill makes it clear that, in certain circumstances, he would have violated [Ireland's] neutrality and that he would justify his action by Britain's necessity," de Valera said in his response, broadcast on Irish radio. "It seems strange to me that Mr Churchill does not see that this, if accepted, would mean Britain's necessity would become a moral code and that when this necessity became sufficiently great, other people's rights were not to count."

Dublin's neutrality should not be mistaken for isolationism. Ireland is a strong supporter of multilateral peacekeeping efforts, with a rich tradition of contributing to UN peacekeeping missions, and Irish troops have served in conflict zones around the world. But nearly eight decades after de Valera's dignified reply to Churchill, Ireland is again at a point where it is being asked to pick, by circumstance rather than actors, sides—this time between the US and China. If the fight against Nazism was a moral necessity, the conflict now brewing between Beijing and Washington is primarily geopolitical. What choice Ireland—or indeed any other country—makes in the confrontation between the United States and China depends upon how the confrontation itself is perceived.

In March 2021, the US National Intelligence Council proposed five scenarios for the distribution of power in 2040, each with corresponding consequences. They are worth looking at.

The first, "Renaissance of Democracies", envisages a future in which open democracies led by the United States and its allies experience a resurgence. Technological advancements driven by public-private partnerships transform the global economy, improve living standards and tackle global challenges. In contrast, China and Russia's increased societal controls hinder innovation.

In the second, "A World Adrift", the international system is chaotic and volatile as major powers like China, regional players, and nonstate actors ignore international rules and institutions. Countries in the OECD (Organisation for Economic Cooperation and Development) face economic slowdown, societal divisions and political paralysis. China expands its influence, but lacks the capacity for global leadership, leaving issues like climate change unaddressed.

"Competitive Coexistence", the third scenario, imagines a future in which the United States and China prioritise economic growth and restore a robust trading relationship, but competition persists over political influence, governance models, technology and strategic advantage. Risk of a major war is low, and advanced economies manage global problems through cooperation and innovation, though long-term climate challenges persist.

In the fourth, "Separate Silos", the world fragments into economic and security blocs centred upon the United States, China, the EU, Russia and regional powers. These blocs focus on self-sufficiency and defence, disrupting information flows, supply chains and international trade. Vulnerable developing countries suffer, and global problems like climate change are inadequately addressed.

In the last scenario, "Tragedy and Mobilisation", the EU and China lead a global coalition, along with NGOs and multilateral institutions, to address climate change, resource depletion and poverty after a global food catastrophe. Richer countries support poorer nations through aid programs and advanced energy technology transfers, recognising the urgency of these challenges crossing borders.

Depending on one's vantage point, the second scenario—in which the international system is plunged into chaos, China significantly strengthens its position, OECD countries have slowed down, China has massively expanded its influence and other nations are beset by social divisions—is the most disturbing. In such a world, can Ireland, as a passive object of international relations, remain neutral and true to itself? Ireland, at any rate, is not only a small state but a middle power, capable, in some respects, of initiating independent international processes. Based on what we know about Ireland's relations with Washington and Beijing, it's not unreasonable to conclude that, in the event of such a scenario coming to pass , Dublin will take on a more active role within the EU, under the principle of collective decision, in areas such as trade, where Brussels has competence. The EU will likely avoid being drawn into the confrontation, preferring economic ties with both the United States and China. Ireland, however, is likely to seek an active role in the new world order.

The deepening rift between the United States and China is expanding from the realm of high politics and hard power to include the domain of "low politics". This involves such areas as infrastructure, communication development, technology, trade, finance and healthcare. In this context, Ireland, which has not joined NATO, has the potential to play a dual role, benefiting itself while also becoming a valuable negotiator for the US when needed, as it did during the Troubles in Northern Ireland.

Given Ireland's formidable lobbying and diplomatic resources, as well as its significant role in global logistics chains, it has the potential to act as a mediator between the United States and China. However, an important obstacle in Ireland's relations with China is the ongoing persecution of the Uighur people. Ireland's historical background and reputation compel it to criticise the Chinese authorities and advocate for human rights, while China, for its part, would regard any mention of this as an infringement on its sovereignty. While this issue might be less prominent when addressing Irish-specific matters, its importance will magnify when Ireland addresses other matters.

Ireland's position in the global power struggle can be evaluated by examining its past responses to shifts in influence and big-power conflicts. Its historical traditions, unity, and welfare have enabled it to shape its agenda based on national interests and maintain its status as a neutral power. Unlike NATO members,

Ireland enjoys security guarantees from the United States through its diaspora, granting it flexibility in decision-making. As Western hegemony faces mounting threats, Ireland may face similar choices as France. But Ireland's vast diplomatic capital should allow it to maintain a degree of neutrality.

In 2024, Ireland plans to enhance its defence capability. By allocating more resources to defence, Dublin aims to address escalating global security threats. Ireland's preference for *independent* security measures, however, signifies its continuing commitment to neutrality and its enduring desire to avoid political and ideological confrontations on the global stage. Despite a harrowing colonial history and internal divisions, Ireland has emerged as a notable "middle power" capable of carving out a place for itself on the international stage. For this once ordinary small nation, achieving true independence has become a conscious necessity rather than a mere luxury, driven by the profound memory of the Great Famine.

I cannot tell if it is this memory of suffering—a heritage Ireland shares with Armenia—or the experience of being, like Armenia, a transnational nation, but in my dealings as a diplomat and a politician, I have generally found the Irish to be wholeheartedly supportive. In the years after Armenia's independence, I spent a good deal of time persuading major Western banks and financial institutions to come to Yerevan. I got the most sympathetic hearing from Irish executives. "Helping your country stand tall and regain its footing is our duty," one kindly Irish director told me. I can count Mary Robinson, Ireland's seventh president who went on to become the UN High Commisisoner for Human Rights, as one of Armenia's dearest friends. Robinson sat on the board of the Aurora Humanitarian Initiative, which recognises the contributions of the righteous peoples and nations that came to the rescue of the persecuted during the Armenian Genocide.

IRELAND

Michael Higgins, the brilliant and erudite current president of Ireland, amazed me in our meetings with his deep knowledge of the cultural ties between Armenia and Ireland, which go back centuries. Despite being situated on the eastern and western ends of the Indo-European world, the two small nations exchanged ideas, particularly in the realm of religion. The medieval Gaelic manuscript *The Book of Lismore* identified Armenia (an "extensive country" with "an abundance of towns and treasures") as the terminus of Noah's Ark. In the eighteenth and nineteenth centuries, Irish scholars fixated on tracing the origin of the "Irish race" concluded, as Ulick Joseph Bourke put it in his hugely popular 1887 pamphlet *Pre-Christian Ireland*, that the Irish came "from Mount Ararat in Armenia". This view did not last, but what did survive in Ireland is an astonishingly extensive collection of the most ancient Armenian manuscripts, which are housed, among other sites, at the Chester Beatty in Dublin. Ireland is not merely a formidable and smart small state. It is also, by virtue of its history, a compassionate, open and global small state.

9

BOTSWANA

A DIAMOND IN THE ROUGH

Picture Botswana at its independence from Britain in 1966. A landlocked country in southern Africa roughly the size of France, it was the second poorest in the world. It had 12 kilometres of tarred road. And out of its population of about 600,000, only twenty-two were university graduates and no more than one hundred had completed schooling. This was the inventory of human resources after nearly a century of European rule. Now consider Botswana's trajectory since it became a sovereign state: in the thirty-five years between 1966 and 2007, Botswana recorded the highest per capita growth in the world. How did Botswana do it?

The birth of Botswana as a modern state coincided with the emergence in the West of what used to be called "modernisation theory", whose proponents posited two claims. First, that authoritarian governments were more effective than democracies in promoting economic growth. Second, that economic growth was a condition for the crystallisation and efflorescence of democracy. The idea that democracy stymied economic growth was as much an article of faith among political scientists of the time as the missionary belief among some American politicians at the turn of the twentieth century that Western-style democracy was the only guarantor of human progress.

Botswana upended such certitudes: it has during its existence radically uplifted the lives of its citizens, improving their quality of life and empowering them with rights, while remaining an uninterrupted democracy. Botswana's political history has been the casualty of the neglect to which small states are accustomed. And yet even the most passionate admirer of its democracy will have to concede that democracy alone cannot explain the country's extraordinary transformation from one of the most destitute nations in the world into the most prosperous and stable republic in Africa. So are we to ascribe Botswana's economic success to its vast trove of diamonds, which account for about a third of the country's GDP and more than 80 per cent of its exports? But if that is so, why is it that natural resources served as a blessing for Botswana alone while acting as a curse in the region and beyond? Perhaps charting Botswana's history might be one way of equipping ourselves to unpack what so many observers consider the mystery of its runaway success. We will see that Botswana's founders, and their forebears, had a long record of protecting and advancing their interests, outwitting those who sought to suppress them, and winning against formidable adversaries.

Botswana—plural for the Tswana community or tribe, which dominates the country—became a British interest only in 1885, following Germany's annexation of Namibia in 1884. Before that, sealed off by Namibia on the north and west, Zimbabwe on the east and South Africa in the south,[1] it was home to several Tswana kingdoms which ruled by a combination of hereditary hierarchy and consultation via popular assemblies of people

---

[1] I have chosen to use current names of Botswana's neighbours.

known as the *kgotlas*. The Tswana, who boast a long history, are thought to have migrated in the 1700s from the south, before assimilating the local communities into the Tswana and spawning a relatively homogeneous society: although there were several sub-tribes and kings—or paramount chiefs—they belonged almost entirely to one overarching community. The kings were figures of political authority and spiritual reverence, but they had no claim to the land, which was commonly owned. Ownership of animals, which always vastly outnumbered humans, was private. And the royal families were by far the biggest owners of the most important animal stock: cattle. Their first contact with Europeans was gentle: by 1818, the London Missionary Society had established itself in the vicinity, and by the close of the 1840s, David Livingstone, the fabled Victorian explorer, anti-slavery advocate and missionary, had befriended the Tswana and even succeeded in converting one of their kings, Khama the Great, to Christianity.

The Tswana were under persistent threat from the Boers. What saved them was their willingness to set aside all differences and unite against foreign threats as one people. It was this gift that helped them defeat the Boers at Dimawe in 1852. But as the scramble for Africa got underway in the 1850s, with Europeans fighting over and dividing up the continent, the Tswana realised quickly that they could not go it alone. In 1853, they approached the British and asked for protection by making their country a protectorate of the crown. They were rebuffed. Colonialism was an expensive business, and Botswana—or Bechuanaland, as it was called—was deemed to possess no innate value to the enterprise. But London's perspective changed once Germany took Namibia in 1894: Britain now needed Bechuanaland to halt the Germans.

In 1885, the British proclaimed the creation of the Bechuanaland Protectorate to protect its inhabitants from "filibustering expeditions" by the Boers. Colonial administrators in southern Africa were not interested in extracting Bechuanaland's resources—they were then unaware of its riches—but nor were they really motivated by the opportunity to enhance the lives of its people. Bechuanaland was such a marginal concern that its official capital city, the place from which the British administered the country, was situated in Mafeking in South Africa. It took a special kind of genius, a British observer mockingly noted decades later, to provide "the Protectorate with a capital sixteen miles outside its own boundaries". But there was a rationale to this: the British had intended to eventually merge Bechuanaland into South Africa. For the time being, however, the arms-length arrangement with the colonial administration worked out rather well for the Tswana, who remained relatively untouched by British rule, and their chiefs, who continued to wield temporal authority.

But how long could this state of affairs last? Cecil Rhodes, the prime minister of the Cape Colony to the south, was already plotting an end to it all. Born in 1853 in England, Rhodes had emerged as one of the most influential figures of his age by piling up fortunes from the diamond and gold mines in southern Africa under the banner of his British South Africa Company. A founder of the De Beers diamond cartel, his fantasy was to recover the American colonies, reconcile the Boers and the British, and create a British-controlled territory that stretched from the Cape Colony to Cairo—a continuous strip of British dominance through Africa—and he was ruthless in pursuing it. In 1893, his company decimated the Ndebele kingdom, seized the land, used the people as labour on mines and settler farms and gave their county a new name: Rhodesia.

In London, home to the bulk of his company's shareholders, Rhodes was a revered figure—a coloniser who was also, as the historian Neil Parsons has written, a hero "of capitalism matched only by the likes of J.P. Morgan and the Rockefellers in America".

When Rhodes announced to a London meeting of shareholders in 1895 that the company owned a "very large piece of the world", they erupted with shrieks of delight. But Rhodes wanted more: he sought to annex Bechuanaland, "the Suez Canal of the trade" in Africa, as he called it, indispensable to his plan to push north. He had already obtained, with the help of a consortium of financiers in the City of London, a Royal Charter to take it over for his company. Its people would be expelled or reduced, as they had been elsewhere, to serfdom.

When news of Rhodes's scheme reached Bechuanaland, a wave of panic, anger and confusion washed over its people. But whereas elsewhere in the British Empire imperial designs gave rise to catastrophic division of leadership and collapse of morale, in Bechuanaland they acted as a unifying glue. Once again, what saved the country from being consumed, in addition to a convergence of conditions beyond their control, was the equanimity and fortitude of its kings, who joined forces to defend their land and people. Where once they had appealed to the local agents of the British crown for protection, now they bypassed the agents of London and made a voyage to the imperial capital, London, to seek the protection of Queen Victoria and her government. It was an extraordinarily bold, creative and wholly out-of-the-box undertaking by the leadership of a small (quasi) state that barely commanded the attention of high officials in Britain. But the three wise kings of Bechuanaland—Batheon of the Bangwaketse, Sebele of the Bakwena and their informal leader Khama III of the BangammaNgwato—were confident that they could outlobby Rhodes at the peak of his power.

Christians and strict teetotallers, the trio enlisted the support of the London Missionary Society and the powerful Temperance Movement during their weeks-long sojourn in England. At numerous public meetings held in towns and cities up and down the country, they patiently put forward their position, winning over ordinary people, politicians, clergy and newspapers, and gradually moving opinion in their favour. Their last meeting was with Queen Victoria, who received them warmly at Windsor Palace and put on a lavish lunch for them. Upon their return to London, Joseph Chamberlain, the colonial secretary, agreed to perpetuate the existing set-up in return for territorial corridors up to nine miles wide from each king for Rhodes's railways. The visitors reluctantly conceded. But Rhodes, by underestimating the Tswana, ensured that they kept everything.

Rhodes nursed a strong rivalry with the prime minister of the Transvaal, Paul Kruger, and in a bid to overthrow him, authorised his partner Leander Jameson, a Scottish doctor who had come to Africa in search of a fortune, to stage a raid into enemy territory. On 29 December 1885, Jameson led a force of 500 company soldiers from Bechuanaland. Rhodes, regarded as a genius in London, believed that the British workers who had flocked for employment on the goldmines in the Transvaal— known as Uitlanders—would rise up against the government. It was a colossal miscalculation. Nobody lifted a finger. Jameson was detained by Kruger. The "Jameson raid", as the London press branded it, threatened to destroy Chamberlain's career because he was suspected of being complicit in it. The fact that a British protectorate—led, among others, by no less a figure than Khama, who had made such an impression on the British public—had been used as a launching pad for the attempted coup scandalised London. Chamberlain, fearful of being implicated in it, immediately annulled the deal he had made with Rhodes.

Here, it would be remiss of me not to mention that Armenia was, in a grim and roundabout way, part of this saga. William Gladstone, the great Liberal prime minister and opponent of colonial expansion, had resigned as prime minister in 1894. His successor, Lord Rosebery, was a close friend of Rhodes and shared Rhodes's vision (Rhodes later named him an executor of his trust). The proximity to a sympathetic prime minister no doubt fuelled Rhodes's rush to claim Bechuanaland. But as his effort got underway, Gladstone launched a forceful campaign to convince his successor to intervene to save the Armenians then being massacred by the Ottoman Empire. "All human beings have the same claims upon our support," the Grand Old Man of British politics thundered in a speech on Armenia in which he went out of his way to emphasise the equality of all human beings before God: the land upon which he stood, Gladstone declared, "is not British, nor European, but it is human". Such a radically humane worldview, contrasting powerfully with the philosophy espoused by Rhodes and Rosebery, was also British. Gladstone's advocacy for Armenia not only embarrassed Rosebery, but made it difficult for him to carry on, and he quit just over a year after taking office, explicitly citing his disagreement with Gladstone over the "Armenian question" as a reason for his resignation. How might things have turned out had it been Rosebery directing the Colonial Office? In the event, Rhodes's career never recovered from the debacle in Bechuanaland.

But the fate of the people of Bechuanaland remained uncertain. Their future was paved with disappointments and unexpected turn of events—the most spectacular and well-known being the energetic attempts by the British administration, under intense pressure from the apartheid government of South Africa, and his own family to stop Seretse Khama, the grandson of Khama the Great and heir to the kingship of the BangammaNgwato community, from marrying Ruth Williams, his English partner, because she happened to be white. Even the Church of England succumbed to pressure and refused to wed the Anglican couple. Seretse—who had abandoned his studies at Balliol College, Oxford, in 1946 to become a barrister in London—and Ruth defied the pressure of opinion in Africa and Europe and married in a civil ceremony in London in 1948. They spent the proceeding eight years dealing with the acrimonious fallout. What set the pair apart, as every observer, sympathetic or not, acknowledged, was their grace.

In 1956, Seretse renounced his claim to the kingship and returned home with his wife. By that point India had been independent for nearly a decade, and the floodgates of decolonisation had opened. Seretse Khama grasped early on that Bechuanaland's fate would soon rest in the hands of its own leaders and people. In 1961, he founded the social democratic Bechuanaland Democratic Party (later Botswana Democratic Party, or the BDP) and threw himself passionately into his nation's emergent politics, already teeming with visions of the future that ranged from socialism to pan-Africanism. In the limited elections of 1965, the BDP won a landslide and Khama was elected prime minister. He pressed for full independence from Britain, which came the next year, with a new capital at Gabarone. Bechuanaland was reborn as Botswana and Seretse Khama, knighted days before independence by a government that had once separated him from his wife, became its inaugural president.

The economic conditions in Botswana at its birth, as I noted in the beginning of this chapter, were dire. Independence was preceded by two years of severe drought and crop failure, devastating agriculture and the majority who lived by it. A fifth of the population depended upon emergency food relief. Foreign aid trickling in from Britain kept things going. It did not, in the circumstances, seem entirely unreasonable to wonder if this new state would survive, much less thrive. Charles King, a correspondent for the *Southern African News Service*, contrasted the elation in the capital, Gabarone—filled with the blue, white and black flags of the new nation—with the despair coursing through the "vast, trackless wasteland that will take the name of Botswana".

Grievances constituted the country's only surplus. And a leader motivated by power, keeping power and evading responsibility could easily have made the country's white minority a target of people's anger—as indeed some of Botswana's neighbours eventually did. Sir Seretse Khama, however, was a visionary statesman, not a revolutionary demagogue. Himself married to a white woman, he placed great emphasis on social and racial harmony, equality of opportunity and civic citizenship. He ensured that white Botswanans engaged with the institutions of the new state by ensuring their presence in visibly important positions. White Botswanans have held prominent jobs since Botswana's founding. The first treasurer of the BDP, Sir Seretse's party, was a white politician called Benjamin Stenberg. During my last stint as Armenia's ambassador before my election as president of Armenia in 2018, my counterpart from Botswana was High Commissioner Roy Blackbeard, a white Botswanan. The first woman to carry Botswana's flag at the opening ceremony of the Olympics, Samantha Paxinos, is a white athlete. Sir Seretse's great early achievement was not to allow Botswana to become a breeding ground for racial resentment. This was no small accomplishment.

Social accord was augmented by political stability. As we have seen, what distinguished colonial Botswana was its unique gift to coalesce when faced with a common challenge. That quality has served it well since independence. Although the BDP has remained the dominant political party, winning every election since Botswana's independence, the opposition parties have acquitted themselves as responsible players. As the political scientist Mpho G. Molomo of the University of Botswana has observed, the "resilience of the multi-party framework that is founded on the basic principles of political freedom and civil liberty" has been strengthened by the "constructive role" played by the opposition parties, who "have provided important checks and balances to make government more accountable and responsive to peoples' needs" without ever paralysing the system or portraying "themselves as alternative governments".

Following the example set by Sir Seretse, politicians—and political parties—have regarded natural resources as national assets rather than as means for self-enrichment. The Mines and Minerals Act of 1967 transferred mineral rights from local tribes and communities to the government. As the scholars Daron Acemoglu, Simon Johnson and James A. Robinson have pointed out, this was one of the most consequential and striking pieces of legislation passed by Botswana's parliament because a large chunk of Botswana's diamond wealth was buried under lands that belonged to Sir Seretse's community. He knew this, and yet chose to forgo a fortune that would have flown to him by ensuring, through legislative means, that the proceeds went to the state treasury. In a region and world where politicians had a reputation for plundering resources, Sir Seretse distinguished himself by pre-emptively giving up what by custom and law belonged to him. The clean political culture incubated by the founding father's high-minded conduct insulated trade and commerce from political avarice and allowed natural resources to be used for the common good once diamonds started to be mined in the 1970s.

Diamonds, of course, went on to form the basis of Botswana's economic and social transformation. But what is distinct about Botswana is its leadership's approach to this mineral. The history of the Democratic Republic of Congo, which half a century ago was mining more than five times the total number of carats then being extracted from Botswana's soil, is a tragic lesson in what has come to be called the "resource curse", which results in plunder, violence and corruption, rather than peace, stability and development. Botswana's success lay in avoiding that deadly trap. Geologists working for De Beers had found diamonds at Orapa, 400 kilometres north of Gabarone, in 1967. (There is some speculation that diamonds had been found as early as 1966, and that this information was shared by De Beers executives with Sir Seretse, who chose to keep it confidential until *after* independence. I have, despite many conversations with Botswanan officials and De Beers executives, not been able decisively to confirm this.) Two years later, in 1969, the government of Botswana founded a joint venture with De Beers in which Gabarone held a 15 per cent stake. By 1975, the government increased its share of the company to 50 per cent. In 2006, Gabarone formed a joint partnership with De Beers to sort and value its production within Botswana, bringing new jobs to the country. In 2013, the government of Botswana persuaded De Beers to relocate its global sales function—De Beers Global Sightholder Sales (DBGSS)—from London to Gabarone. Thus far in this partnership, De Beers has mined more than 700 million carats—and Botswana has kept 80 cents on every dollar made by De Beers. It is difficult to find a deal of this kind in the annals of enterprise.

Thanks to the political culture and robust institutions erected by Sir Seretse, and nurtured by his successor Quett Masire, mineral revenues have financed heath, education, and infrastructure projects—and welfare projects directed at poorer sections of the society—that have made Botswana the envy of the continent and a model for small states everywhere. The country written off at birth was able to raise itself into the league of the prosperous economies and stable democracies within a few decades after its independence in large part because, as Robert Guest, the *Economist's* foreign editor, noted in his 2004 book *The Shackled Continent*, even as its economy grew faster than any other in the world, "cabinet ministers have not awarded themselves mansions and helicopters—and even the president has been seen doing his own shopping".

Investing in citizens is the smartest choice a state can make, and Botswana stands out here. Primary education is free and universal and, as Karin Alexander and Gape Kaboyakgosi have noted, 85 per cent of Botswana's population live within a five-kilometre radius of a health facility and almost the entire population has access to potable water. In a subcontinent afflicted by the consequences of AIDS denialism, Botswana provides free access to antiretroviral drugs to those diagnosed with HIV.

Botswana's rise from destitution into the ranks of upper-middle-income states required more than internal stability. It also called for shrewd external management. Remember that Botswana at independence was landlocked by racist white minority regimes—South Africa, Namibia (then South West Africa), Zimbabwe (then Rhodesia)—that were inimical to the black democracy in the middle. Botswana's window to the world beyond this was the narrow border with Kenneth Kaunda's majority-ruled Zambia. Geographical limitations were compounded by colonial-era arrangements: since 1910, Botswana had been part of the South African Customs Union Agreement, which made it dependent on its hostile neighbours' customs unions, transport facilities, and import and export markets. If this was not bad enough, as a member of the Rand Monetary Union, dominated by Pretoria, Botswana also had no control over its monetary policy. Its train network, meanwhile, was controlled by Rhodesian Railways. As Sir Seretse acknowledged, "our survival as a nation depends almost entirely on our neighbours whose policies are diametrically antithetical" to Botswana's. The foreign policy Sir Seretse devised for Botswana, in the words of Gilbert A. Segkoma, "defied progressive analytical concepts". A principled pragmatist, Sir Seretse deftly combined economic engagement with political dissension.

In practice, this meant that Gabarone traded with and via Pretoria without maintaining formal political ties with its government. Botswana also vocally condemned the apartheid policy of segregating and debasing human beings on the basis of skin colour. Gabarone gradually delinked itself from South Africa, most notably in 1976, when it launched its own currency. But its gains were under constant threat. A year before that, Gabarone had forged formal relations with Beijing, receiving in return aid, expertise and the development of Botswana's railways. Between 1982 and 1987, China refreshed a 120-kilometre stretch of Botswana's railway line at an expense of $20 million.

In 1985, South Africa ordered a military raid on Gabarone to kill exiled members of Nelson Mandela's African National Congress. A dozen people, mostly women and children, were slain. There was international outrage, but at home the event precipitated military reforms. As a neutral power and member of the Non-Aligned Movement, Botswana had acquired weapons from the West and from Moscow during the Cold War. After the attack by South Africa, however, it intensified procurements from the United States. But this did not indicate a reorientation. Despite being lured by Moscow and Washington, Botswana remained studiously non-aligned. Officers of the Botswana Defence Force, including Sir Seretse's son, Ian, received training at Sandhurst, and the budgetary allocations to defence that followed were generous. By the 1990s, a nation that had begun with a rudimentary police force had one of Africa's most professional armed forces, firmly under the government's control. Reconfigured to serve a deterrent purpose, the military remained subordinated to diplomacy, especially after the end of the Cold War.

Gabarone's emphasis since the 1990s has been on maximising its influence in the region by being an active participant in multilateral fora. As a successful democracy, it has also been able to press other states in the region. Ian Khama, who served as president from 2008 to 2018, went so far as to violate the unspoken rule on neutrality in African affairs when he exhorted

Robert Mugabe of Zimbabwe to step down in 2013. Two years later, he castigated Burundi's Pierre Nkurunziza for seeking a third term in contravention of the term limit. In 2016, he rebuked Joseph Kabila, the president of the Democratic Republic of Congo, for not holding elections. Khama's stern words landed on their targets because he governed a country whose democratic credentials were in comparison beyond reproach, and unlike Western nations, Botswana wasn't tainted by military misadventures. In 2018, when his own second term came to an end, Khama, ignoring the genuine and heartfelt pleas of rural constituents to continue, stepped down.

Khama's resignation, leading to the election of his vice president Mokgweetsi Masisi as the new president, resulted in political tension. Khama has accused his successor of displaying authoritarian tendencies, and the government has filed cases against Khama, who now lives in South Africa. All of this is mild compared to what has happened nearby, and Botswana's economic prospects remain bright—in fact, the war in Ukraine, tainting Russian diamonds, has expanded the market for Botswanan gems, and Gabarone recently renegotiated an even more lucrative deal with De Beers—and yet, as other states have demonstrated, political strife is easier to ignite than to douse. Minor differences can, if they are not quickly resolved, fester and engulf nations. Botswana's founders, inheriting one of the most intractable economies in Africa, bequeathed to their successors one of the most successful small states in the world. For the sake of Botswana—and the world—they must not squander their patrimony.

10

JORDAN

THE KING AND THE PEOPLE

In February 2020, when King Abdullah II of the Hashemite Kingdom of Jordan embarked on his visit of Armenia, protocol dictated that I receive him at the palace. My relationship with King Abdullah, however, had been cultivated over time. I had interacted with and got to know him well during my visits over the years to attend World Economic Forum summits in Jordan. Besides, his tour of Armenia was historic—the first by a Hashemite monarch. I set aside the strictures of protocol and received him directly on the tarmac of the airport. It was dinnertime and we drove straight to a restaurant called Derian, an establishment with a special connection to the royal visitor and his family.

Derian was the labour of love of an Armenian family from Aleppo that had lost everything in the Syrian civil war. Once successful and wealthy, they had arrived in Armenia with nothing and started from scratch a small restaurant, if it can even be called that, equipped with only five seats near a car wash. The food was so delicious that word spread rapidly. In 2015, I visited

Derian with a friend from the Armenian diaspora. We instantly became its admirers and recommended it to our friends, and they to their friends. In this way, Derian grew into an institution. But it wasn't the food alone that prompted me to take King Abdullah there on the February evening.

The family behind Derian, like countless other Armenians, felt indebted to the king and his family—going all the way back to his great-great grandfather Hussein bin Ali, the Sharif of Mecca—for all they had done to shelter them and protect them from persecution. Moreover, the Hashemites had given generous plots of prime land by River Jordan, where Jesus was baptised, to Christian denominations for the construction of churches. When Armenia found itself embroiled in the turmoil of war and grappling with the challenges of a pandemic, King Abdullah offered solidarity. His decision to invite me to Amman on a state visit in November 2020, at a time when he was not receiving foreign guests, demonstrated not only his affection for Armenia, but also his determination to demonstrate that the conflict in the Caucasus was not driven by religious differences. It was a gesture I will never forget.

Our dinner at Derian turned into hours of engaging conversation, punctuated by the melodies of an Arab band. For the duration of his stay in Armenia, King Abdullah's deep and abiding respect for all religions was evident and his visit provided a unique perspective on the Hashemite dynasty. In King Abdullah one encountered a blend of royalty and humility, a descendant of the Prophet Muhammad who remained remarkably grounded.

More recently, my return to Jordan to attend the royal wedding of Crown Prince Hussein to Princess Rajwa brought new joys as I witnessed a traditional ceremony that exuded the richness of Jordan's culture. The wedding stood out for its inclusivity, with a significant portion dedicated to ordinary people and representatives of various religious minorities. It was a testament to Jordan's commitment to valuing diversity—a nation where coexistence is celebrated. Amman, bustling and cheerful, was a sight to behold. Years ago, I had dined at an Armenian restaurant called Levant in the city. This time around, I invited several guests to the same restaurant, only to find it had expanded significantly. I jestingly told King Abdullah that one day, I would take him to an Armenian restaurant in his own country. While I am far from an authority on Jordan, my encounters have left me with a deep admiration for this modern nation.

* * *

Jordan is one of the best adverts for the force that sustains small states: the will to survive. "Many obituaries of the Hashemite kingdom of Jordan have been prepared for instant use", the British journalist and historian Peter Mansfield wrote in his study of the Arabs, noting that "the external and internal forces gathered against this last of the Anglo-Arab monarchies were so strong and numerous that its survival seemed impossible". And yet, more than 75 years after its foundation, due in large part to the dexterity, perseverance and sheer indefatigability of the Hashemite dynasty, Jordan lives, while "the obituaries gather dust on the files". This is no small achievement for a tiny state that began as a destitute emirate in an oil-rich neighbourhood, was swelled by refugees, demoralised by assassination, bloodied by civil war, imperilled by a state within a state and challenged by threats of coups d'etat.

The Hashemite dynasty or the House of Hashim, which traces its origins to Prophet Muhammad, has a grand lineage. Its name is derived from Hashim ibn Abd Manaf, a highly respected leader of the Quraysh tribe in Mecca and the great-grandfather of Prophet Muhammad, who was born in the Hashemite clan of the Quraysh tribe in Mecca around 570 CE. Following the Prophet's departure, in 632 CE, a schism arose in the Muslim community over the question of leadership. A faction known as the Shi'a (meaning "supporters" or "partisans") believed that the rightful successors to the Prophet were his close relatives, principally Ali, who was married to the Prophet's daughter, Fatima, and had been his cousin and companion. The other faction, known as the Sunni, believed that the leaders should be elected from among the Muslim community. Ali, the fourth caliph, had two sons with Fatima: Hasan and Hussein. While neither inherited the caliphate, the descendants of Hasan, the older of the two children, succeeded by the tenth century in establishing a hereditary custodianship over Mecca, Islam's holiest city, and the surrounding Hejaz. At some point before or during their rule, which continued into the twentieth century under Ottoman rule, they became Sunni. But as direct descendants of Prophet Muhammad, the Hashemites, addressed as Sharif in recognition of their pedigree, were highly respected by both sides.

In the early twentieth century, the Hashemite family played a pivotal part in the Arab Revolt against the Ottoman Empire. Led by Hussein bin Ali, the Sharif and Emir of Mecca and the King of Hejaz, the objective of the uprising was ultimately to break free from Ottoman rule to create an independent Arab state. Although revered by Muslims, he also inspired the loyalty of Christians. Once the Ottoman administration launched a policy of genocide against its Armenian subjects and tens of thousands of Armenians began fleeing for their lives, it was Hussein bin Ali who mobilised Muslims to stand with their Christian brethren. In 1918, as reports of persecution of Armenians proliferated, he issued a decree to all Muslims in the Arab world. I kept a copy of it, which I read out to King Abdullah II, Ali's great-great grandson, during his historic visit to Armenia in 2020:

> From Al-Husayn Ibn 'Ali, King of the Arab Lands and Sharif of Mecca and its Prince to The Honourable and Admirable Princes—Prince

Faisal and Prince Abd al-'Aziz al-Jarba—greetings and the compassion of God and His blessings ... What is requested of you is to protect and to take good care of everyone from the Jacobite Armenian community living in your territories and frontiers and among your tribes; to help them in all of their affairs and defend them as you would defend yourselves, your properties and children, and provide everything they might need whether they are settled or moving from place to place, because they are the Protected People of the Muslims (Ahl Dimmat al-Muslimin)—about whom the Prophet Muhammad (may God grant him His blessings and peace) said: "Whosoever takes from them even a rope, I will be his adversary on the day of Judgment." This is among the most important things we require of you to do and expect you to accomplish, in view of your noble character and determination.

Nearly a century after that proclamation, I bowed in gratitude on behalf of the Armenian nation before King Abdullah, the custodian of the Armenian and other Christian places of worship in Jerusalem and the direct descendant of Hussein bin Ali. It was under Hussein's leadership that Arab nationalism, growing out of the Arab revivalism that had begun towards the end of the nineteenth century, intensified during the First World War. There had been tribal revolts against Ottoman rule in 1905 and 1910. By 1916, Hussein, supported by his resourceful sons Abdullah and Feisal and backed by British assurances, was at the head of a full-blown armed uprising against Turkish rule. A series of victories resulted in the liberation of Amman, Aqaba, Jerusalem and Daraa. But the reasonable expectation of Arab sovereignty was frustrated by two factors or, as the Arabs saw them, betrayals: the first was the Sykes-Picot Agreement which divided the Ottoman Empire's territorial possessions among France, Britain and imperial Russia. The clandestine contents of this treaty, signed as early as 1916, were exposed by the Bolsheviks, who declined Russia's share of the war spoils. The second factor was 1917's Balfour Declaration that effectively promised a Jewish homeland in Palestine, which the Arabs understandably considered theirs.

Following Turkey's defeat in the war, as Jewish migration to Palestine picked up pace and the former Ottoman Empire was carved up between Paris and London, Arab nationalist sentiment was inflamed. Their part in helping the Allies to victory was trivialised and their lands suddenly had new French and British overlords. In 1920, a gathering in Damascus of Arab notables from Greater Syria—which comprised Palestine, Jordan, Lebanon—declared King Feisal the king of Syria. His brother, Abdullah, was named king of Iraq. The Arab Kingdom of Syria, which included on paper Palestine and the territory that later became Jordan, lasted only four months; in July 1920, Feisal was expelled by the French, who asserted their "mandate" with a show of force. The British, fearing the consequences of failing to placate incensed Arab opinion, made Feisal the king of Iraq the following year. But what of Abdullah, Feisal's older brother whose appointment to the kingship of Iraq by the gathering in Damascus the British had effectively thwarted? More resourceful than the British had imagined, he went to Transjordan, the region on the east bank of the Jordan River which the British were planning to incorporate into Palestine, and from there proceeded to Amman with the stated aim of restoring order. The British, outpaced and scarcely able to use force against an ally, had no choice. In 1921, they accepted him as the Emir of the place, but under British tutelage. Transjordan would be a protectorate. Its de facto (and later de jure) extrication from Palestine provoked outrage among Zionists, who conceived of an Eretz Israel that stretched from the "river to the sea".

By 1924, when Ali, the oldest son of Hussein bin Ali, took over the reins of Hejaz, the three heirs to the House of Hashim—Ali, Abdullah, Feisal—were confirmed as kings of three Arab states: Hejaz, Transjordan and Iraq. But only in Jordan would the Hashemite standard survive. For in 1925, the Ibn Saud dynasty seized Mecca and Ali had to renounce his throne. In Iraq just over a quarter century later the young heir to Feisal was assassinated by the Baathists. Jordan certainly did not escape the turmoil and bloodshed resulting from nationalist fervour and political upheaval in the region. In 1951, King Abdullah of Jordan was assassinated at the entrance to the Al Aqsa mosque in Jerusalem by an Arab radical. But Abdullah had used his time in power to consolidate Jordan's statehood. He had succeeded in absorbing Aqaba into Transjordan as early as 1925, and even though the 300,000 or so inhabitants of the new nation were largely homogeneous—Arabs accounted for more than 90 per cent of the population—generating in them fidelity to a national identity that transcended layers of tribal and familial loyalties was no easy task. It was compounded by the rough-hewn living conditions—Amman, chosen as the capital in 1921 against the relatively more developed Al Salt, was little more than a village of 2,000 denizens—and scarcity of resources, most important of all water. Besides, for all practical purposes, the British controlled the foreign policy and military of the fledgling Protectorate.

But the years up to 1946, when Britain granted full independence, were also crucial because the institutions of statehood, or the groundwork for them, were laboriously laid down by King Abdullah, who also oversaw land reforms. Full independence finally came in 1946. This momentous event was followed, two years later, by a shattering war between Israel and an assortment of Arab states. No sooner had the United Nations voted to partition Palestine than Jewish forces hastened to make significant territorial gains. In the process, as the Israeli novelist Yizhar Smilansky and more recently the historian Benny Morris have documented, Jewish militias staged horrifying atrocities in Palestinian villages. The killings and expulsions of Palestinians enraged Arab opinion. Sharing the longest border of any Arab nation with Israel, Jordan was the frontier state in the Arab-Israeli conflict. It had most to lose from the fallout. In the 1948 war, Jordanian troops, trained by Britain, limited their activity to the corpus separatum of Jerusalem (or Al Quds to the Arabs) and areas granted to Palestinian Arabs by the United Nations' partition plan. The fighting culminated with Egypt taking the Gaza Strip, Israel seizing West Jerusalem (among other territories), and Jordan occupying the West Bank (its name indicating its location, on the western bank of the Jordan River) and East Jerusalem.

The armistice lines that went up after the war remained in place for two decades. For Jordan, the acquisition of East Jerusalem—home to the Al Aqsa mosque, the third holiest site in Islam—was a consolation of sorts for the loss, a quarter of a century before, of Masjid al-Haram in Mecca and the Masjid an-Nawabi in Medina, the first and second holiest places in Islam, to the Ibn Sauds. But emotional relief was accompanied by a demographic deluge. Suddenly, the population of the tiny country spiked from 400,000 to more than 1.3 million. How was the Hashemite Kingdom, itself callow, to integrate the West Bank's large Palestinian population? How was it going to make the relatively better educated and urbane fellow Arabs nursing a just grievance about the loss of their homeland reconcile themselves to their tragically diminished status? Since Palestinians vastly outnumbered the Jordanians, failure to win them over threatened the newly constituted statehood of Jordan. In the winter of 1949, King Abdullah chose to speak directly to the Palestinians and their leadership and proclaimed himself their king in their midst. Although he advocated and followed a policy of pragmatic moderation towards Israel and Zionism, the following year, having joined the other Arab states in an armistice agreement with the Israelis, he annexed the West Bank by a parliamentary resolution, inducted Palestinians into his cabinet and changed his country's name from Transjordan to the Hashemite Kingdom of Jordan. Only Britain (and, later, Pakistan) recognised the annexation, and it inflamed opinion in fellow Arab states, which felt that King Abdullah was, by virtue of annexing the West Bank, effacing the Palestinian quest for their own state.

There is another way of looking at this, of course: by giving the Palestinians the choice of Jordanian citizenship, he was helping them exit the diplomatic and bureaucratic limbo in which they had been trapped following the UN partition plan and the Arab-Israeli war. Far from snuffing out the Palestinian cause, Jordan became its loudest advocate in later years. It was in Jordan that Palestinians would be most wholesomely integrated. So much so that, today, Queen Rania of Jordan is of Palestinian origin, while Crown Prince Hussein, the future king, is half-Palestinian. In the aftermath of the 1948 war and the subsequent annexation of the West Bank, however, the atmosphere was so febrile and tensions ran so high that King Abdullah was felled by an assassin's bullet as he attended Friday prayers at the Al Aqsa mosque in July 1951. His teenage grandson, Prince Hussein, was also struck but survived miraculously: the bullet was deflected by a medal pinned on his chest that very morning by King Abdullah.

This little miracle would prove immensely consequential for Jordan. The succession that followed Abdullah's death clearly indicated his success as king. There was some drama: there was intense competition for the throne between Talat, the Crown Prince and designated heir, and his younger brother Naif, and the latter even attempted to stage a coup, but Talat took over the reins and oversaw the adoption of a relatively liberal constitution; Talat, however, abdicated just over a year later, due to illness, in favour of his son, the young Prince Hussein, who owed his life to the medal given to him by his grandfather. What is remarkable about this sequence of events is not its minor ups and downs, but rather how quickly its many differences were resolved. Hussein, crowned in August 1952, went on to rule Jordan until his death from cancer in 1999—a nearly five-decade-long reign characterised by political stability and economic and social progress.

This is not to say that this period was free from trouble. If anything, the eighteen-year-old Hussein assumed the throne just as all the major political currents—the Cold War, Arab nationalism, Arab-Israeli antagonism, radical left nationalism, Arab expansionism—converged upon his young and small state. It is a measure of his leadership that he succeeded not only in surviving but also in steering his country safely through all these crises. The beginning, however, was so perilous that the perennial question about Jordan's survivability was again aired by commentators. The forces of Arab nationalism, energised by the assassination of King Abdullah, regarded his grandson and successor as a pushover. The elections of 1956 resulted in the victory of the Nationalist Socialist Party; Suleiman Nabulsi, who became prime minister after being invited by King Hussein to form a government, appeared too preoccupied by the ideological currents emanating from Egypt to be trusted with the job of shoring up the Jordanian economy. The king initially went along with his prime minister, while demonstrating, when required, his ability to outmanoeuvre anyone who underestimated him. In 1956, the monarch decided to Arabise the Jordanian military by dismissing British officers, including his family's long-time friend Sir John Bagot Glubb ("Glubb Pasha"), and handing the command to General Radi Annab, the first Jordanian to command the Arab army. Educated at Harrow School and trained at the Royal Military Academy Sandhurst, the young king took personal command of the Bedouin-dominated armed forces—a decision that proved fateful in foiling a coup attempt the following year. When mostly non-Bedouin units of the army appeared poised to strike in 1957, King Hussein, who had just turned 21, personally appeared at the barracks in full uniform to assert his authority and quash the growing rumours of his assassination. (The king's cousin, King Feisal II of Iraq, was assassinated the following year in a violent coup in Baghdad.) The government was dismissed, and the Royal Hashemite Court grew into the nucleus of power and centre of decision-making. What made it novel, however, was its accessibility. King Hussein opened his palace to the public and made it a policy to personally receive and meet *every* last petitioner to the Royal Court. The king dispelled the notion of himself as a distant authority and became, as Jordanians say to this day, the "people's monarch".

The internal stability that followed was tested by external events, chief among them the Cold War and Arab-Israeli discord. For his part, King Abdullah, situated between his Arab brethren and Israel while hosting a significant Palestinian population, recognised the difficulty and importance of forging a harmonious and sustainable path between the two competing sides. Alert to the futility of conflict and appreciative of the indispensability of dialogue, he made the bold decision to open channels of communication with Israel as early as 1963 in the hope of finding a mutual arrangement of peaceful coexistence while upholding the dignity and rights of the Palestinians. It was a statesmanly initiative, taken long before others entertained it, and carried the potential to produce a lasting settlement to one of the most enduring altercations in memory. Unfortunately, its promise was torpedoed by a cross-border military raid by Israel on the town of es-Samu' in Hebron on the West Bank in November 1963. Staged in apparent retaliation for an attack on the West Bank border by Palestinian militants in which three Israeli soldiers were killed, the Israeli action resulted in the deaths of 21 Jordanian soldiers and the destruction of 118 houses, a school, a hospital and a mosque.

Israel's onslaught was devastating, disproportionate and, as the Israelis themselves later acknowledged, unwarranted. The militant Palestinian factions responsible for the attack on Israeli soldiers were equally hostile to the government of Jordan, which contained a number of high-level Palestinian ministers and officials. The Jordanian administration was seeking to demobilise them as part of the broader effort to find a peaceful solution to the Arab-Israeli discord and, more pointedly, the Palestinian crisis. As Yitzhak Rabin, who headed the IDF at the time, said candidly, Israel had "neither political nor military reasons to arrive at a confrontation with Jordan" and antagonise its monarch. But that is what the Israeli attack, occurring on King Hussein's thirty-first birthday, achieved in doing. It was, in the words of the Israeli scholar Moshe Shemesh, "a turning point in Jordan's attitude towards Israel, from a state of guarded coexistence to one of disappointment and pessimism". It ruptured the Jordanians' faith in Israel's claim to want a non-violent settlement to their problems and pushed the kingdom firmly into the camp of the Arab states then spoiling for a fight with Israel.

Once there, Jordan, though averse to war, found itself dragooned into the 1967 war orchestrated by Egypt and Syria. The result was catastrophic: Israel not only prevailed, but also captured East Jerusalem and the West Bank. Jordan lost a vast swathe of territory, but gained a large quantity of refugees as Palestinians under Israeli fire again fled their homes for Jordan. Military honour was partially restored in 1968, when the Jordanian military succeeded in pushing the Israelis out of the town of Karameh. Jordan's equation with Palestinians—or, more accurately, a bellicose wing of Palestinians—deteriorated as Amman pushed back against attempts by the Palestine Liberation Organisation and other militant organisations to establish a state within a state. A civil war erupted as the Royal Jordanian Army cracked down on the extensive Palestinian *fedayeen* network.

By the early 1970s, various armed groups were driven from the country and the authority of the state asserted.

The expulsion of Palestinian militias was accompanied by solidarity with the hundreds of thousands of impoverished Palestinians who had sought refuge in Jordan. Amman continued to extend its hospitality to dispossessed Palestinians by granting citizenship to anyone who asked for it, and the economy flourished as remittances from Jordanian expatriates working in oil-rich Arab states rose in the 1970s. Education and real estate were the prime beneficiaries of this boom. One consequence of prosperity was the growth in population, which nearly doubled between 1970 and 1980, shooting up in that decade from 1.7 million to 2.3 million—half of them citizens of Palestinian origin. This, in turn, had serious political implications once oil prices fell in the early 1980s; remittances, which accounted on average for about 15 per cent of the GDP, dwindled; and unemployment, which had dropped to 3 per cent in 1980, shot up to 20 per cent by 1989. Jordan's forex reserves were almost depleted. Overwhelmed by external debt, faced with a balance of payments crisis and on the brink of defaulting on its debt obligations, Amman went to the International Monetary Fund. The IMF, in exchange for loans of $275 million over an 18-month period and an option to reschedule a part of Amman's $6 billion foreign debt, devised a drastic plan to restructure the economy and remove what it saw as impediments to growth.

The menu of adjustments included privatisation of state-owned enterprises, contraction of subsidies on food and fuel, and a freeze on hiring by government bodies. Prices of food, beverage, tobacco, telephone calls and even water for irrigation increased by between 10 and 15 per cent. Even though King Hussein had successfully negotiated the maintenance of an annual subsidy of $120 million on staples such as rice and bread, the pain of austerity, coming after a decade of relative ease, ignited riots in the country within days of its implementation. Rather than react with force, the king responded to the unrest by reviving the democratic process that had been put on ice as Jordan was besieged by a catalogue of security challenges, internal and external, in the preceding decades. On a visit to Washington when violence erupted, Hussein returned to the kingdom and did what monarchs seldom do: he went to villages and towns, gathered people together, sat among them and listened to them. In the process, he converted a current of deep disaffection into a wave of abiding affection for him. He felt sufficiently confident in the allegiance of his subjects of all origins to relinquish during this period Jordan's claim to the West Bank (although the crown would keep the custodianship of the Holy Places).

King Hussein's great challenge had been averting crises by finding a balance between domestic and international expectations of him that were often irreconcilable. As Henry Kissinger put it in his memoirs, *White House Years*, King Hussein "sought with dignity and courage to reconcile the roles of Arab nationalist and America's friend. A pro-Western monarch in the vortex of Arab radicalism, he maintained his independence as well as the respect of rulers in the region." Foreign unrest followed almost immediately after he had succeeded in allaying the unrest at home as Iraq invaded Kuwait. Amman, as the largest trading partner of Baghdad, was caught in a difficult position. An overwhelming majority of Jordanians supported Iraq. And yet, contrary to the popular but incorrect view at the time, Jordan did not condone Iraq's actions through silence; if anything, King Hussein worked hard to bring them to a swift end through active diplomacy and numerous personal appeals directed at Saddam Hussein. And it would not be inaccurate to state that, after Kuwait, Jordan was the non-aggressor state that suffered the most because, as had happened in the past, a million refugees from the war passed through Jordan, and at least 300,000 ultimately settled there, intensifying the strain on the state and its limited resources. By some estimates, Jordan lost upwards of $3 billion in revenues as sanctions on Iraq led to the collapse of trade.

The disquiet over Iraq ended in 1994, when Jordan, after lengthy negotiations, became the second Arab state after Egypt to sign a peace treaty with Israel. The so-called Wadi Arab treaty brought to an end the state of war that had existed between the Hashemite Kingdom and the Jewish state since the Arab-Israeli war of 1948. The twilight of Hussein's reign had begun. In 1992, the king had had surgery to remove cancerous tissue. The cancer returned six years later. From his hospital room at the Mayo Clinic in Minnesota, the monarch sent a poignant hand-written note to his brother, Crown Prince Hassan: "My general condition is better, although the fever is recurring an average of three times a day, and treatment by antibiotics is continuing without stop." He was diagnosed with non-Hodgkin's lymphoma, and died a year later, in 1999. The man who had taken the reins of his country at the tender age of eighteen, and was dismissed by observers as a milksop, had grown into a widely respected leader who had surefootedly led his people through a cascade of crises.

One of the longest serving heads of state by then, King Hussein had also raised Jordan's profile internationally: the country that was written off repeatedly had come to be regarded by the late 1990s as an indispensable force of moderation in the region and a key to peace in the Middle East. His funeral was an illustration of his—and by extension his country's—stature in international politics. Representatives of fifty states poured into Amman to pay their respects. Among them were Boris Yeltsin, the ailing and ageing president of Russia who made his first public appearance after months of illness; every living American president at the time: Bill Clinton, Jimmy Carter, Gerald Ford, George H.W. Bush; the president of Syria, Hafez Al Assad, who had once attempted to shoot down the monarch's plane; Yasser

Arafat, the leader of the Palestine Liberation Organisation, who bowed twice before the funeral cortege; and a stream of Israeli leaders, including Prime Minister Benjamin Netanyahu, his foreign minister Ariel Sharon, the Labour Party leader Ehud Barak, Shimon Peres and even the perennially bellicose Yitzhak Shamir. In one of his last public remarks, at a summit in Maryland organised by President Clinton to find a settlement to the Israel-Palestine dispute, King Hussein, urging the two sides to end the conflict, told them that they had all seen "enough destruction, enough death, enough waste" and none of them had the "right to dictate through irresponsible action or narrow-mindedness the future of our children or their children's children". In death, he brought together leaders who had spent their lives fighting each other. As his funeral procession moved through the streets of Amman on an artillery cortege, a band of Scottish pipers played a military tune, mourners broke through cordons to touch him, and church bells rang in sorrow and gratitude from an ancient Christian community which the king—and his family—had protected.

* * *

The last decision of the departed monarch had been to name his son, Abdullah, the heir to the Hashemite throne. The transition from soldier to ruler was smooth, radiated continuity, and underlined, as the scholars Beverley Milton-Edwards and Peter Hinchcliffe have noted, "the extent to which the Hashemites have earned their legitimacy as the ruling family of Jordan". King Abdullah II, educated in America and Britain and trained, like his father, at Sandhurst, had served almost all of his professional life in Jordan's military as major-general. (His brother, Feisal, commanded the air force. And their sister, Aisha, served as a brigadier.) Ascending the throne at thirty-seven, he did not have the luxury of a learning curve. His reign has been marked by a multitude of upheavals—from the so-called War on Terror to the invasion of Iraq and the Arab Spring to the civil war in Syria, which brought 600,000 refugees to the Hashemite Kingdom, and the coronavirus pandemic.

Like his father, King Abdullah II has been a steadying force. He has not deviated from the principled support Jordan has long given to the Palestinians; nor has he shut the door to refugees. At the same time, he has presided over serious political reform—a glacial process that has involved drawing conservative and progressive elements into agreement—that bears the stamp of his own socially liberal vision. In a significant electoral overhaul, the kingdom was divided into eighteen electoral districts, with proportional representation and an open list of candidates. Eighteen seats were set aside for female representatives, seven for Christians and four for other minorities. A series of amendments to the constitution in 2021 obliges the state to protect women and disabled persons and help the youth advance, compels the government to subject irregularities in public spending to thorough scrutiny and places prohibitions on lawmakers from gaining favourable contracts with state-owned enterprises. These reforms, though slow brewing, are hugely significant and were achieved without bloodshed.

Jordan, bordered by Iraq, Syria, Israel and the West Bank, continues to be seen by the West and in the region an indispensable linchpin of security and stability. It continues, at the same time, to forge extensive partnerships with the world beyond. Since his ascension, King Abdullah II has visited China eight times and has built strong personal relationships with the Chinese leadership. Bilateral trade between the two nations peaked at almost $5 billion last year, although India and the United States remain the two largest export markets for Jordan, which remains, for reasons of geography, a country of major importance to Washington and the West. Shaped by regional conflict, Jordan is unlikely to want to become embroiled in the emerging Cold War between Washington and Beijing.

In June, I travelled to Amman to attend the wedding of Crown Prince Hussein to Rajwa Al Saif. It was a match that bound Saudi Arabia with Jordan. As Saudi citizens jostled with Jordanians to catch a glimpse of the royal couple, I saw the old rivalry between the Ibn Saud and the Hashemites dissolve in a union of love. After wishing the couple well, I walked the streets of Amman to speak to ordinary people, almost everyone waiving the Jordanian flag with pride. Apparent in their genuine happiness and warmth was the long distance Jordan had travelled from its uncertain beginning to its current position. Here, in a region riven by so much strife, was an oasis of stability that granted shelter to those in need and strove to provide dignity to all. That, as anyone familiar with the turmoil of history will testify, is no small achievement.

11

ARMENIA

HAYASTAN

I must begin by clarifying that the chapter that follows is not an exhaustive story of Armenia—a subject that merits its own book—or a comprehensive distillation of the causes of its successes and failures. Rather, it is a short historical overview, intended to serve as an introduction to my country, interspersed with my own broad personal reflections that are the product of a lifetime of engagement with Armenia via science, academia, diplomacy and politics.

Although Armenia had great advantages and tremendous potential compared with the small states we have examined, it lacked some of the key attributes necessary to realise them—attributes which, as we have seen, were fundamental to the success of other states. Because I cannot disclose everything, I shall identify just some of them, while accepting that I have played my part in the successes *and* failures of Armenia. This chapter is also, necessarily, personal: I was placed in the privileged position to serve Armenia by the fateful choices of my forebears. I hope their story, inextricably tied to mine, can illuminate my nation's journey.

* * *

In the summer of 1946, a train bearing young Armenians set off from Tehran to Yerevan. The carriages echoed with the sound of musical instruments, songs, laughter. It was a journey defined by joy and hope. The battlefields of the Second World War had claimed 300,000 Armenian lives—a catastrophic number for a small nation. At the war's end, the Soviet Union went to great lengths to lure back members of the Armenian diaspora, who numbered among the most industrious workers and best engineers, shoemakers, musicians, mathematicians, scientists and soldiers, to repopulate the deserted homeland. The fact that Armenia was part of the USSR did nothing to diminish its sanctity in the hearts of patriotic Armenians scattered around the world. The train from Tehran was part of a great wave of voluntary repatriation—perhaps the only one of its kind—to reclaim and rebuild Armenia. Among the numerous passengers on board were my parents: Zhenya Chukhajian, a strong-willed 21-year-old determined to do graduate work in Yerevan, and her friend Vartan Ter-Sarkissian, a 27-year-old architect of great renown leaving behind a promising career with the Swedish construction company Skanska for an unknown future in Armenia. That train journey is the reason for my existence; if it weren't for that, I wouldn't be here and you wouldn't be reading my book. When they arrived in Nakhichevan, they saw children jump on the food discarded by the passengers. This sad spectacle did not dampen their patriotism. Both of them hoped that this would be the last in a series of migrations that had brought them together.

My father, born in Anapa on the northern Black Sea coast, had grown up between the Sea of Azov and Kharkiv in

Ukraine, an Armenian subject of a vast Russian Empire lurching imperceptibly towards its demise. The Ter-Sarkissians ("Ter", which literally translates as "Lord", was an honorific given to families descended from clergymen in the Armenian Apostolic Church) had dispersed across the world. One branch went on to prosper in Singapore, founding, among other institutions, the Raffles Hotel. Others settled in Europe and America, making careers in Hollywood. My paternal grandfather, who had fled with his family from Erzurum in Ottoman-ruled western Armenia to the Russian Empire to escape religious persecution, left with his family for Tehran following the Bolshevik revolution. Iran, apart from being the only state whose passport he could secure at the time, was also home to an old Armenian settlement. In 1605, the Persian Emperor Shah Abbas the Great had settled thousands of Armenians in New Julfa, just outside Isfahan, and granted them a monopoly of the lucrative silk trade. The Armenian community's reputation for hard work and integrity, acclaimed by the *shahenshah* himself, followed them into the twentieth century.

My maternal grandfather, a successful trader, had made a more circuitous journey to Tehran. One of his relations was Tigran Chukhajian, a famous conductor and founder of the first opera in the Ottoman Empire. The family's name was widely known and highly respected. But artistic accomplishment and business acumen were no guarantors of immunity from religious oppression. In 1915, they moved to Armenia, then part of the Russian Empire; then, fleeing the Bolsheviks, they migrated to Turkmenistan, where they settled for some time in Ashgabat, before finally moving to Tehran. It was there, in the early 1940s, that my parents first met. They were members of a promising post-war generation of Armenians; they were young, astute and well educated. Each of them had the opportunity to move to the West, where there was a dense network of friends and family to receive them, and live a measurably more comfortable life. They chose to move to Armenia. They arrived at this decision separately, without consulting each other. Some may find their submission to the pull of the homeland at the expense of their promising careers strange. But it is precisely such affection and commitment, all-consuming and transcending distance and time, that has sustained Armenia over the long and arduous centuries of its history.

My parents married in 1950. What followed was a harmonious division of labour: my father continued his practice, and my mother, who had by then obtained a degree in psychology, devoted herself to making a happy, contented home. My younger sister, Karine, and I were the beneficiaries of this arrangement. The honorific "Ter" was excised from our family name when my father went to get a passport. "We are a communist nation," the official told him. "There are no lords here." My father, for all his anti-communism, agreed with this wholeheartedly. Ours became the only branch of the Ter-Sarkissian family to go thereafter by the name Sarkissian.

Our home, built by our father in Yerevan, was filled with highly distinguished figures in the arts, literature, architecture who discussed history and politics late into the night. It was clear to my sister and me that our father was the natural centre of this circle. Though reserved and sometimes forbidding, he could be expansive with us. He particularly loved showing me the buildings in Yerevan, the ancient Armenian city rebuilt in the shape of the sun in the 1920s by the architect Alexander Tamanyan. The pink stone, my father would tell me, was formed from volcanic ash. At night, as we gazed at stars together, he, guiding me by his hand, showed me Venus, Mars, Jupiter. Proficient in German, English and French, and fluent in Russian, he taught me languages and trained me in mathematics and chess from when I was four years old. I more than admired my father: I revered him. But just as

I began to form an idea of the world and develop a sense of self anchored to his personality, he was diagnosed with cancer. I did not fully appreciate its significance in the beginning as I saw my parents engage in mutedly animated conversations and travel to Moscow and Leningrad for treatment. I often bunked off school and spent the days with my grandmother, who hypnotised me with her endless supply of stories of Armenians and their travails and triumphs—the arrival of Christianity, the victories of Tigranes, the achievements of the Cilician kingdom, the age of the Russian Tsars, the greatness of William Gladstone, the coming of the Ottomans—all of them, I later learnt, true.

In 1964, not long after I celebrated my tenth birthday, my father passed away. I had spent many evenings standing guard and talking to him as he received treatment. That is what I most intensely, painfully missed in the days and weeks following his departure. But I felt instinctively that I could not succumb to despair. My family—my mother, young sister, elderly grandmother—needed me. I had, without knowing it, made an internal transition to adulthood. My mother's grief, so profound that it was almost inexpressible, was compounded by the enormous responsibility of raising all by herself two young children. She too chose not to show it. Instead, she took two jobs to support us, often working shifts that exceeded sixteen hours a day. Fortunes faded; our family's days of glory and happiness became a thing of the past, part of my fond memories and the lore that my wizened and wise grandmother narrated to me in the evenings. The personal story became, in my mind, a parable of the national saga.

* * *

Armenia is one of the world's most antique civilisations, the first state to embrace Christianity, and has inhabited the land where it currently stands against all the odds for millennia.

197

Chronicling its history in the fifth century CE, the historian Movses Khorenatsi felt the need to clarify that, "although we are small and very limited in numbers ... and many times have been subjugated by foreign kingdoms, yet too, many deeds of bravery have been performed in our land which are worthy of record". Armenia's achievements were always braided together with an appreciation of its geographic limitations. Located on the intersection of Europe and Asia, it became, over the centuries, what Gibbon called a "theatre of perpetual war" between great empires: Roman, Greek, Persian, Parthian, Arab, Ottoman, Russian. The autochthonous kingdoms, governments, and ways of life rising and dissolving on its soil endowed it with a unitary cast that was sufficiently robust to withstand the ravages of so many competing armies.

The kingdom of Urartu, born in the ninth century BCE and stretching all the way from the Euphrates to Lake Urmia, was the first united polity to emerge from the Armenian highlands. Its language, now extinct, was suffused with Armenian. Arzasku, its first capital, is lost, while its second capital, Van, is currently part of Turkey. But a link to Urartu persists in Yerevan, which owes its name to the palace of Erebuni, built by King Argishti in 782 BCE at the height of the kingdom's prosperity on a site just outside Armenia's modern capital. Urartu was sacked and seized by the Iranian Medes in the sixth century BCE, and the Medes themselves were overthrown by the Persians; but those who survived and proliferated there were speakers of Armenian, an Indo-European language, who called themselves "Hai"—children of Hayk, a descendant of Noah in Biblical lore and patriarch of Armenia in the national history set out by Movses—and their land "Hayastan". Hayastan functioned as a confederation of principalities which, through consensus, chose a king. Monarchs were not clothed in divine authority; they were treated as first among equals. With the victory of Alexander the Great over the

Persians in the fourth century BCE, Hellenistic civilisation infused the culture of what would go on to become, from a Western vantage point, the easternmost edge of Christianity.

By the second century BCE, as Rome emerged as the pre-eminent power in the distant west and Parthia developed into a formidable force in the east, Armenia, bound to Rome by treaty, engaged in deft diplomacy, relentlessly propitiating, bargaining, finessing and counterbalancing to ensure its survival. In their pursuit of autonomy, its rulers were permanently on the lookout for alliances and had cultivated an excellent sense of timing. In the first century BCE, as Rome and Parthia were weakened, the Armenian king Tigranes II lost no time in forging a partnership with Mithirades, the spirited foe of the Romans, whose daughter he married. Defeating Rome and Parthia in a series of wars, Tigranes—now addressed as "King of Kings" and "Tigranes the Great"—united all the Armenian territories under his crown and established his capital at Tigranekert before conquering northern Syria, southern Anatolia, Mesopotami and Phoenicia, and reigning over a unified empire that ran from the Black Sea to the Mediterranean. Rome dispatched its legions led by Lucullus and then Pompey. Betrayed by his own son, Tigranes surrendered to Pompey in 66 BCE following a series of battles. Although he lost the Empire, he was recognised as the king of Armenia. To regard this period as Armenia's "golden age" is to equate greatness with conquest. To me, its import lay, rather, in the fact that, in the age of ancient empire and by the fight-or-become-extinct logic that governed it, Armenia, through a combination of skill and courage, raised itself into the ranks of the most powerful and formidable states of the era.

The end of Tigran's dynasty, in 1 CE, was followed by the rise of the Arshakuni dynasty, whose first ruler, King Tiridates, was crowned by Emperor Nero in Rome in 66 CE. A relatively stable and balanced period ensued until the Sassanid dynasty emerged in the third century CE in Persia as a result, one way or another, of the Roman Emperor Trajan's ill-advised attack on Parthia more than a century earlier. The Sassanids, fiercely Zoroastrian and determined to impose their beliefs, were implacably hostile to Armenia. And Armenia, which had taught itself to survive between Persia and Rome, was again forced into making an alliance with Rome. Henry Kissinger's observation that America has interests, not friends, was true also of Rome and Persia. In 387 CE, the two quarrelling empires partitioned Armenia between themselves. And yet this boundary did not divide Armenians, who were now bound by an identity forged in the crucible of faith.

In 301 CE, Armenia had accepted Christianity as the state religion—the first in the world to do so. The Apostles Bartholomew and Thaddeus were the first to preach the gospel to Armenia—which explains why the Armenian national church is of apostolic origin—but the actual story of the country's conversion to Christianity is far more interesting. Gregory, the son of a nobleman who was said to have assassinated the father of King Tiridates III, was taken to Cappadocia (now central Anatolia in Turkey) and hidden by relatives. There, growing up amid Christian missionaries, he accepted Christianity. Years later, when the threat of a blood feud appeared to have dissipated, Gregory returned to Armenia and began preaching his new religion. Tiridates III got wind of this. He captured Gregory, had him tortured and banished to the dungeon (*khor virap*), where a widow kept him alive for the next 15 years. The king went on to acquire a reputation for cruelty, especially against Christians. In one instance, he had 39 Christian women executed. But then, in the words of Agathangelos, who chronicled the king's deeds, Tiridates III "took on the appearance of a wild boar, and dwelt among the beasts". Conscious of his degeneration, he pleaded for a cure, whereupon he was advised by his sister to set Gregory free, which he did. Gregory, Agathangelos tells us, cured the king, and the monarch and his court accepted Christianity and proclaimed it the state religion.

The distinctiveness conferred by faith was reinforced by the creation, in 405 CE, of the Armenian alphabet by the theologian and linguist Mesrop Mashtots. The alphabet Mashtots devised, containing thirty-six letters and written from left to right, corresponded phonetically with the sound of the spoken Armenian language and is in use to this day. It is this script, perhaps more than any other single element, that preserved the Armenian identity. The canon engendered by it became a national carapace into which Armenians, especially after their dispersal by circumstance, could retreat. Language and faith, having become the twin-bases of the Armenian identity, had the power to unite a riven people—a truth most powerfully demonstrated at the Battle of Avarayr in 451 CE, the seminal event in the annals of Armenia. That year, the Persians waged a fierce battle to impose Zoroastrianism on the Armenians in the belief that their weakened and divided people would submit. To their astonishment, they found Armenians unifying against the common threat and mobilising behind the nobility. Led by Vartan Mamikonian, a member of a sprawling martial family that had set up roots in India, Armenian forces fought a gallant battle against the belligerent Persian proselytisers at Avarayr. Mamikonian died on the battlefield, became a saint, Armenians retained their faith and the battle became the most fabled chapter in Armenia's national memory.

Then came the era of Islam, the most significant development in the region and beyond. Its Arab armies destroyed the Armenian capital Dvin in 642 CE. The Armenians, led by the Bagratuni dynasty, defeated the Arabs at the Battle of Vardanakert in early eighth century CE and drove them out of the country, before the Arabs regrouped and liquidated a good slice of the Armenian nobility in the cathedral of Nakhichevan a few years later. Notwithstanding the bloodshed, what is striking is that Armenia went on to develop a more harmonious relationship with Muslim Arabs than with Christian Byzantium. Some historians have observed that the threat from the Arabs, who levied a religious tax on the Armenians, may have stimulated an economic revival. "The nobility and peasantry found themselves obliged to abandon their autarkic, rural economy, and to produce a surplus of raw and manufactured products for sale." Cyril Toumanoff, the pre-eminent historian of the Caucasus, has written:

> Thus commerce and urban economy ... recovered; the middle class revived; new cities like Ani, Kars, Balesh (Bitlis), Artanuji, rose beside the old, such as Artaxata, Dvin, Theodosiopolis, Tiflis, Partav (Bardha'a). Caucasia once again became the nexus of trade-routes connecting Europe and Asia, and the prosperity of the mediaeval period was founded.

An economic golden age of sorts began in Armenia, led by the Bagratuni dynasty and King Ashot I, by the mid-ninth century CE. Their capital, Ani, was "the city of a thousand and one churches": a highly sophisticated centre of culture, religion and commerce on the intersection of prized trade routes, with many hospitals, palaces and public buildings protected by a double line of fortifications, where, as the historian Aristakes of Lastivert, who had witnessed much destruction in his lifetime, wrote, "Princes with joyous countenances sat on the princely thrones; they were clad in brilliant colours and looked like spring gardens ... The sound of flutes, of cymbals, and of other instruments filled one's heart with the comfort of great joy". Today, Ani, inside Turkish frontiers, is known as the "ghost city": a reliquary of decay and ruin. Its state speaks to the decline of Armenia after the Bagratid era, which ended with the sack and destruction of Ani by the Seljuk Turks in 1064 CE.

Armenia, plunged into a protracted period of torment and tribulation, never recovered from that blow. Armenian power, however, did not yet fade. It shifted 1,400 kilometres to Cilicia, where modern-day southern Anatolia is situated. This is perhaps the only mediaeval instance of sovereignty being relocated and re-established in a different territory. Cilician Armenia, beginning in the eleventh century CE, lasted until 1375 CE. To secure itself against Christian Byzantium and the Muslim Caliphate, Cilicia sought to forge impracticable alliances with a distant Mongol power and with the Crusaders. A period of stability and prosperity, described by some as the Armenian Silver Age, followed as Cilicia established itself as a centre of trade and culture. The Catholicos Nerses IV, the head of the Armenian Apostolic Church, achieved wide renown for his haunting poetry. The physician Mkhitar Heratsi made significant advances in surgery, treating patients from the Christian and Muslim worlds, and published his *Relief for Fevers*. But the alliance with the Crusaders proved the undoing of Cilicia's internal cohesion once Rome began applying pressure on the Armenian Church to submit to the Catholic church. A minuscule minority made the conversion, the forefathers of the small Catholic population of Armenia today, but the overwhelming majority rejected that demand. The discord peaked when the line of succession resulted in the ascension to the throne, in 1342 CE, of Constantine II (born Guy de Lusignan) of the Poiters-Lusignan dynasty. His reign, threatening to turn Armenia effectively into a Frankish kingdom, provoked an uprising and culminated in his assassination. Before his successors could restore order, Cilician Armenia was overrun and reduced by the Mamluks in 1375 CE.

Armenians did not perish. They kept the flame alive in Cilicia and in the old Armenian heartland—home to the Mother See of Holy Etchmiadzin and seat of the Armenian Pontiff or Catholicos of All Armenians—which became a battleground for the rival armies of Sunni Ottoman Turkey and Shia Muslim Persia. Armenians themselves had become, as the late Christopher J. Walker memorably put it, "suppliants, a minority dependent on the goodwill of the ruling power, with almost no power to defend their own interests". The Persians were measurably more tolerant of Armenians and other religious minorities than the Ottomans. But it is the extended conflict between the Sublime Porte and Persia, lasting from the fifteenth to the sixteenth century CE, that physically fractured Armenia into western and eastern halves. This division, lasting to this day, was not organic; it was the by-product of a struggle between imperial powers. The theme of great power contest continued to determine Armenia's fate into the twentieth century even as the cast of great powers itself changed.

Decimated at home, the cause of Armenia endured abroad. From Europe to India, the Armenian diaspora worked vigorously in the eighteenth century to disseminate ideas for restoring Armenia. The monastic order founded by the abbot Mekhitar in 1701, and granted a permanent home by the Venetian government on the island of San Lazzaro in 1715, preserved and produced Armenian ecclesiastical scholarship, provided refuge and education to students (among them Lord Byron, who, arriving at the monastery in 1816, left after having learnt to read and write classical Armenian), set up a branch in Vienna and functioned as the voice of Armenia, the home of "eastern Christianity", in the West. What made the Mekhitarist order remarkable was the fact that it was Catholic. Its labour was a clear demonstration that Armenian identity had transcended religious differences. Around the same time, the first Armenian journal, *Azdarar*, was put to print and published in Madras by India's Armenian community, which had a continuous presence in the country for 4,000 years. (Armenia, too, hosted a large Hindu colony set up by a pair of Indian princes in 2000 BCE—a fact we know from an ancient Syriac text translated and published by the Mekhitarist order in 1832.) As early as the 1770s, two Armenians in India, Movses Baghramian and Hakob Shahamirian, published highly influential books calling—and setting out a blueprint—for a democratic Armenia governed by a constitution. Such ideas naturally took a long time to gain traction.

The nineteenth century began in the Caucasus with the annexation of Georgia by Russia following the atrocities of Qajar Iran, whose founder, the eunuch king Agha Mohammad Shah, had massacred his way through Tbilisi in 1795. In 1823, Persia ceded Yerevan and Nakhichevan, among other possessions in the Caucasus, to Russia, which administered the two regions as an Armenian province. The period that followed was characterised by intellectual efflorescence, institutional reform and political ferment. The most consequential change concerned language. Armenian had developed over the centuries into two distinct forms. Classical Armenian (*grabar* or *krapar*), literary and liturgical, was used by the church and the clerisy. Despite its limited utility, it enjoyed a high status; those who couldn't master it, and they were a majority, were considered crude. The so-called "Yerevan dialect" (*ashkarabar* or *ashkharapar*), on the other hand, was regarded with a measure of scorn for supposedly being the argot of the lowly. This state of affairs was not only a repudiation of the unifying role played by the Armenian language; it had become a curse that was stunting the intellectual growth of Armenia. As a young teacher, Khachatur Abovian noticed that students preferred Russian to incomprehensible Armenian. Educated by the Armenian church and a celebrated alumnus of the university at Tartu, Abovian became an advocate of (and a martyr to) the cause of *ashkharabar* Armenian. His 1841 novel *The Wounds of Armenia* was not only a literary masterwork that inaugurated modern Armenian literature; it was a pioneering work because it was the first book of its kind to be written in vernacular Armenian.

Abovian's work sparked a literary, artistic and even political-activist effervescence in service of the idea of reviving the Armenian nation and regaining its lost sovereignty. Mikayel Nalbandian, a friend and fellow traveller of Alexander Herzen, Mikhail Bakunin and Nikolay Ogarev, and Raffi (Hakob Melik Hakobian) were the pre-eminent figures in this movement. A secular feeling found forceful expression in the literary ferment of the time. As Raffi wrote ruefully:

> O forefathers! I drink this glass, but not as a toast to your remains. Had you built fortresses instead of monasteries with which our country is full, had you bought guns and ammunition instead of squandering fortunes on holy urns, had you burned gunpowder instead of incense at the holy altars, our country would have been more fortunate than she is today.

Nalbandian's verse, *Mer Hayrenik*, was adopted as Armenia's national anthem in the twentieth century. Wherever one stood, this much was clear: just as the Mekhitarist order attested to the religious versatility of the Armenian identity, so the acceptance of *ashkharapar* affirmed its linguistic plurality.

In the nineteenth century, however, the establishment of Russian power in the Caucasus was seen by the British, not wholly without reason, as a possible prelude to a Romanov push into India. To check Russia, Britain proceeded to augment the military power first of Persia and then of Ottoman Turkey. The Great Game as it unfolded in the Caucasus bubbled with deceit, intrigue and confusion. The supreme irony for modernising Armenians who pitched the West as a model for their compatriots was that the pre-eminent Western power, Britain, was a major backer of the Ottoman government, the prime persecutor of the Armenians. Ottoman oppression of its Armenian subjects intensified in the aftermath of the Russo-Turkish War of 1877, in which the Russian army was commanded by half a dozen Armenian generals, and London, despite gallant protests by the great Liberal leader William Gladstone, was not able to halt the massacres that followed. This is not to say that conditions under Russian rule were ordained to remain safe and secure for Armenians. Foreign rule, no matter how seemingly lenient, is always parlous—it is certainly no alternative to self-governance—a fact demonstrated by the rapid unravelling of the quasi-autonomy of Armenia once Prince Grigory Golitsyn appeared in 1896 as Russia's plenipotentiary in the Caucasus.

Thanks to the caprices of one individual, official Russian attitudes to the Armenians, animated up to that point by some notion of Christian concord, dissolved suddenly into racial antipathy. Golitsyn's hatred for the people he was dispatched to administer ran so deep that he declared there would be "no Armenians left in the Caucasus" by the time he was finished, "except a few specimens for the museum". In 1903, a year before that remark, Russia had seized the properties of the Armenian church. Two years later, Armenian bodies piled up in Baku, Nakhichevan and Karabakh as Azerbaijanis, incited by the authorities, went on a murderous rampage. Officials looked on; in Baku, they occasionally joined in the slaughter. In Karabakh— the oldest continuously inhabited Armenian territory, which Armenians call Artsakh—the Armenians were prepared and able to defend themselves. The more radical among the politically conscious Armenians, whose number had proliferated by then, engaged in reprisals against officers who had exacerbated the bloodshed. The governor of Baku was assassinated. And yet the hostility against Russia eventually cooled with the appointment of Count Vorontsov-Dashkov, a highly enlightened and impartial figure, as viceroy to the Caucasus. Indeed, Armenian tribulations in the Caucasus were eclipsed by the Armenian suffering in the Ottoman Empire.

The Hamidian Massacres of the late nineteenth century—so named for the "Bloody Sultan" Abdul Hamid II—had shaken Armenia and Russia. Hamid saw Armenians as the instruments of the foreign powers determined to destroy the Ottoman Empire. Having assured France, Russia and Britain—all of whom had pressed him to advance reforms to safeguard the Armenians— he set his dreaded Hamidiye regiments loose on his defenceless and disarmed Armenian subjects in 1894. Tens of thousands of Armenians were slaughtered over three years. William Gladstone, who had stepped aside after serving four terms as Britain's prime minister, waged an heroic campaign to mobilise international action. Sadly, the massacres under Hamid were only the overture to the calculated carnage against Ottoman Armenians that began in the middle of the second decade of the twentieth century. Faced with the threat of the Russian Army and seeing Armenians as a fifth column, the Young Turks decided permanently to eradicate Armenians from the lands on which Armenian civilisation had flourished more than a millennium before the Turks had set foot on them. The campaign began on 24 April 1914 with the detention of 235 prominent Armenians of Istanbul's Armenian community—poets, politicians, writers, intellectuals—who were split up, loaded into trains, and taken to distant prisons and killed. The decapitation of the community's leadership was followed by mass arrests, separation of men and women, deportation and death marches. Henry Morgenthau, the US ambassador to the Sublime Porte, described what he witnessed in a cable to Washington six months after the slaughter began:

> It is extremely rare to find a family intact that has come any considerable distance, invariably all having lost members from disease and fatigue, young girls and boys carried off by hostile tribesmen, and about all the men having been separated from the families and suffered fates that had best be left unmentioned, many being done away with in atrocious

manners before the eyes of their relatives and friends. So severe has been the treatment that careful estimates place the number of survivors at only 15 percent of those originally deported ... there seems to have been about 1,000,000 persons lost up to this date.

Russian troops, entering historically Armenian cities, found them cleansed of Armenians. The Armenian population of Ottoman Turkey, which was 2 million in 1914, had fallen below 200,000 by 1918. A million and a half Armenians were slaughtered in the intervening period. The word "genocide" was later coined by the Jewish jurist Raphael Lemkin to convey Turkey's campaign of extermination against the Armenians. Some of those who survived the genocide found refuge in Iran and Arab Muslims havens such as Lebanon, Syria, Iraq and Egypt; others fled to Transcaucasia, where they regrouped and joined in the effort to defend Caucasian Armenia. In 1918, following the collapse of the Russian Empire and the withdrawal of Bolshevik Russia from the Great War, Armenia declared independence.

My grandparents belonged to the generation of Armenians who were born or came of age during this brief historical recess in which Armenians succeeded in exhuming the statehood they had long ago squandered. But before the first Armenian Republic could be admitted to the League of Nations, Mustafa Kemal, who would go on to lead the successor state to the Ottoman Empire, ordered his nationalist forces to devastate its territories, rendering the fledgling state unviable. Once the Treaty of Lausanne returned Anatolia to Turkey, the prospects of Armenia's survival seemed bleak, and Yerevan, facing total destruction, acceded without resistance to the Russian demand to join the future USSR in return for Moscow's promise to protect Armenia's frontiers. The guarantees were misleading. Rather than preserve Armenian lands, the Bolshevik government formally ceded them to Ankara. Mount Ararat, the sacred emblem and deity of Armenians, ended up inside Turkey's newly expanded borders.

* * *

I was born in Soviet Armenia, the "second republic" as my parents' generation called it, in June 1953—right in the middle of the USSR's momentous transition from Stalinism to the Khrushchev Thaw. I first glimpsed Stalin in stone. A colossal statue of his, one of the largest ever raised, towered over Yerevan. His reign of terror was beginning to give way to optimism as I entered school. Armenians radiated a new kind of confidence. When I was nine, I saw the statue of Stalin being taken down; five years later, I witnessed a 22-metre-tall monument to Mother Armenia—designed and sculpted by Ara Haroutunian and Rafael Israelian, two very close friends of my father—go up on the same spot. In the spring of 1965, I witnessed an enormous crowd—of up to 100,000, some said, the first and largest demonstration in Soviet history up to that point—outside Yerevan's Opera House demanding formal recognition of the Armenian Genocide. I listened to speeches, songs and harrowing testimonies of survivors that continued late into the night. In 1926, the Communist Party had decreed against the commemoration of the Armenian Genocide. This time the Soviet government not only recognised the Medz Yeghern—as we call the Armenian Genocide—but also ordered the construction of a solemn memorial to its victims outside Yerevan.

The passing of my father had made me conscious of my responsibility to my family, and over time this feeling expressed itself in fierce competitiveness. The arena in which I could compete best in the Soviet Union was education. I was drawn to the sciences—particularly physics—and did well. My academic performance was not the result of some unaccountable, inherent genius; it was the product of some talent, of course, but mostly conscious striving, by me, but also by my mother, who worked even harder to support me. It was difficult not to feel even at that age that, rather than pray for miracles, people could and should endeavour to shape their own fate. They may not always succeed, but they would at least qualify as captains of their souls. This belief in personal responsibility informed my outlook.

I gravitated towards the limitless world of theoretical physics and astrophysics at the Yerevan State University. And in the 1980s, as my papers on theoretical physics began being published at home, circulated in the Soviet Union and read abroad, I received an invitation from Sir (now Lord) Martin Rees of the Institute of Astronomy at Cambridge University.

In Cambridge, it was impossible not to feel transported to a higher plane. From my big office with its own personal computer to the libraries that contained oceans of knowledge, everything was available to me. Then there were the periodic lectures by and interactions with Nobel-winning scientists who treated everyone as their peers. Working on the theme of the universe's structure, I would occasionally spot squirrels on the tree outside my window. It felt sometimes that I was in heaven. When friends asked me what I thought about London—its buildings, monuments, avenues, cars and department stores—I invariably disappointed them by saying none of that impressed me because all of it fitted into my conception of the place. What stirred me was the *freedom* of the place. In the Soviet Union, my life had been determined for me. I knew its trajectory: I would do more research, earn some prizes, acquire a respectable position in the academy, save some money, buy a car, build a dacha, retire and then die. What was distinct about the West was its uncertainty—uncertainty which promised *possibility, probability and opportunity.*

* * *

The USSR had valuable things—its educational system was enviable and outstanding—but the political structure, even in the era of Perestroika and Glasnost, stifled creativity and destroyed enterprise. This fact was grimly illustrated for me by the fate suffered by Alexey Pajitnov after my return to the Soviet Union. A colleague of ours at the prestigious Academy of Sciences of the Soviet Union, Pajitnov had invented the popular video game *Tetris*. We did not at first think much of this creation. As scientists with passes to the ASSU, we constituted something of a national elite because we had a relative measure of autonomy and constant access to computers. And developing video games emerged as a widely practised hobby—a brainy pastime to make things to show off to and share with friends and colleagues.

I had co-developed a game called *Wordtris* at about roughly the same time as *Tetris*. It had emerged from a project in the 1980s at the Computer Centre of the Academy of Sciences to invent a fax machine capable of translating information from one language into another during transmission. I was a young professor of theoretical physics at Yerevan State University and head of the department of mathematical modelling of complex systems, and my partners on the fax machine project, Sergei Utkin and Vjacheslav Tsoy, were scientists based in Moscow. We used the applications developed there in an educational game in which the player would have to make words from letters raining down from above. After displaying our creation to friends, we forgot all about it and got on with our lives. While I had been away in Cambridge, rumours went out in Moscow that American entrepreneurs were sniffing around the Soviet Union for video games. Rather than being clandestine, their trips were facilitated by Electronorgtechnica, or Elorg—the foreign trading company run by the KGB. *Tetris* was acquired by the Americans. But the tales we heard of fabulous wealth passing hands were not reflected in its creator's way of life. What should rightfully have been his was pocketed by the Soviet state, which had a monopoly on the copyright. Pajitnov later fled the Soviet Union for the better life that was his due. What had transpired taught us that there was a vast market for video games beyond the frontiers of the Soviet Union—but we did not want the *Tetris* story reprised.

In 1988, the Soviet authorities agreed to let me travel to the United States to conduct research at Harvard and Berkeley. I flew out with copies of the code for *Wordtris*. I did not bother to try to hide them because hardly anyone knew code language. Once in the US, I reached out to a network of Armenian diaspora lawyers, who advised me that we could protect our interests if we vested the copyright of the game in a US-based company. They even suggested a generic name. I proposed *Armenica*—a portmanteau of Armenia and America—and incorporated it in the States. I then flew to California to give a demo of our game to Spectrum Holobyte, a company affiliated with the video game publisher Mirrorsoft and owned by Robert Maxwell. I never met the mysterious Maxwell, but Spectrum was sufficiently impressed by *Wordtris* to offer to come to Armenia between 1988 and 1989 to see the whole game. Fortunately, while in Cambridge I had saved up my stipend to purchase an IBM PC XT machine. With its monochrome graphic display and 10-megabyte hard-drive, it proved a precious private asset in our command economy. For the next month, Sergei and Vjacheslav moved into my house in Yerevan, where we tweaked, tinkered with and perfected the game on my machine. We made it bilingual and even incorporated music into it. The final product was a sublime work of art. *Wordtris* was not our name for it. We called it Lavengro —Romany for "wordsmith".

The Americans, however, had other ideas. Their emissary, travelling as a tourist to elude the KGB, liked what she saw and invited me back to the United States to sign the deal. On returning to California in 1988-89, I was told that our game would be christened *Wordtris* and sold together with *Tetris* as the "*Tetris Gold*" group of games. I protested, not least because I feared it would mean further enriching Elorg, which owned the name *Tetris*. But we were assured otherwise. The game developed almost as an act of self-amusement by three Soviet scientists was then tossed over to a team of 300 video game developers to be revised and rewritten. What they reproduced before putting it in the market was nowhere near as beautiful as what we had created, but we could not complain. The deal had emancipated us financially. And it was an incredibly uplifting moment on a deeper level. My sons, Vartan and Hayk, were the first recipients of the prototype developed by Nintendo, *Wordtris* became a beloved game from the United States to Korea, holding the No. 1 spot for a long period, and the late Steve Jobs prodded me afterwards to rework the game to be included on the Apple Mac as an educational programme. But my interest in video games, intensified by the adventure of developing and selling *Wordtris*, faded away once the Soviet Union collapsed and Armenia became an independent state in 1991.

* * *

For Armenians, a nation debilitated by centuries of persecution, the USSR had provided stability and security, while also, as is the wont of imperial powers, planting the seeds of prospective strife. Those seeds blossomed in Karabakh/Artsakh—the historically Armenian territory awarded to Azerbaijan by Stalin as part of his design to disrupt cohesive national and ethnic communities—just as the Soviet Union was coming apart. Anxious to advertise its authority, Moscow rejected every reasonable democratic bid by the local population—pleas, protests, resolutions, referendums—to transfer Karabakh to Armenia. Mikhail Gorbachev's refusal even to mediate, creating the perception that the state was indifferent to the Armenians, resulted in the pogroms of Armenians in the cities of Sumgait and Baku between 1988 and 1990. Lithuanians, Latvians and Georgians were also exposed to serious violence during this period. There was much that was admirable about Gorbachev, but to praise him for presiding over the "peaceful" dissolution of the Soviet Union is to airbrush the fact that a great deal of blood was in fact spilled.

On 21 September 1991, I cast my ballot in the referendum on Armenia's independence from the Soviet Union. When I emerged from the polling booth, I saw city squares deluged by ecstatic crowds. Cars honked jubilantly through the streets. The elderly joined children in waving the national flag. The rapture that surged in our hearts contained in it the haunting strains of an ancient nation that was being reborn. But Armenians at the time felt this freedom was going to be incomplete as long as Artsakh remained captive to the Soviet frontiers inherited by Azerbaijan. War broke out.

The war years were bleak. When I flew home from London, all that was visible from the plane was the tarmac. Everything else was pitch black. Yerevan, known in the USSR as the "city of lights" because its streets and magnificent buildings remained always lit, was plunged into darkness between 1991 and 1996. Trees, revered by Armenians, were felled for fuel. Families cooked meagre meals with wood and children read by candlelight. Bread was rationed to 250 grams per person a day. There wasn't a flower in sight, hospitals ran on a few hours of power supply, there was a flood of refugees and the cold claimed many lives. The nuclear power plant that had supplied Armenia's energy had closed in the aftermath of the devastating 1988 earthquake. It hadn't been affected, but the people and the authorities thought emotionally, not rationally, taking for granted the gas supplies from Russia. In the early 1990s, Armenia became excessively dependent on foreign sources, some of them hostile, for its energy needs.

Crucial pipelines running through neighbouring Georgia were sabotaged by our adversaries.

And yet, against all the odds, Armenia prevailed. Why? Because the entire nation believed in and dedicated itself to the national cause. Armenians, shaped by their historic memory, were more determined than their adversaries. From Russia to Central Asia and Europe to North America and South Asia, Armenians everywhere believed that they could build a successful state in their newly independent homeland—and joined forces to protect and fortify it. This explains why Armenia surged ahead of Azerbaijan at the time in building a professional army. Armenian identity did not need to be legitimated with rhetoric— it expressed itself in action.

The responsibility for what the soldiers had sacrificed so much to win was transferred to politicians: could they convert the battlefield gains into a peaceful settlement?

This was the question at the forefront of my mind when I became prime minister of Armenia in 1996. My experience as Armenia's maiden ambassador to London reinforced my belief that Armenia could only resolve the friction with its neighbour through diplomacy. We had been here before. The history of Cilicia held valuable lessons for Armenia. For almost 300 years, that Armenian state had survived and thrived by its diplomacy. Its internal cohesion, resting on a confident Armenian identity, enabled it to concentrate its energies on preserving its statehood. It forged alliances with powers near and far and engaged with friend and foe. When Levon Ter-Petrosyan, Armenia's inaugural president, invited me to become prime minister, two factors informed my decision: first, he offered me a carte blanche to clean up and reform the system, which was already heading in a worrying direction; second, since Ter-Petrosyan was a scholar versed in the history of Cilicia, I was optimistic that he would draw the right lessons and that we could give shape to a smart government policy, particularly in the foreign arena.

On taking office, there was a profusion of issues that demanded my attention. The government, however, had to prioritise. The provision of uninterrupted power 24 hours of the day to every Armenian household and business took obvious precedence, and, with great effort, we were able to meet the challenge. Creating a healthy and stable banking system was fundamental to bringing stability to the economy, and we reformed dozens of laws to simplify the sector. I worked hard to bring HSBC to Armenia, and the banking behemoth's choice to make Armenia the first post-Soviet home of its services was a vindication of our efforts. Since independence, media freedom in Armenia had been choked by the Soviet-era Ministry of Press Information. One of my first acts on taking office was to conclusively abolish this department. I then launched the United Armenian Agency, an autonomous organisation to act as a bond between the Armenian diaspora and the homeland. This office, proving indispensable in Armenia's plan to acquire assets abroad, later became the Ministry of Diaspora (before being reduced, in 2019, to a high commissioner's office for diaspora affairs). Prominent figures in the diaspora gave definitive pledges of financial support to purchase for the republic significant energy assets located abroad and create profitable joint partnerships, including in oil and gas. Alongside the United Armenian Agency, I established the Armenia Development Agency—a one-stop shop to sell Armenia abroad and bring investment into the country. These institutions, acting as magnets for investments by such colossal brands as Glaxo Wellcome, BMS, Coca Cola, among others, formed part of a broader vision to fire up Armenia's economy. I approached the World Bank to replace its poverty reduction programme for Armenia with a developmental programme, and initiated a new phase of privatisation linked to investment, rather than the Russian-style privatisation connected to vouchers that had resulted in the loss of valuable national assets. I then drew up a comprehensive blueprint to put Armenia on the path of peace, stability and prosperity.

In 1997, I travelled abroad to attend a World Bank meeting and to interact with potential investors. On the way back from Washington, DC, to Armenia, I stopped in London, where I had organised meetings with Jacques de Larosière, an old friend and the head of the European Bank for Reconstruction and Development. Having spent three months working 18-hour shifts seven days a week, I had shed weight and was fatigued, and arrived at the meeting a few minutes late. De Larosière stared at me as if I had committed an unpardonable sin. I apologised, shook hands, helped myself to some coffee and settled down to discuss business. "Armen," de Larosière said gravely. "I said I am sorry," I replied. "No. Armen," he said. "I am not upset with you. I am worried about you." I was puzzled. "Have you looked at yourself?" he asked. "You look like a shell of yourself." I was a little tired, I told him, but otherwise I was well. He promised to sign the deal—a major loan to Armenia—but on one condition: I would have to see a doctor that very day. I agreed, and he relented. The next morning, I was diagnosed with cancer and given a slim chance of survival.

My first thought was about my family—I had earned just about enough to ensure they would be well looked after—and my second thought was about Armenia. There was a surge of emotion in my heart and my mind, but I did not buy into the prognosis. *I can beat this*, I told myself, and decided to keep the news to myself, return to work, receive treatment privately and implement the programme because we could not afford to miss this window of opportunity. Then, one evening, as I was in the middle of my treatment, I saw my son watching over me as my protector. It was exactly what I had done when my father was being treated nearly four decades before. It was time for me to resign and go abroad for intensive treatment. The president rejected my resignation and offered to act as a caretaker prime minister himself while I was away. I demurred: it was not clear how I was going to fare, and Armenia needed certainty. I then went abroad to start treatment. It was a journey filled with disappointment and sorrow, not because of the illness which necessitated it but because of the abrupt termination of the laboriously worked out plan and vision for the country. Submitting myself to specialists, I asked them to attack the cancer as aggressively as it was humanly possible. One afternoon, there was a surprise knock at my door. When I opened it, my mother was standing outside. Having travelled from Armenia, she collapsed on seeing me. I had lost so much weight by then that I looked like a reed. I told her the truth. And with the support of my family—my mother, my sister, my boys Vartan and Hayk, and most especially my beloved wife and friend Nouneh—I endured the treatment and its side-effects for months and months and finally pulled through.

While I returned to academia and worked as a businessman in the West, I remained involved in Armenian affairs, serving, pro bono, long stints as the country's ambassador to London. Then, in 2005, just before she died, my mother wrote me a letter. A stroke had robbed her of speech, but she was just about able, with some effort, to use her hands. And she had decided to expend some of her valuable reserves of strength on telling me about my inheritance. I was not going to get much from her by way of material wealth, she informed me. But by the choices she had made, she was leaving me with something infinitely more valuable: a family, and our homeland. At the twilight of her eventful life—during which she had witnessed a world war, endured an exodus, tended to the victims of persecution, healed the casualties of unspeakable trauma and raised two children—she had revisited and reviewed her choices in life and had felt wholly vindicated. *Armenia* was her bequest to me. She had sacrificed so much to ensure that our ancient homeland from which so many of our forebears had forcibly been driven out was to be my inheritance. My parents had been my touchstones. But had I been worthy of their sacrifice? I cannot be the judge of that. What I can say is that Armenia, always the animating force of my life, became even more important to me after her passing.

In 2018, after a five-year pro bono spell as ambassador in London, I returned to serve as Armenia's fourth president. Three years earlier, the constitution had been amended by referendum to vest executive authority in the prime minister's post. But in my negotiations with the outgoing president, Serzh Sargsyan, who nominated me for the presidency, I was offered a strong role in the nation's foreign policy, foreign investment, science, cultural affairs and education. My demand to eradicate the barrier between Armenia and the diaspora—to allow its members to serve in the Armenian government—was grudgingly accepted. It was an opportunity to do some of things I had been thwarted by cancer from doing almost a quarter century before.

On 2 March 2018, I was elected to the presidency with 90 per cent of the vote in the National Assembly and inaugurated just over a month later, on 9 April, as Armenia's fourth president. But then President Sargsyan, rather than take his place as an elder statesman, decided to take up the newly empowered post of the prime minister, despite having made a promise earlier to the public not to do so. Unsurprisingly, the anger simmering away beneath the surface exploded into large-scale protests led by Nikol Pashinyan, a journalist turned lawmaker.

Days after my election, the streets of Yerevan were clogged with tens of thousands of protestors. Armenia was caught in a crisis that could only be resolved through concession, compromise, or carnage. Ten years earlier, near the spot where the protestors now stood, the blood of Armenians had been spilled by force. The Armenian Genocide Day, observed every year on 24 April, was days away. If Armenians engaged in fratricide, they would not only disgrace themselves—they would also defile the memory of our ancestors. I was determined not to let this happen. Although my role was largely ceremonial, I was adamant that something had to be done. On the morning of 21 April, a Saturday, I decided to walk to Republic Square in the heart of the city to meet the protestors. My security detail was deeply worried because they could not guarantee my safety. I explained to them that the people massed beyond the presidential palace were our compatriots. I could not conceivably justify remaining as their president if I feared them. So I walked out of the palace and into the crowd and shook hands with the people. The word spread through the crowd. Seeing that their First Citizen was not some distant and aloof figure, they spoke freely and cheered as I strolled through the crowd, forming a line behind me. It was a turn of events none of us had anticipated. Even my wife, who was abroad at the time and following events back home on the television news, was stunned by what she saw. Eventually, I met Pashinyan, surrounded by a hundred thousand people, and reached an agreement with him to hold talks the next morning. This breakthrough, averting bloodshed, had been worth every risk. And I felt returning to Armenia had been the right decision.

On 23 April, I summoned the national leadership—the prime minister-elect (I had not yet ratified his election), the deputy prime minister, the speaker of the national assembly, the Catholicos and the head of the Constitutional Court—for a meeting that was broadcast live on TV. I explained the severity of the situation and told them that we could not allow our nation to descend into violence on the day commemorating the Armenian Genocide. Three hours later, Sargsyan resigned. Instead of a bloody confrontation, the so-called "Velvet Revolution" culminated in a non-violent transfer of power in the weeks that followed. I was filled with pride and gratitude that Armenians had risen above division. On the morning of 24 April, as I laid down a wreath at the Genocide Memorial and said a prayer, the country was at peace.

The *Financial Times* declared that I was "basking in the afterglow" of this success, "acting as a father figure to a young, reform-minded government". In truth, I was deeply concerned about the future of the country in the absence of urgent reforms to root out corruption, involve the diaspora in state affairs and achieve a balanced distribution of authority between state institutions rather than allowing power to become concentrated in one office. But reform, a non-starter, ceased even to be a talking point once the Covid-19 epidemic shut down the country.

Then, on 27 September 2020, at the height of the pandemic, Azerbaijan launched a full-scale war against Armenia in Artsakh. The government was caught by surprise. The fighting, which unfolded over the following forty-four days, was ferocious. Thousands of young Armenian soldiers were killed in action. It would be inaccurate, however, to say that they died fighting Azerbaijan's forces alone. Baku's war effort was superintended by Turkish officers and boosted by Turkish weapons, particularly Bayraktar II drones. Although I had no constitutional authority to direct the response to the war at home, and was not invited by the government to be involved in the decision-making, I flew to Brussels and held meetings with NATO secretary general Jens Stoltenberg, EU foreign policy chief Josep Borrell, and European Council president Charles Michel and demanded an explanation from them. The fact that a NATO member was actively engaged in a military campaign in the Caucasus had such deadly ramifications that there should have been wide condemnation. There was none of that, sadly. From Europe to North America to South Asia, I activated my contacts and received offers of help. But the war was effectively over before assistance could be mobilised.

On 9 November, Prime Minister Pashinyan signed a ceasefire agreement mediated by Moscow, nominally Armenia's military partner. The implication was clear: it was the beginning of the end of Artsakh. There was an eruption of rage in Armenia. How could a people who had been lulled into the belief that they were the superior power account for this defeat? The blow was so painful that it was hard to think objectively. And yet a cool-headed analysis made it clear that the result of the war was not an event; it was a process: the culmination of twenty-five years of failure to turn victory into peace.

* * *

On 10 November, a day after he signed the ceasefire agreement, I called on Prime Minister Pashinyan to resign in favour of a technocratic government. This public call was intended to allow the country to metabolise the new reality and formulate a path forward. We needed to unite as a country—utilise the remainder of the government's term to stabilise the economy, instil confidence in a deeply shaken populace, amend the constitution to remove the imbalance of power that had directly harmed Armenia, and subject it to a referendum—and not engage in a divisive contest that would polarise the country.

The war, exposing a deep decay, had also revealed the perils of a system with power concentrated in one office. It was imperative to fix this. By convention, constitutional changes only come into effect with the election of a new president, and I offered to resign my post in order to put a new constitution into motion. The prime minister made a public pledge in March 2021 to alter the constitution by November of that year. While waiting for him to act, I convened the Summit of Minds in the spa town of Dilijan in October 2021, bringing to Armenia prominent business, political and tech leaders in the hope of demonstrating to a demoralised nation a year after the war that it still had tremendous potential. Immediately after the conference, I flew to Saudi Arabia—a country with which Armenia had no diplomatic relations. The visit, organised with the help of the good offices of the UAE's leadership, was intended to show by example that new partnerships could be forged to boost Armenia's security. I was also keen to signal, especially since Turkey and Azerbaijan had given the war a religious tint, that Armenia had no antipathy towards Islam. In fact, the first country I visited after the war had been Jordan, at the invitation of His Majesty King Abdullah II, where I had stressed to the Armenian community that their homeland and church had a proud history of harmony with Islam. Having floated a presidential initiative called Advanced Tomorrow (ATOM), an ambitious cyber and scientific innovation hub, I travelled through Asia that autumn to sell the idea to governments and to attract private investment.

By the end of the year, it had become apparent to me that the constitution, placing all executive power in the prime minister's hands, was not likely to be changed. The status quo was surreal: there were no checks and balances, authority was exercised by one individual, the diaspora was banned from participating in the state and the president was expected to act as the head of the state without any tools or power. Not only could I do little by remaining in what had been reduced to a purely ornamental office—I felt I could be more helpful as a civilian. I told this to the prime minister during a phone call in January 2022 in which I informed him of my resignation. Choosing to communicate directly with the people, I shared my decision on Facebook rather than announcing it, in the traditionally detached manner, on state television.

* * *

The constitutional change of 2015, taking Armenia from a presidential to a parliamentary system of government, ignited a debate about whether the country was the Third Republic, born from the Soviet Union's demise, or a continuation of the First Republic. I was invited to comment on this not long after becoming president. I felt it was a trivial debate, not least because recent events had left me more concerned about the future of Armenia as it existed—its security, demography, economy and democracy—and had a disquieting feeling that we were on another dangerous crossroads of history.

Perhaps it was this mood that brought to mind the rumination of Yeghishe Charents, the greatest Armenian poet of the twentieth century, who, in one of his most haunting verses in the aftermath of the Genocide and the collapse of the First Armenian Republic, had asked: *Am I going to be the last poet of my country?* And so, in my response to the question, I said in earnest that I did not know the answer, nor indeed did I know if I would be the last president of the Third Republic of Armenia—already creaking under the burden of the failures of its own history—or if I would go on to become the first president of the Fourth Republic, built on new strong ideas fit for the twenty-first century.

To grapple sincerely with this question, one would have to go back to the 1990s, specifically to the period following Armenia's victory in the Artsakh war.

In 1994, when a ceasefire was declared, Armenia was the decisive victor. This achievement was the product of national unity, dedication and perseverance. But the elation that followed the war could not take away from the fact that Armenia had to wrestle with some fundamental questions about the nature of the state—questions it had been too distracted during the war to ask and to answer. Having begun as the most coherent nation in the Caucasus, against a backdrop of civil strife in Georgia and defeat in Azerbaijan, Armenia was confronted by the challenge of peace immediately after winning the war.

There was reason for optimism: Levon Ter-Petrosyan, the Third Republic's first president, had academic credentials that promised a rational approach in forging a path forward. Armenia had other enviable advantages, too: a united populace at home; a committed diaspora abroad; national assets in the form of factories and production plants raised during the Soviet era; a skilled workforce; a nuclear power plant and hydropower capability; and national resources such as gold, silver and mineral mines.

All that Armenia needed was a strategic national vision—a programme, a model—of the kind of state it was going to be. This would underpin and inform the nation's perception of, and long-term goals for, itself. Armenia had to arrive at decisions on contentious and consequential issues. How would it define its national identity? How would it sustain its internal cohesion? How was it going to achieve closure on the harrowing memory of the Genocide?

Addressing issues of national identity, mission and vision, and producing a strategy for the state, were essential to protect the interests of Armenia's citizens at home and Armenians all over the world. A clear and considered response would have essentially shaped the future written constitution of the state— its most significant laws, the structure and balance of power, the institutions of the government and a national plan of action— and bequeathed to Armenia a Bible of national and state values to guide Armenia's quest for resolution to every and each national, state and military problem.

There were several successful models of different states that Armenia could have drawn from. We could, for instance, have looked to the Israeli model or the Irish one, or even the more complex Singaporean example. We could have turned to the Cilician model from our own history. Perhaps best of all,

Armenia could have forged an *Armenian* model guided by the best examples of all of them.

Taking the Israeli path would have required Armenia to channel all resources into the singular pursuit of preserving Artsakh's independence, creating new settlements in that territory, and being prepared to accept an interminable confrontation with our neighbours Azerbaijan and Turkey. Had we gone the way of Ireland, another nation with a vast diaspora, Armenia would have had to concentrate its energies on internal recovery after a long period of external rule and building a successful democracy and modern economy.

Had Armenia chosen, say, the Cilician model—perhaps the most practicable—it would have had to be resourceful, imaginative, diplomatically agile, and open to trade and relations with its own diaspora. It would have had to forge alliances from west to east and north to south, push Azerbaijan to a settlement from a position of power and make it a partner and become a hospitable harbour for trade and business. An Armenian model would have necessitated learning from the mistakes of others, rather than making them ourselves, and drawing on their successes. Whatever model Armenia chose would have determined the quality of our democracy and our attitude to free markets and free enterprise, free media, the security of Armenia and Artsakh, and the search for a lasting resolution for the latter.

Unfortunately, instead of emulating others or designing our own successful model, Armenia ended up with what I'd call a "no-model model"—giving rise to a state bereft of long-term strategic planning, clear vision of where it was headed and what it wished to achieve, and whose actions amounted merely to reactions. This hollowness meant that we also squandered a very important ingredient of modern politics: pragmatism. Instead of building a strong small democratic state anchored to a global diasporic nation, with full engagement and involvement of the diaspora in the social, economic and political life of the republic, we ended up with a closed model with constitutionally enforced barriers that dramatically limited the diaspora from contributing to the Armenian homeland.

Armenia's greatest national asset was and is its people, both at home and abroad. A state animated by strategic thinking would have engaged with the diaspora, devised means for the diaspora to participate in the nation's affairs and constitutionally codified its rights. The Soviet Union, as we have seen, had striven to court the Armenian diaspora as early as the late 1940s. The Third Republic of Armenia, however, chose to erect barriers between the diaspora and itself. In 1999, my late friend James Wolfensohn, then the president of the World Bank, warned me that Armenia was doing serious harm to itself by shunning its diaspora. Being Jewish, Wolfensohn had a keen understanding of the importance of diaspora. "If you keep this up," Wolfensohn said, "Armenia will become a Disneyland at best for your diaspora, nothing more." It was difficult to disagree.

One result of Armenia's choices was that some of the world's most successful individuals in the fields of science, politics, business, banking, military, intelligence, among others, could play no part at all in the governance of Armenia. Instead of courting the best specialists in the diaspora to develop and improve our intelligence and military, we rested on our laurels. Instead of turning Armenia into a transparent and incorruptible oasis of high-tech innovation, open trade, judicial independence, the rule of law, entrepreneurship and business development, where locally incorporated companies could own international assets and engage in global business ventures, Armenia became a small and insular oligarchic state.

Post-Soviet Russia and other republics were replete with major assets in need of investors and buyers; Armenia—for all its reputation for economic shrewdness, and despite being blessed by an affluent diaspora eager to help the mother country—did not pursue the possibility of acquiring them. If it had, Armenian companies would today be counted among the world's top exporters of oil and gas, just as the Dutch Shell and the French Total are.

Sadly, Armenia was engaged in an imitation of discussion on such questions as the pros and cons of political systems—parliamentary or presidential—and the best resolution to the Artsakh issue—in a phased manner or at once. This was naturally unproductive. On the issue of Artsakh, we were engaged in interminable approximations of deliberations on the minutiae of self-determination and territorial integrity, when political pragmatism dictated that converting victory into peace was Armenia's highest priority.

Azerbaijan at the time had a clear and pragmatic three-pronged plan: first, to build a pipeline to take oil and then gas from Azerbaijan to international markets; second, to use the revenues to modernise the military; third, to use the modernised military to force a settlement to the Artsakh issue. The success of this strategy hinged on laying the infrastructure for the pipeline, which required Armenia's acquiescence. This gave Armenia leverage and created an opening in the late 1990s for Yerevan to negotiate with Baku for a comprehensive settlement, which would include the construction of the oil pipeline, possibly even via Armenian territory; a lasting solution to the Artsakh dispute; and guarantees of peace that would lead to stability, security and prosperity in the region.

It is with this in mind that I had, in a speech in the mid-1990s at the Zbigniew Brzezinski Centre in Washington, DC, described Armenia as a "Caspian State". What I had meant was that Armenia could be a serious player in the future of the geopolitics of the Caucasus and the export of the region's natural resources.

The Third Republic, tragically, did none of this. Instead, commencing on a path that was devoid of substance, it hurtled from historic victory to disastrous defeat over three wasted decades. Among small states, there are monarchies and quasi-monarchies, and presidential, semi-presidential and parliamentary systems. What is common to all successful small states is clarity about the national vision that steers the state. Armenia's politicians did not possess that clarity.

The Third Republic of Armenia is now a thing of the past. But will Armenia's new reality force it to be sober, accountable and purposeful? Will the corruption, isolationism, myopia, duplicity and deception that overwhelmed the successes, victories and promise of the Third Republic be confined to the past— and pave the way for an open, honest, efficient, organised, self-confident and true-to-self Fourth Republic? The fate of this unique country—at once an ancient civilisation, a small state and a global nation—may depend on how we Armenians answer these questions.

12

CONCLUSION

SAVING THE WORLD?

I have lived many lives—a diplomat, a politician and a businessman. But first and foremost, I am a scientist—a theoretical physicist. The world we inhabit today is vastly different not only from the Soviet Union in which I was born—it is significantly different, too, from what we left behind a few years ago. In 2020, people across the globe were told by their governments to shut down their normal social and working existences for several months because of the pandemic. Four years on, the political and geopolitical arenas that welcome us out of our self-imposed restrictions are not what we expected nor experienced in the previous eight decades since the end of the Second World War, let alone the past thirty years since the end of the Cold War.

Welcome to the dawn of a new era—an era in which the post-war traditional boundaries that once defined our global interactions are being redrawn, and where the power dynamics that once governed nations, states and institutions are evolving into something entirely unprecedented. Owing to its complex and multi-faceted nature, this era is characterised by a paradoxical blend of shrinking distances and expanding influence. In this transformed landscape, individuals armed with mobile gadgets wield unprecedented power, Small States are significant players, and the prospect of peace and stability—or war and destruction—is within their grasp.

Gone are the days when globalisation was simply a matter of institutions and governments working across borders, and when global trade was largely ordered by the rules of multilateral organisations. The dynamics have shifted. While states might be moving away from a rules-based globalisation, they find themselves engaging with it in subtler, more nuanced ways. As globalisation moves from the purely physical to the virtual realm, it is easier than ever before to reconfigure or bypass the rules. This change, among others, is driven by the power of individuals—those equipped with nothing more than smartphones and an internet connection.

These devices, once mere communication tools, have transformed into instruments of change, granting people the power to influence events on a global scale. From trade to cybersecurity and eco-activism to cryptocurrency, from citizen journalism amplifying unheard voices to social media igniting mass movements, individuals now possess the means to amass wealth, disrupt state policy, spark uprisings, expose corruption and shape public opinion like never before. Central to this evolution is the undeniable reality that, thanks to new technology, our world is rapidly "shrinking". Physical distances remain, yet the connectedness fostered by technology renders them less significant. In this interconnected realm, information travels instantaneously, cutting across borders and reaching people around the globe.

The rise of Small States further exemplifies this phenomenon. These states, previously overshadowed by their larger counterparts, have emerged as formidable actors on the global stage. The increasing numbers of successful Small States, and their growing presence and impact, challenge the traditional notion of power existing solely within big nations. Small States, forging dynamic relationships with large players, have harnessed the ability to dance the intricate dance between confrontation and mediation. An intriguing consequence of this technological and scientific revolution is the transformation of the world and politics. Our new world, which is powered by what I call "quantum politics", is in some senses the antithesis of the classical world. Just as science made the leap a century ago from classical to quantum mechanics, so the world and politics have transitioned in this century from a classical to a quantum stage. If the classical political world was organised by traditional forms of connections—religious, ideological, national, institutional—the quantum age is shaped and reshaped constantly by, among other forces, individuals connected by technology.

In the past, elections were held every five to six years, providing politicians with ample time to enact policies and engage with their constituents. Today, the political landscape is in constant flux, as politicians are evaluated every moment through online comments, polls, and social media posts. This shift has intensified the scrutiny of politicians and their actions. To manage public opinion in this new digital age, politicians now maintain dedicated social media departments that craft carefully curated narratives and messages. Politicians are acutely aware that a single misstep or controversial statement can lead to a career-ending public backlash. Beyond politics, technology has revolutionised everything from transportation to energy and space travel. A simple tap on a screen allows us to summon a taxi or rideshare service, order food of our choice, organise a holiday and become a shareholder in a public company. This change has not only empowered consumers with more choices but has also spurred the growth of services and generated employment opportunities for millions.

Even space exploration, once the exclusive preserve of great powers, has been democratised in the digital age. Small States such as the United Arab Emirates have successfully ventured into the cosmos. Indeed, the UAE's accomplishments in space exploration exemplify how technology has opened up new vistas for nations that were previously unable to participate in such endeavours. On the darker side of the ledger, the concept of objective truth has become distorted by technology. What now matters most is not the objective reality of a situation but rather what the majority, often influenced and manipulated by technology, believes. This phenomenon has given rise to a post-truth society, where perception often trumps facts. Technology's ability to rapidly disseminate information on a national or global scale has led to a massive inception of ideas. Viral content can shape public opinion and cause social and political upheaval, illustrating the power that technology and its wielders exert on our collective consciousness. Our understanding of concepts such as democracy, truth, common sense, diplomacy and trade must catch up with the new reality engendered by technology.

In this period of rapid scientific and technological evolution— or "R-Evolution", a term I coined to convey the pace of change— survival will depend upon the willingness to learn and be adaptable. The dominance of large powers has depended on three factors I call MET: military, economic and technological.

1. *M*: In the realm of military power, the United States still remains an unrivalled behemoth. No other nation possesses the capability to match the sheer might and reach of the American navy and air force, which can be deployed virtually anywhere. The reasons behind this dominance are twofold. First, the United States has invested heavily in its military infrastructure,

maintaining a technologically advanced and robust armed forces. Second, few countries have the financial resources or political will to achieve such a level of military might. The one area where the US is vulnerable is nuclear weaponry; here Russia has parity with America. The traditional form of nuclear deterrence has been the principle of "mutually assured destruction"—the belief that the fear of a counterstrike will prevent the first use of nuclear weapons. It remains unclear whether this can still hold in the quantum age.

2. *E*: Economic dominance presents a different picture. Currently, there are two economic powerhouses, the United States and China, each vying for supremacy. This contest, however, is not a static situation. India, with its burgeoning economy, is poised to join their ranks in the near future. Japan has already been there. Beyond that, a multipolar world beckons, where several middle-ranking nations will possess significant economic influence and emerging economies will gradually close the gap with their Western counterparts. Indeed, measured by GDP per capita, the top-performing states are successful Small States. Their prosperity demonstrates their adept economic management.

3. *T*: In terms of technology, the United States, China, Russia, Japan, India, among other large powers, enjoy certain advantages, particularly in the fields of cyber and internet technology. But here again the rise of smaller states and entities promises to disrupt traditional dominance. These smaller players are quickly emulating the technological prowess of their larger counterparts, enabling them to challenge established norms. Artificial Intelligence (AI) is set to accelerate this transformation, levelling the playing field and creating parity. In the seventeenth century, when Newton advanced his laws of motion, the number of individuals engaged in advanced mechanics probably did not

exceed one thousand in a global population of 600 million people. That number had probably climbed to about 10,000 scientists by the time of Albert Einstein. Today, roughly seven decades after Einstein's passing, there are millions of people in almost all regions of the world engaged in complex scientific research. If you could find Newton in a thousand and Einstein in ten thousand, imagine how many talented people you could find in hundreds of millions. And these individuals are not solely the treasure of large states. Indeed, as we have seen, Small States such as Estonia, Israel, and Singapore have demonstrated that they can lead, and sometimes even surpass, their larger counterparts in the technological field, which will flatten further with the spread of AI.

The old order has given way to a new paradigm, one where Small Powers, whether individuals, states, or online entities that sometimes act as "virtual Small States", are playing an increasingly pivotal role. Platforms such as Google and Facebook, and individuals like the late Steve Jobs, Bill Gates, Elon Musk, among others, have demonstrated an unprecedented ability to shape global policies. The power they and others in the tech world have and wield is monumental and more decisive than some states, as their actions rise above the confines of boardrooms and reach and reshape global public opinion.

The rapidly evolving quantum world we find ourselves in today is a realm of uncertainties, contradictions and possibilities. It is a world where states simultaneously retreat from and engage in globalisation, where individuals with smart devices rewrite the rules of the game and where smart Small States emerge as powerful catalysts of change. As survivors, Small States are naturally averse to global conflict and hold the potential to steer our world towards peace and stability. As we chart this intricate landscape, one thing becomes evident: a future shaped by the collective endeavours of smart Small States is likely to be a less violent one. Their ability to navigate complexity, mediate conflicts and champion peace underscores their indispensability to maintaining stability.

But if they are to play a part in "saving" the world, Small States must be successful on their own terms. Success does have a standard recipe, but in my opinion—which is forged in the crucible of experience—the following three ingredients are fundamental because they can define the character and determine the fate of Small States.

1. A Strong Foundation of Identity and Purpose

Small States wishing to embark on the path of success must first cultivate a robust national identity. This identity draws strength from history, traditions and culture, providing a sense of belonging and unity among citizens. The states we have studied in the preceding pages either mined history or crystallised a modern basis for a national identity.

2. National Mission and Strong Leadership

A defining factor for these states is the presence of a national mission. Strong leadership plays a pivotal role in guiding citizens towards a shared national purpose. This mission serves as a guiding light, directing, as the Small States we have examined demonstrate, the efforts of the populace towards common goals.

3. Articulated Vision and Strategic Planning

Translating a national mission into reality requires a clear and articulated vision. Strong leadership must lay out a roadmap for achieving the desired objectives. It is not enough to have a goal;

the journey to that goal must be well-defined and understood. This vision, when communicated effectively from the top, rallies the majority of citizens, ensuring that they are on board with the state's course of action. Nor is strategic planning limited to internal affairs; it must also extend to inter-state relations. Small States with an eye on success must strategically navigate the complex web of international diplomacy, leveraging relationships to their advantage.

Besides these principal ingredients, the success of Small States will also depend, to varying degrees, on other factors.

Crafting a coherent state structure, including choosing between presidential or parliamentary systems, which is crucial to avoid inconsistencies as seen in Armenia, which oscillated between parliamentary and presidential systems. Maintaining a balance of power with strong institutions, such as an independent judiciary and a capable legislature, prevents abuse of power. A harmonious relationship between the leadership and the populace is most effectively fostered through democracy. Democracy naturally aligns the interests of the government with those of the people and thus minimises the effort required to maintain this concord. Nevertheless, Small States that are not democratic from the start can succeed by gradually adopting democratic principles while prioritising development. Transparency is a cornerstone of success for Small States. By actively demonstrating a commitment to combating corruption, Small States earn the trust and confidence of their citizens. Israel and Singapore showcase how transparent systems, coupled with proactive measures against corruption, build confidence and contribute to overall prosperity. To thrive, Small States must confront realities honestly. They must discard delusions and reject deception and elect to be candid in all their dealings. Pretence and dishonesty are incompatible with sustained success. The commitment of leadership to open communication with their citizens breeds trust, and facilitates informed decision-making and creates and strengthens a shared sense of purpose. In the pursuit of success, Small States must pragmatically assess their advantages and disadvantages. This involves recognising the nation's assets, be they natural resources, strategic geographical positioning, or the talents and contributions of their people, at home and in the diaspora. Pragmatism should extend to recruiting the best minds for governmental roles, and creating, through training and investment, a pool of capable and talented individuals who can steer the nation forward. Foreign relations too must be guided by pragmatism. This entails forging alliances and partnerships that align with the nation's interests and objectives, rather than being driven solely by ideological considerations. Successful Small States adopt economic strategies and industrial policies that maximise their resources and capitalise on their strengths. To enhance their global influence, Small States should focus on developing a highly skilled and professional diplomatic corps. Ireland, having invested in nurturing a cadre of diplomats with international exposure and education, serves as an exemplary model. Its diplomatic corps acts as a bridge between the state and the international community, effectively advancing Dublin's interests and strengthening its presence on the world stage. To fortify themselves further, Small States should work hard on creating a global network of support to enhance the nation's standing and image.

In other words, the success of Small States hinges on a carefully orchestrated symphony of elements. A strong national identity, strong leadership, a clear mission, an articulated vision, balanced power structures, democratic values, transparency, honesty and pragmatic approaches collectively contribute to their success. While each small state's journey is unique, these ingredients offer a recipe for success that transcends geographical boundaries.

THE SMALL STATES CLUB

In a world characterised by division and diversity of ideologies, a distinct category of nations stands out not for their territorial expanse or specific ideologies, but for their consistent success on the global stage. These are the Small Smart States—a unique club bound not by geography, ideology, structure, or demographics, but by their shared success stories. Small States, by their nature, exhibit shared characteristics. They are survivors. They thrive on stability, security, peace and sustained development. It is this very success, underpinned by a common set of attributes, that positions them as potential saviours of our dangerously polarised world. By banding together, these states can not only create a platform to exchange invaluable insights, but also contribute to rescuing the world from its extreme instincts.

Unity in Success, Not Size

The defining characteristic of the Small States Club is not their geographical extent or population, but the prosperity and achievements these states have realised. The absence of rigid territorial, ideological, structural, or demographic confines is what sets them apart. Their shared story revolves around success in various spheres—from technological innovation and economic performance to social development—and these nations shine as exemplars of what can be attained with the right approach.

The Power to Salvage and Share

Their collective success grants these Small States a unique power —the capacity to contribute to global solutions individually or together. Their achievements aren't just isolated victories; they contain potential answers to the challenges humanity confronts. By coming together, these nations can pool their collective wisdom and resources to address pressing issues that do not see borders.

A Platform for Shared Wisdom

The concept of a Small States Club is not just about leveraging the success of its members for global betterment; it's also a platform for the exchange of ideas. These states, despite their varied origins, can share experiences, strategies and insights that have propelled them to success. It is a collaborative endeavour where triumphs and failures alike can serve as lessons for others.

A Call to Save the World

Nor is the notion of the Small States Club merely a convenient club or alliance—it is also a call to action. These states, armed with attributes that have led them to success, are being summoned to join forces for a greater cause. They are uniquely equipped to be the vanguards of change and models for others, driving solutions that can have far-reaching consequences for the better.

Championing Diversity in Solutions

One of the most remarkable aspects of the Small States Club is its inherent diversity. Without being bound by common ideologies or structures, these nations represent a rich tapestry of approaches to governance, economics and development. This diversity translates into a cornucopia of ideas that can be adapted, modified and applied to various contexts around the world.

THE SMALL STATES CLUB

A Future Shaped by Unity

The Small States Club can stand as a testament to the power of collective action. Its member states, drawn together by a higher purpose of stability, security and development, have the potential to save the world from conflict and chaos by uniting their strengths. But more immediately, a club of this kind can serve as a conclave for dialogue and an instrument of de-escalation for conflicting small states—a deterrent to violent discord and a platform for stability. The club can function as a dynamic forum for the exchange of ideas and views, and eventually evolve into a larger organisation of successful small states—let's call it S20—that represents the interests of small states at forums such as the G20 and beyond.

But if small states resist the prospect of uniting to formulate a moral, logical and pragmatic basis of mutual cooperation, then they leave themselves—as they have long done—vulnerable to petty local feuds, geopolitical machinations, conflict and war. As the world races to a point of greater disorder, small smart states can choose to remain perilously disunited—or they can take steps to unite in a Small States Club that can protect their interests, serve the common good of humanity and act as an inspiring model for others.

BIBLIOGRAPHY

Avi Shlaim, and William Roger Louis. *The 1967 Arab-Israeli War: Origins and Consequences* (Cambridge ; New York: Cambridge University Press, 2012).

Chan, Kwok B, and Chee Kiong Tong. *Past Times: A Social History of Singapore* (Times Editions, 2003).

Fomin, Maxim, Alvard Jivanyan, and Séamus Mac Mathúna, eds. *Ireland and Armenia: Studies in Language, History and Narrative* (Washington, D.C.: Institute for the Study of Man, 2012).

GärtnerHeinz, and Erich Reiter, eds. *Small States and Alliances* (Vienna: Österreichisches Institut Für Internationale Politik, 2000).

Ghazarian, Jacob. *The Armenian Kingdom in Cilicia during the Crusades* (Routledge, 2018).

Gilbert, Martin. *Israel : A History* (New York: Rosetta Books, 2014).

Gunilla Eriksson, Ulrica Pettersson, and Springer International Publishing Ag. *Special Operations from a Small State Perspective: Future Security Challenges.* (Cham Springer International Publishing Palgrave Macmillan, 2018).

Guo, Yvonne, and J J Woo. *Singapore and Switzerland* (World Scientific, 2016).

Ilan Pappé. *The Forgotten Palestinians* (Yale University Press, 2011).

Ingebritsen, Christine. *Small States in International Relations* (Seattle: University Of Washington Press ; Reykjavik, 2006).

Jesse, Neal G, and John R Dreyer. *Small States in the International System* (London: Lexington Books, 2018).

Josey, Alex. *Lee Kuan Yew : The Crucial Years* (Singapore ; London: Marshall Cavendish, 2013).

Jung, Joseph. *The Laboratory of Progress* (Taylor & Francis, 2022).

Kuan Yew Lee. *The Singapore Story : Memoirs of Lee Kuan Yew* (Singapore: Marshall Cavendish Editions, 2015).

Kwa Chong Guan, Derek Heng, Peter Borschberg, and Tan Tai Yong. *Seven Hundred Years: A History of Singapore* (Marshall Cavendish International Asia Pte Ltd, 2019).

Maass, Matthias. *Small States in World Politics: The Story of Small State Survival, 1648-2016* (Manchester University Press, 2017).

Mansfield, Peter. *The Arabs* (New York: Penguin Books, 1978).

Mathisen, Trygve. *The Functions of Small States in the Strategies of the Great Powers* (Universitetsforlaget, 1971).

Mehran Kamrava. *Qatar Small State, Big Politics, Updated Edition* (Ithaca: Cornell University Press, Baltimore, Md, 2015).

Michael Quentin Morton. *Masters of the Pearl* (Reaktion Books, 2020).

Milton-Edwards, Beverley, and Peter Hinchcliffe. *Jordan: A Hashemite Legacy* (Routledge, 2009).

Mohammad Morsy Abdullah: A Modern History. *The United Arab Emirates* (Routledge, 2020).

Morris, Caroline, and Petra Butler, eds. *Small States in a Legal World.* (Springer, 2019).

Morton, Fred, and Jeff Ramsay. *The Birth of Botswana* (Longman Publishing Group, 1987).

Parsons, Neil. *King Khama, Emperor Joe, and the Great White Queen* (University of Chicago Press, 1998).

Raun, Toivo U. *Estonia and the Estonians* (Hoover Press, 2002).

Rosemarie Said Zahlan. *The Origins of the United Arab Emirates: A Political and Social History of the Trucial States* (Routledge, 2017).

Rouben Paul Adalian. *Historical Dictionary of Armenia* (Scarecrow Press, 2010).

Salibi, Kamal S. *The Modern History of Jordan* (British Academic Press, 1993).

Sandis Sraders. *Small Baltic States and the Euro-Atlantic Security Community* (Springer Nature, 2020).

Schiff, Eric. *Industrialisation without National Patents* (Princeton University Press, 2015).

BIBLIOGRAPHY

Shapira, Anita. *Israel : A History* (Waltham, Mass.: Brandeis University Press, 2012).

Susan Williams. *Colour Bar : The Triumph of Seretse Khama and His Nation* (London: Penguin Books, 2016).

Vladislav Zubok. *COLLAPSE : The Fall of the Soviet Union.* (S.L.: Yale University Press, 2021).

Walker, Christopher J. *Visions of Ararat* (I.B. Tauris, 1997).

INDEX

Umm Al Quwain, 73, 74
UN High Commisisoner for
Human Rights, 158
UN Security Council, 11, 15,
152–3
Union of Soviet Socialist Republics
(USSR), 1–4, 5–10, 67, 91,
113, 114–16, 143, 194, 210–12,
231
Armenian independence,
214–15
collapse of, 92
video games, 212–14
United Arab Emirates (UAE), 12,
15, 45, 55, 59–60, 70, 88–9,
224, 234
Arab union, 71–4
contradictions, 85–8
elections, 75–7
socio-economic development,
77–85
See also Abu Dhabi; Dubai
United Arab Emirates Space
Agency, 81
United Armenian Agency, 217
United Jewish Agency, 100
United Kingdom (UK), 9, 74, 87,
93
United Nations (UN), 39, 140,
181–2
See also World Economic
Forum
United States (US), 33, 35, 38,
101, 102, 145, 146, 158, 173,
213–14
vs. China, 40–1, 87–8, 111,
155–7

and Estonia, 123
as an export market, 191
federation, 73–4
Ireland's economic
transformation, 149–51
Ireland's integration, 153–4
Irish independence, 151
and Qatar, 51–2
"R-Evolution", 234–6
Switzerland and, 142–3
See also World War I; World
War II
"unity in diversity", 28
University of Botswana, 169
University of Tartu, 123
Unterwalden, 127
Urartu, kingdom of, 198
Uri, 127
US National Intelligence Council,
155
US State Department, 123
Utkin, Sergei, 212, 213
Utub tribe, 44
Uyghurs, 124

Valais, 141
Van, 198
Vanda Miss Joaquim, 39
Vardanakert, Battle of, 201–2
Vartan, 214, 219
Vatican, 10
"Velvet Revolution", 221
Victoria (Queen), 165–6
Vienna, 204
Vietnam War, 143–4
Vorontsov-Dashkov, Count,
207

Dr Armen Sarkissian served as the president of Armenia from 2018 to 2022 and as its prime minister between 1996 and 1997. Widely regarded as Armenia's most respected statesman on the international stage, he holds the distinction of being the longest serving ambassador of any country to the United Kingdom.

Trained as a scientist, Dr Sarkissian co-invented the bestselling videogame Wordtris in the 1980s, before being appointed Armenia's maiden ambassador to Britain following his nation's independence from the Soviet Union in 1991.

In a distinguished and varied career spanning four decades, he has gone on to found vast business and philanthropic networks in major capitals around the world, and has held top leadership positions in international organisations such as the East West Institute, Euro-Atlantic Security Initiative, Global Leadership Foundation, the World Economic Forum and others. A highly sought-after speaker on matters of international security, leadership, nation-building, and East-West relations, he is the founder of Eurasia House International and the Founding Director of the Eurasia Centre at Cambridge University's Judge Business School.

Dr Sarkissian is married to Nouneh Sarkissian and they have two sons.